DIPLOMATIC DANCE

DIPLOMATIC DANCE

The New Embassy Life in America

— GAIL SCOTT —

Fulcrum Publishing
Golden, Colorado

This book is dedicated to three important men in my life:

My father, Dr. Michael A. Puzak,
who wanted me to be a champion in everything I endeavored to do;

My uncle, Colonel J. Scott Kurtz,
who encouraged me to be a lady;

My grandfather, Charles Merrill Kurtz, Esq.,
who taught me to be a good storyteller.

Library of Congress Cataloging-in-Publication Data

Scott, Gail, 1944–
Diplomatic Dance : the new embassy life in America / Gail Scott.
p. cm.
ISBN 1-55591-345-8
1. Diplomatic and consular service—United States. 2. United States—Foreign relations—1993- 3. Embassy buildings—Washington (D.C.) I. Title.
JZ1480.S38 1999
327.2—dc21

99-17985
CIP

Cover design: Metro Graphics
Designer: Bill Spahr

Printed in the United States of America
0 9 8 7 6 5 4 3 2 1

Fulcrum Publishing
350 Indiana Street, Suite 350
Golden, Colorado 80401-5093
(800) 992-2908 • (303) 277-1623
www.fulcrum-books.com

Contents

Acknowledgments

Over the years of interviewing authors and reading their books, I always wondered why everyone had such long thank-you lists. Now, after more than three years of being preoccupied with this one project, I understand how important any author's support system really is. Month after month, you face only your computer in self-imposed solitary confinement. For me during that time, away from the excitement of the parties and the interviews, it was these people who were my precious "lifeline."

First, I must thank my family, who always encouraged me, except for Bagel, our beagle, who only is interested in things that are edible. My mother, Betty Kurtz Puzak, listened long-distance to my first chapters. My daughter, Indrani, with classmates from all over the globe, constantly reminded me that today's college graduates think the whole world is their neighborhood. Meanwhile, my best friend, Fred, put up with the towering piles of newspapers and long weekends of writing but learned to really "savor" the endless embassy buffets.

Which reminds me how *caloric* this book has been: not to read but to write. Book writing can be very sedentary, lonely work. But I was lucky to have two fitness gurus who kept me moving in between chapters: in Georgetown, the everyday gorgeous Jennifer Neufell, and in Naples, the perky slave driver Sheila Frasher.

Second, my staff of student interns (mostly from Georgetown University's School of Foreign Service) kept changing, but I learned something from each one of them. Sean O'Connor was only a freshman but was already smitten with Washington's power corridors. Nicole Giugno literally wrote my intern manual and then showed everyone else how to do it. Shawn Rabin brought delightful wonder and charming nerve to the phone and to our parties. Christina

Kline, Ashleigh Searle and Karolin Kuyumcuyan, charmers all, got me on ambassadors' calendars and the countries' vital statistics in our directory. Pete McMahon organized me and my office as he, Amy Johnson and Devyani Puri moved me into a new computer and onto the Internet while booking another round of interviews. Vajravorn 'Na' Tasukon, son of a Thai diplomat and a Thai Ministry of Foreign Affairs' scholar, and multilinguist Anna-Maria Kaneff, couldn't stay long but added greatly to the spirit of this book. And at the end, Anjalina Sen gathered the pictures and permissions with impressive style while former state department intern Stephanie Kaplan brought her own expertise to our *diplomatic dance.* Without this help from these energetic and enthusiastic students, this book might never have made it onto the dance floor.

Third, I especially appreciate "my professional team," who supported and helped me from the very beginning. Foremost, Sandy Trupp, now head of Ruder-Finn's Washington office of Planned Television Arts, first thought of the project, talked me into doing it, and kept talking until I finished it and then helped us tell the world about it. Bob Baron and Sam Scinta of Fulcrum Publishing patiently waited out in Golden, Colorado, while I recovered from knee surgery, traveled twice to Asia, pouted through computer breakdowns and dried out my notes from two office floods. My Fulcrum editor Daniel Forrest-Bank was equally patient with his expert but kind suggestions, while Charlotte Baron was Fulcrum's *diplomat extraordinaire* and Rebecca Langridge, our cheerful marketing specialist. Fulcrum's Bill Spahr designed an elegant and graceful interior. Special thanks to Kathy Klinesmith at Metro Graphics for her wonderful cover design. Albert Mogzec, Washington's diplomatic photographer, was always on the scene and ready to help. My personal marketing guru Bob Stack, who always shoots for the moon and, as usual, got terrific results. Also, with great ideas and infectious enthusiasm, my friend and colleague Susan Nichols made sure everyone-who-was-anyone in Washington joined our diplomatic dance.

And finally, I especially appreciate all my *original* "dancing partners," diplomats and embassy staffers, who first opened the doors and let me in. I enjoyed working with Christiane Hohmann, the first female East German diplomat to serve in Washington, who was trained in Germany's new united diplomatic corps; ever-helpful press secretaries Yrjö Länsipuro and Jarmo Mäkelä and charming Cultural Counselor Anneli Kristiina Halonen of the Finnish Embassy; quintessential Social Secretary Amanda Downes of the British Embassy; good-humored Press Counsellor Mikhail Shurgalin, who patiently took me around all the Russian properties; proactive Croatian Press Secretary Marijan Gubric, who "graduated" to a special assignment with

President Franjo Tudjman; Singapore's savvy former First Secretary for Information Jean Tan; South Africa's helpful Debra Steiner, Maridel Araneta and Allen Wright; Dane Jørgen Grunnet, who introduced me to embassy intrigue close-up; Australia's smooth spokesperson Sandi Logan; Brazil's good-humored Ana Paula Silva, who is the ambassador's chief-of-staff; Canada's Director of Public Affairs Terry Colli, who has served five consecutive ambassadors over 20 years; Ecuador's persuasive Press Counselor Teodoro Maldonado and ever-helpful Monica Gross, the ambassador's private secretary; Romania's cheerful former Press Secretary Simona Miculescu; Austria's Director of Press and Information Martin Eichtinger, who can *really* dance; Japanese Press Officer and newlywed Aya Yoshida (née Nakamura); Belgium's efficient Cultural Attaché Andrea Murphy; Egypt's Lorna Jacobson, social secretary, and Patricia Alikakos, the ambassador's private secretary; and Spain's Social Secretary Diane Flamini, who is a story herself.

I also especially appreciate the wonderful and wise assistance I had from Larry Kolp of Meridian House International and Cissy Anderson, current president of the Hospitality and Information Service (THIS), the Meridian volunteer affiliate, which welcomes and enriches the lives of Washington's foreign diplomats. And, finally, I want to thank our protocol friends at the state department, who are *always* right: Lawrence Dunham, assistant chief of protocol, and Maria Sotiropoulos, the protocol officer who is first to welcome each new ambassador when they arrive on American soil, even if it's the middle of the night.

When I started more than three years ago, one particular ambassador was especially kind and helpful. I shall always remember how Ecuadorian Ambassador Edgar Teran-Teran talked with me for over two hours, as if we were old friends. His wisdom and candor made that first interview a great primer for all the other ambassadorial interviews to follow. An international lawyer, Ambassador Teran still commutes to Washington on business and to keep an eye on his beautiful daughter, Maria Teresa, who I'm happy to call my friend.

Most of all, I want to thank the gracious ambassadors and their spouses from all over the world, who, by inviting me into their public and private lives behind those closed embassy doors and telling me their stories, brought our *diplomatic dance* to life.

Thank you, each of you, for joining our *diplomatic dance.*

Meridian House, the heart of Meridian International Center and site of the annual Meridian Ball. Photo courtesy of the Meridian International Center.

Preface

Growing up, I always thought the world was one place. I could call many places home. At Halloween, I used to dress up in different native costumes. In fact, I still do. But, when I was a little girl, instead of only collecting candies, I took along UNICEF's little orange box.

Each spring, my mother took me on Goodwill Industries' famous embassy tours here in Washington. I vividly remember going to a fancy tea at the 34-room French residence and thinking I just might like to be a diplomat.

For my seventh-grade autobiography, "Thirteen Milestones," I explained to my teacher, Mrs. Dieffenbach, why I loved living in Washington: "It's such an international city you even see women in saris crossing the street."

So, it should have come as no surprise that I would grow up and one day wear a sari myself, not as dress-up for Halloween but as the wife of a Sri Lankan–born journalist. To me, the world was one place with interesting, beautiful differences depicted in my German grandfather's bright yellow *National Geographic*s and my Czech grandmother's hearty golubcies and perogies.

After all my years in Washington, I still get a kick out of the festive air surrounding state visits. You don't have to be at the White House to participate. Sudden, unexplained traffic jams often mean that a motorcade, with foreign flags flying, is just around the corner. Look up at your nearest lamppost and see which country's small flag is hanging next to ours, decorating Washington's long avenues.

In Georgetown, where I live and wrote this book, the motorcade may be the president coming to speak at the university or our neighbor, Madeleine Albright, coming home late at night from another exhausting trip.

Ironically, it is our beagle, Bagel, who knows our secretary of state "intimately." To the dismay of the secret service, Bagel's favorite stop on her nightly walks around the block is Madeleine's. Her flowerbeds and front stoop are irresistible to our hound dog. Once, Bagel even made it through her front door for a party, bolting past the secret service and dancing in between the arriving guests' legs. We amuse ourselves by imagining Bagel's secret service code name.

From the beginning of my research, I realized two things: first, that the endless embassy party circuit would definitely leave me with a wider waistband, and second, that the world was changing so fast that even the ambassadors were playing catch-up. I certainly was. To update my world view, I armed myself with a daily dose of CNN, *The Washington Post, The New York Times,* and *The Wall Street Journal,* followed with a weekly chaser of *The Economist* and regular cruises through embassy websites. In the middle of my research and writing, the White House sex scandal hit Washington and foreign news was pushed off the front pages except for the Asian financial crisis. As a former TV anchorwoman myself, I witnessed the network news anchors struggle each night to keep some sense of world affairs in their evening newscasts.

Twice during these two and one-half years, I interrupted myself to bake and take homemade chocolate chip cookies halfway around the world to my daughter, Indrani, who was studying and working in Nepal and India. Each time I left the United States and returned, even though I still experienced jet lag, I saw signs of the hemispheres coming closer together. And, each time, I was sure the world was spinning faster.

Early on in my research, I enlisted mostly Georgetown University School of Foreign Service undergraduates to drop in between classes, eat my cookies, and help me fax, phone, and cajole. Often, not until we spoke French or Spanish or Turkish or Hebrew or Hindi to embassy staffers did we get results. Many embassies, even though they officially had press officers, seemed afraid to have any contact with us. Obviously, they were the gatekeepers of old and wanted the embassy gates to remain closed. Only a handful of curious and media-savvy ambassadors personally responded to my original letter, while one staffer called to inquire, "How much does it cost to be in your book?"

Mostly unknown to each other, dozens of embassy staffers, some diplomats themselves, made an incredible difference in helping us convince their ambassadors and spouses to "dance" with me. Then, they got us interesting material and pictures and never complained about our endless fact and quote checking.

Often my research assistants asked, "But when are you going to start writing?" and, "How are you ever going to decide who goes in the book?" To their total wonder I answered, "This book will write itself," and "The countries will help me choose them."

And, that's exactly what happened. Some stories were so compelling, some ambassadors so fascinating, some press officers so helpful, some countries so intriguing, some regions so important, that they couldn't possibly be left out.

When I told my friends and acquaintances that I was writing a book about diplomacy, they politely wondered how I would even begin to tackle such a huge topic. So I created a parlor game, "What's the first thing you do if you're writing a book about diplomacy?" Trying to be helpful, they had dozens of serious suggestions.

Never did one person give mine, "First, you go shopping." I created a closet of "embassy uniforms" that I could don instantly before the taxi arrived. For someone who loves to entertain and give parties, I surprised even myself by often wishing for a quiet night at home after too many engraved invitations and national day buffets. Finally, I understood why the ambassadors cherish nothing more than "a night off."

When I started my research, I thought I knew how this book would turn out. But I learned much more than I ever could have imagined. And yet, I am still fascinated by this constantly changing *diplomatic dance.* I hope you will be too.

The Viennese Opera Ball organized by the Austrian-American Alliance for the children and supported by the Austrian Embassy. Photo by Glen Mayne.

Introduction

I come from a family of storytellers and I want to take us on a whirlwind tour around the world—from Sweden to Sri Lanka, Britain to Brazil, Spain to Singapore—without leaving home. Together, we'll peek beyond the impressive residence gates and lackluster visa offices to get an honest report of what diplomatic life is like in the world's number-one post on the verge of the millennium.

Of course, some of the fun of visiting and reporting on embassies is the feeling that you're actually in those countries when you step through their gates. The formal British butler, with expected pomp, took my coat and showed me up the rich, red-carpeted marble staircase. But the young and zealous Israeli security guards kept me in a little room for 20 minutes while their own ambassador impatiently waited for me until they were satisfied with my credentials.

Champagne and warm-from-the-oven jam cookies turned my first Swedish interview into a party, but a simple cup of Ceylon milk tea took me back to Sri Lanka, instantly. The Finns' imported smoked salmon and iced vodka always makes me wish for their sauna. Long ago, the fashion-conscious Fendi sisters first introduced me to the irresistible old-world charm of Firenze House, the Italian ambassador's residence, where there's always good wine and lots of flirting. In comparison, China's cafeteria-style buffet consists of long, long tables laden with dozens of disposable aluminum roaster pans full of Chinese specialties and "Great Wall" Chinese wine to wash it all down.

Little lamb chops and meat pies are "finger food" at New Zealand's garden party, where icy beer brings out endless "Kiwi" and "Aussie" jokes, but next door in Britain's expansive formal gardens the best French champagne and thousands of blossoms have made the quite proper and quite pricey

Queen's Birthday Party the legendary embassy party in Washington. At France's big Bastille Day bash, the huge crowd stormed the Marriott buffet tables and pulled down giant vases of red, white and blue flowers and flags for souvenirs after creating so much noise during the ambassador's long speech in French that they had to close the bars.

Other countries, like Jordan and Kuwait, never serve liquor, and nonsmokers may find it hard to breathe when Danes smoke their short but potent King cigarettes or the Lebanese or the Turks get together to celebrate and smoke. At Russian receptions, military and naval uniforms are always in abundance, and the giant German national days are full of oompahs and wursts. And, of all the embassy events I attended, the Vatican's Holy See party had noticeably the fewest women.

Differences among countries abound and that's the fun of it. But these differences—in history, wealth, power, religion, education, weather, art, music, food and formality—often create competing and conflicting styles not just in entertaining but in diplomacy. And that's what *Diplomatic Dance* is all about.

Curiously, this book has had a life of its own from the beginning. Just the title alone, *Diplomatic Dance,* intrigues and prompts ambassadors to smile, laugh and even admit their latest move on the diplomatic dance floor.

Diplomacy, the political art of negotiating between countries, has always involved intricate steps. And although the diplomatic scene in Washington remains for the most part refined and polite, today it is more complicated and convoluted than ever before. As we approach the millennium, many of the "dances" have changed dramatically and so have the partners. This is due to dynamic developments in global politics, global economics and global communications.

Political Musical Chairs

With the fall of the Berlin Wall and the end of the Cold War, the breakup of the former Soviet Union and Yugoslavia and the evolving tapestry of African nations, there are approximately 170 individual dance cards today. And, the constantly changing music keeps everyone on their toes. Even the "velvet divorce" between the Czechs and the Slovaks resulted in two ambassadors, two agendas, two embassies and two residences where once there was only one.

Although NATO is a *four-letter* word to Russia, three former Soviet Bloc members (Poland, Hungary and the Czech Republic) were ecstatic to be invited into the peace-keeping force's "circle dance" last year. That left Eastern European sisters Slovenia, Romania, Bulgaria, Slovakia, Macedonia, Croatia and the three Baltics feeling like wallflowers. They each hope to be asked to "dance" by NATO next time. But so do Caucasus and Central Asian states such as Kazakhstan, Tajikistan and Uzbekistan.

Indians and Pakistanis, Israelis and Palestinians continue to fight instead of dance while "the Emerald Tiger"of Ireland has become peaceful and a desirable economic partner. Meanwhile, Canada flirts with Cuba. Iraq threatens to crash the party. As the world's sole superpower, the United States dances in the spotlight—sometimes alone.

Surprisingly, ambassadors from some of the smallest, least-known countries often have the broadest global views. Jayantha Dhanapala, the former ambassador from Sri Lanka, a small independent island nation southeast of India with its own internal unrest, is currently the United Nation's under-secretary-general for disarmament. He chose to leave Washington's diplomatic dance to help "select the music worldwide." Ironically, now he, a Sri Lankan, is in the unusual position to cajole huge, independent India and smaller but proud Pakistan to voluntarily join the nuclear nonproliferation pact.

"It's a whole new world," admits a graying FBI agent at Germany's festive Oktoberfest. "The countries we used to call our enemies are now our friends and our old friends are the ones we're spying on now," says the senior spook who has spent his life protecting diplomats.

Ambassador Walter Cutler, who was twice U.S. Ambassador to Saudi Arabia, is currently the president of Meridian International Center, a Washington nonprofit organization that promotes international understanding through the exchange of people, ideas and the arts. He agrees that "life was simpler" during the Cold War. "We had a sense of mission then, and today, with the new diplomacy, we are still adjusting, still feeling our way."

He vividly remembers when, because of the break-up of Yugoslavia, Meridian had to quickly alter the name of an art exhibition it was circulating to American museums from "Prints of Yugoslavia" to "Prints of Former Yugoslavia."

Similarly, in 1990, Meridian facilitated a visit by a group of talented young lawyers who had come from the Soviet Union to work for several months with American law firms and judges. Before they returned home their country suddenly dissolved into a dozen new republics. "At our farewell reception," Cutler recalls, "they insisted on redesigning their own name tags, proudly taking colored crayons to draw the flags of the new countries to which they were returning but in which they had *never* officially lived. Such is the pace of change in our post–Cold War world."

Countries who used to be courting each other, dancing a waltz or a tango together (like the United States with Iraq), are not even on speaking terms any longer, much less considering each other suitable partners. Russia and the United States shrewdly suggest new steps to each other while newly independent states, like teenagers on a first date, awkwardly try out steps for the first time.

"Of course," the Russian ambassador enthusiastically agrees. "Some [countries] are doing a *tap* dance," he adds, with a chuckle and a wink. For sure, the diplomatic dance floor has never been so crowded, and the old ballroom so full of new liaisons.

ECONOMIC JITTERBUG

Mix together the Asian financial crisis, Europe's first move to a common currency, cross-border mergers like Chrysler and Mercedes, and political rumors that China is secretly seducing partners, and the tangle of global economics begins to resemble a ballroom where everyone is dancing to their own tune and no one knows exactly which new steps will be the winning combination. Yet international economic interdependency is real; foreign business wakes us up, affects our stock markets and our take-home pay.

Many of today's embassies echo the evolution in the corporate community: downsized, smaller but more efficient staffs working on slender budgets and expected to cover even more territory—especially international trade—with higher profile and bigger marketing punch. And definitely, more security. With the demise of the Cold War, embassies are often the front line of industrial espionage, seeking high-tech information so crucial to the developing economies in our rapidly changing world.

In this most prestigious and pressurized post, ambassadors in Washington work hard and play less and less. Today's top diplomats are truly on 24-hour duty for political and commercial negotiating.

"Fifty years ago, as ambassador, I wouldn't be involved in business issues at all. But now they are absolutely high on my lists," says former British ambassador Sir John Kerr. "My job is largely PR, encouraging investment, telling everyone how lively the British economy is and how open," says this high-profile ambassador who spent much of his time in the United States making economic allies on the Hill and speaking at economic conferences across the country.

Many ambassadors who are neither economists nor successful business executives privately told me they find commercial diplomacy an aspect of their job for which they aren't necessarily prepared. With the exception of a few—such as Japan's Ambassador Saito, who directed economic relations with the United States in the 1970s; Jamaica's Ambassador Bernal, who is an economist and banker; Turkmenistan's Ambassador Ugur, who went to Harvard Business School and was an active entrepreneur; and Uzbek's much-published economist, Dr. Sodyq Safaev—many of Washington's top diplomats are not formally acquainted with the business world and many were not trained as career diplomats.

In fact, many of them are scientists, doctors, lawyers or teachers, chosen by their newly independent nations because they weren't affiliated with the Communist Party or another former regime and are therefore "clean." For example, former Slovakia's former Ambassador Branislav Lichardus and his wife, Dr. Eva Kellerova, are their country's preeminent medical research scientists, and Ukrainian Ambassador Shcherbak is not only a physician but a well-known novelist. Interestingly, the diplomatic corps' former vice dean (second in seniority), Saint Lucia's former Ambassador Joseph Edmunds, is a nematologist—a scientist who studies worms. Not as odd as it sounds when you consider he was formerly chief technical advisor to the banana industry that is the economic backbone of his Caribbean island.

Communication Fast Dance

Global technology—the computer, the Internet, the satellite dish and cable news—has irreversibly changed this antique profession of envoys with dossiers and diplomatic pouches full of secrets into today's "public diplomacy" of outspoken leaders, with CNN itself as the global playing field.

"CNN is the enemy of today's ambassador," proclaims Egypt's Ahmed Maher El Sayed. "We are always behind. Often, I am awakened in the middle of the night with a call from home. I turn on CNN immediately to see what's happened while I was sleeping."

In comparison, Britain's first minister, sent to America in 1791, didn't send a dispatch home until 1793, two years later! At the time, Washington, the new capital, was considered a swampy political outpost, inferior to the "more civilized" Philadelphia.

Before House Speaker Newt Gingrich resigned, he made a major address to Georgetown University School of Foreign Service students, in which he predicted unprecedented, revolutionary changes in diplomacy over the next two generations.

He warned these students, who are "studying to someday be an ambassador," that they are "literally studying a job which will be transformed while you're studying it." Entitled "Diplomacy in the Information Age," Gingrich's speech outlined how already "secretaries of state act the way ambassadors once acted" and state governors and even city mayors "routinely lead missions across the planet" to negotiate business deals for their "constituents" back home. He suggested that everyone from the secretary of state and the president to foreign leaders and their ambassadors regularly hear it and see it first on CNN and sometimes hours, even days later through regular diplomatic channels.

In *Diplomatic Dance,* we'll discover what modern top diplomats have done to keep up with our global economy, speedy travel and instant communication to avoid becoming relics, dinosaurs—and their embassies, irrelevant and obsolete social structures between countries that serve only form, not function.

Among Washington's approximately 170 embassies, competition is fierce for trade deals, media coverage, State Department empathy, Capitol Hill connections, Pentagon attention and, most importantly, White House accessibility. Then mix ancient ties, old jealousies and new liaisons and you have another recipe for international intrigue among the countries themselves. The EU (European Union), the G8 (the United States, United Kingdom, Germany, France, Canada, Japan, Italy and Russia), the OAS (Organization of American States), the ASEAN (Association of Southeast Asian Nations), the SARC (Southeast Asian Regional Countries) and the OAU (Organization of African Unity) are only some of the well-known groups. But I also found the OECS (Organization of Eastern Caribbean States), which together rents the old Finnish Embassy, proudly flying five separate flags in front but sharing the same conference room, library, fax and copier inside.

However, my favorite new faction is the very unofficial group of a dozen or so female ambassadors who have been trying to meet as an informal support group. Secretary Albright invited them to New York when she was U.S. Ambassador to the UN but hasn't found time to do so as this country's first female secretary of state.

In *Diplomatic Dance,* I have included a huge directory (see appendix 1) that lists each foreign embassy or legation in the United States and how to contact them via mail, phone, e-mail, fax or even visit them on the World Wide Web. (Even though the United States doesn't presently have full diplomatic relations with Cuba, Iran or Iraq, they can be reached through appropriate channels.) For each country, the directory lists its location, capital city, languages, religions and currency. The date of their national day tells when each embassy celebrates its nation's independence. (Often, offices are closed on that day, and the embassy holds its biggest party of the year, much like the Fourth of July in the United States.)

The wealthier the nation the more likely it has additional consulates in other American cities to handle tourism and trade inquiries. (Webpages may one day make such offices less necessary.) Sometimes, the visa offices are in a separate location from the embassy. And just in case you need to be in direct touch with the ambassador, I have added a protocol guide to help you be polite and do it just right.

Austrian Ambassador Helmut Tuerk and Mrs. Tuerk, who have returned to Austria where he will be serving as his country's highest-ranking, nonelected public official. Photo by Marshall Cohen.

It is my hope that you will enjoy not only this tour behind the gates but that you will also keep this book around as a handy reference for future travel, business and study. As we globetrot together, we can't help but appreciate more about the rest of our world and discover how each of us can become more of a world citizen.

Some of the countries I chose to highlight are powerful, some are still struggling. Some are old friends and others are only on the newest maps. But each tells an important part of the story. For instance, Sweden's diplomats serve as major negotiators for other countries, Israel's ambassadors never wait in line and Latvia's leading man is a former Chicago marketing and PR executive who gave up his American citizenship to represent his parents' homeland. Thailand's First Couple graciously epitomize diplomatic teamwork while Macedonia's attractive single ambassador postpones her private life to fight for her country's very name. And, Croatian Americans traveled from all over America to reconstruct and decorate, by hand, their new national home on Massachusetts Avenue.

With all this competition and jockeying for position, diplomacy has become a very creative business. Ambassadors host tennis tournaments; drive cross-country to attend the national political conventions, showing their children the states on the way; help rebuild Washington's cherished C&O Canal;

lend their names and chefs for charity events; and turn their embassies and residences into art galleries and multipurpose rooms to attract attention. For example, colorful and clever banners regularly hang from the Finnish Embassy, inviting you inside to see their latest exhibit.

One ambitious ambassador, Austria's Helmut Tuerk, even "took his show on the road" to 50 states and all U.S. territories and had a two-story-high teepee from Montana's Chickasaw Nation in his backyard to prove it.

"When you're from a small country it's hard to get attention," says former Ambassador Turek, who reasons, "The large countries get attention because of their size and sheer weight. And countries causing problems get attention for other reasons. We have no ambition to join the list of troublemakers, so we must make contacts in other ways."

As a "marriage broker" for Austria's myriad small businesses, this indefatigable diplomat knew every state's governor, business leaders and Native American tribal chiefs. He no longer had to wait in line at the State Department or Commerce Department for help. In addition, when he went to Capitol Hill his colorful memories enabled him to chat with each congressional leaders about their home state's wonders: fly fishing in Idaho, mountain biking in Colorado, crawfish eating in Louisiana or lobster trapping in Maine.

In Washington, the steady stream of social functions still require white tie, black tie and the signature diplomatic dark-blue suit or silk dress. "Casual" or "lounge suit" only means "not black-tie." But the era of grand balls, high tea for the ladies and leisurely tennis is giving way to smaller "working" dinner parties and working nights and weekends for conscientious ambassadors.

The former dean for 25 years of the oldest and largest school of international relations, Georgetown University School of Foreign Service, Peter Krogh says that even with today's belt-tightening, social entertaining by "attractive and effective diplomatic couples" can still be highly influential "in shaping international perspectives." He adds, "The information age notwithstanding, that role is still there to be played by diplomatic couples capable and determined enough to seize upon it."

"When I took up the deanship," he continues, "there was a handful of ambassadors who stood out … and who exerted significant influence in the nation's capital. Their prominence and effect were a direct function of the personal and professional qualities—and utter devotion to duty: Ashraf and Amal Ghorbal of Egypt, Berndt and Wendy von Staden of the Federal Republic of Germany and Willy and Ulla Wachtmeister of Sweden. The power of these husband-and-wife teams was formidable. Their embassies created salons which figured centrally in the development of foreign policy in Washington." To Dean Krogh, such "stars" today are Helmut and Monica Tuerk, for whom the size of their country is disproportionate to the influence they wield—by virtue of their skill—in the nation's capital.

Ambassador Cutler of the Meridian International Center agrees that "personalities count in diplomacy" so much that an ambassador or a spouse alone, by virtue of their personality, energy and creativity can become popular and gain precious access to powerful people in Washington. "Hence, even an ambassador who represents a country with relatively little clout on the global scene can gain access, and access is the name of the game."

While the trend is away from the lavish embassy parties of the past, many countries still feel the need to buy expensive Washington mansions or build new embassies to make their presence better known. And old "Embassy Row" on long, dramatic Massachusetts Avenue can no longer accommodate the new countries and all the new buildings. Major national bunkers hunker down near Intelsat over on International Drive in Upper Northwest Washington, D.C. There you'll find Israel, Ghana, Jordan, Bahrain, Kuwait, Singapore, Austria, Egypt and, as this book goes to press, Bangladesh and Brunei are building there. Germany and Russia sit atop their own separate hilltops while passersby and architectural critics debate their façades.

France, unsurprisingly, sits alone in a gated sylvan setting in upper Georgetown, while the Canadians enjoy their monumental view of America's ceremonial Pennsylvania Avenue. Ironically, the wealthy Saudis chose a former insurance building across from the Watergate complex and near the Kennedy Center rather than build their own. (It is said they wanted the marble building mostly for its deep, secret vaults.)

Meanwhile, back on Massachusetts Avenue, the Finns are still relishing their green glass house—an architectural curiosity, the epitome of today's "public diplomacy" and one of the few new embassies built recently on old Embassy Row. As I write this, down the hill just off Massachusetts Avenue on Whitehaven Road, the Italians are crafting their spectacular palazzo and the Turks are moving in across from Japan. Georgetown has become home for the Royal Thai Embassy while the big Ukrainian Consulate sits near picturesque Key Bridge on M Street. Macedonia and Venezuela rent Georgetown office space down by the Potomac, but dreams of a new Royal Swedish landmark on the riverfront floated away when popular Swedish Ambassador Henrik Liljegren left for Turkey.

In writing *Diplomatic Dance,* discovering distinguishing features of each country and its ambassador was a goal, along with discussing the effects of global trends on this ancient profession. Politics is the obvious topic, but I often found ambassadors relieved and delighted to discuss almost anything else. At the beginning of my research, Japan's Ambassador Saito was happy to talk about Japan's economic successes, but upon my return after the Asian financial crisis hit Japan, he had a much less rosy picture. However, he was proud that Japan didn't have to "downsize" its embassy staff the way other Southeast Asian countries were forced to do.

During interviews with the ambassadors and their families and staffs, I tried to move the conversation beyond the "country line" and latest crisis or conflict into a more private discussion of what their daily business and private lives were really like. I was looking for their answers to the universal human problems: finding their way back to former professions; facing retirement or a move to a lesser, unexciting post; balancing parenthood and career; keeping and making friends while relocating often; creating a private life in a public profession; staying up-to-date, but not exhausted, with today's instantaneous information overload; finding time and ways to relax and exercise; and, especially for the female high-ranking diplomats, dealing with sexism and power plays of a formerly all-male bastion while deciding whether to date or not. To my delight, the ambassadors often surprised me with their candor, warmth and humor.

Diplomatic Dance has given me an exciting three years. I hope you have as much fun and learn as much as I have. For where else in America can you dress up and go on a whirlwind trip around the world in just one night? It is like the Concorde without the jet lag.

So fasten your seat belt and welcome aboard—and don't forget your dancing shoes.

DIPLOMATIC DANCE

1

The United Kingdom of Great Britain and Northern Ireland: Still the Standard

Arriving at the British Embassy, everything is just as it should be—in perfect order and in complete control. Over the phone, the ambassador's social secretary, Amanda Downes, had told me which entrance to go to. At the side gate, Derek Hexley, the jolly security guard, congratulates me on my old governor green Jaguar and tells me exactly where to park—in the special place reserved just for Ambassador and Lady Kerr's private guests.

As I enter the porte-cochere, John Shand, the butler, is there to open the door at exactly the right moment and take my coat. No need to knock and stand in the cold. He leads me up the impressive twin staircase, carpeted red, and at the top, Amanda Downes meets me and shows me into the ambassador's morning room, where Lady Kerr greets me in front of a perfectly made fire. She is wearing a mint-green skirt and sweater with matching cardigan, pearls and a warm smile. The butler offers tea just before the ambassador, Sir John Kerr, KCMG, Her Majesty's Ambassador to the United States, enters with just a bit of flourish, and we all sink down into the chintz-covered sofas across from each other, making perfectly polite small talk about the weather and the sprinkle of snow outside. The stage is set.

The reporter in me is trying hard not to be too charmed but, as an American, it is hard to resist feeling like a walk-on in Masterpiece Theatre's *Upstairs, Downstairs.*

The first thing I notice about this otherwise ever-so-proper ambassador is how he doesn't sit up straight and instead lounges on the sofa, leaning way back as if he were about to take a nap. The mother in me wants to tell him to sit up straight. Maybe he's doing it just to distract me. If so, it works. Throughout our 45-minute interview he remains in this almost prone position while everything else about him appears perfect: his handsome hand-stitched pinstripe, his nicely starched pink shirt, his pink-and-grey rep tie, and his impressive Oxford cuff links on his natty French cuffs.

He lights the first of many cigarettes and the interview begins.

"My job, as I see it, is not to mess it up," he says only half jokingly. "Britain and America have a very good relationship with very deep history, so there's not much damage that could be done even by the most incompetent." The doctor's oath, "try not to do any harm," is his guide. "I tiptoe cautiously," he says.

He speaks very quickly, often emphasizing an important point by stopping to smoke, taking his hand away in a royal swirl. Lady Kerr, in the meantime, sits quietly, listening and leafing through their family album, which she brought to show me.

Washington is not new to this career diplomat and his family. After first posts in Russia and Pakistan, Sir John's work on NATO and other defense issues often brought him to Washington over the next fifteen years. And from 1984 to 1987, he and his family lived in the U.S. capital when he was head of chancery and politico-military counselor. In 1990, after another stint in London, he served as Britain's permanent representative to the European Union in Brussels. The "KCMG" after his name stands for Knight Commander, Order of St. Michael and St. George.

We sit beneath a handsome portrait of "Monty," as Sir John refers to British war hero Field Marshall George Montgomery, the Viscount Montgomery of Alamein. It was painted by President Dwight Eisenhower, the supreme commander of European Allied Forces in World War II and Montgomery's contemporary. Another American, Walter Annenberg, U.S. ambassador to the Court of St. James, gave it to the British Embassy. Ambassador Kerr rescued the portrait from upstairs where it was hanging in the private quarters, because he thinks it "nicely symbolizes" the close relationship between the two countries.

Even though the Americans and the British were once archenemies, Ambassador Kerr sees three main ties that continually keep us together. "First, is our common language. Our silly British sense of humor is a wonderful weapon and even though you don't understand it, you still like it," he says with a glint in his eye. Next, of course, is "our military, defense relationship ever since Churchill and Roosevelt were really pretty close. And, now our economic ties." I remember him telling me earlier, "When the chips are down, we know we'll be there for each other."

"We are the biggest foreign investor in the United States, more than 130 billion dollars. London is the world's banking center. There are more American banks in London than in New York. BP, Standard Oil of Ohio, MCI,

Former British Ambassador Sir John Kerr and Lady Kerr in the residence garden. Photo by Didi Cutler.

Holiday Inn, Burger King, Brooks Brothers, Seven-Eleven, and Dunkin' Donuts are British. And if we can do Dunkin' Donuts, we can do anything."

We all laugh and take a sip of tea.

"Fifty years ago, as ambassador, I wouldn't be involved in business issues at all. But now they are absolutely high on my list." Washington is the largest of the twelve British posts in America that this modern diplomatic manager oversees. If he's in town, he's usually on Capitol Hill about two days a week. But many weeks he spends several days on the road visiting the other posts and speaking at business conferences, colleges and universities, and to major newspaper editorial boards as well as doing interviews on radio and TV. "People are very kind, and if you are the British ambassador you get a platform. With the snow coming down, I think I'll be giving a lot of speeches in Texas." We all laugh.

"The queen and the government want us to do this, spread the word. My job is largely PR [public relations], encouraging investment, telling everyone how lively the British economy is and how open. If an American businessman needs to establish their business in one place in the European Union, they can go to fifteen different countries from England, reaching three hundred and seventy million people. We're the best and the cheapest for any telecommunications. The English advantage is that we are by far the most open, London is the biggest capital market. Plus, we have wonderful food and amazing weather," he says, smiling.

"My main job is on the Hill," says the seasoned ambassador, who admits to being "fascinated" by our Congress, which he monitors on C-Span and the Sunday political interview shows.

"Our first British minister, sent to the U.S. in 1791, didn't send his first dispatch until 1793 and that was a description of the American people and what makes them tick." With today's worldwide news coverage and the technology explosion, the home office knows about foreign events as soon as ambassadors do. "We look for the news behind the news, the analysis. We are here to spot a trend, sometimes even before you do."

To this ambassador, not surprisingly, "form" is important in diplomacy. "There are rules of business, and we shouldn't bother the cabinet level if it can be solved at a lower level. Our embassy team has to be very good to get posted here," suggesting that his staff "clears away" most day-to-day matters. "When a diplomat asks to see top people, we are not coming to pass the time of day. We are not here to waste great men's time."

Lady Kerr, an Oxford graduate like her husband and the daughter of an Olympic athlete who was a Rhodes scholar and a Wiltshire schoolmaster, has now been through her picture album several times, intermittently nodding nicely. I am anxious to include her more in our conversation and talk about how she's made what's been called "Washington's second most important address" feel like home. "Brussels was a home," she says honestly of their previous post. "This is more like a hotel."

"But," the ambassador diplomatically adds, "this clever design, with the building having been built sideways onto Massachusetts Avenue, creates the illusion that it's much smaller than it really is and you feel like you're out in the country." He gestures widely, "especially out there on the terrace in April."

She adds, "We've seen all sorts of birds and little animals, including a baby fox and an opossum."

Later, Kerry Blockley, the gardener—or chief horticulturist as he's officially titled—tells me the difficulty of dealing with each new ambassador and wife who want to put "their own footprint" on the vast garden, which itself is one-half the size of the residence. According to Blockley, at least the Kerrs are easy to please, because "they want to hear the mower going and don't mind us working while they're sitting on the terrace, unlike the last ambassador who didn't want to hear or see any work being done"—a difficult request with eight acres that need constant manicuring.

Besides the embassy being their home, "this is a public house as well," Sir John explains. There are hundreds of overnight guests each year who are cared for by the residence staff of 21 employees. Houseguests include not only

The author, Sir John Kerr and the late Princess Diana at the American Red Cross Land Mines Event. Photo courtesy of the American Red Cross.

members of the royal family but cabinet ministers and senior members of Parliament. Prince Philip, Princess Margaret, Prince Andrew and even Prince Charles would stay upstairs across the hall from Ambassador and Lady Kerr's bedroom, but her royal majesty would never sleep here. The queen would stay at Blair House, America's "best guesthouse," located across the street from the White House, because if she were here, it would be for an official state visit.

The late Princess of Wales, after her royal breakup with Prince Charles, preferred to stay down the street at the Brazilian residence with her good friend, Lucia Flecha de Lima, the wife of the Brazilian ambassador. However, the much beloved "People's Princess" would lunch at the embassy and adored having Sir John as her "official" escort. He always joked, "I'm the guy with the Rolls Royce."

"People like to come here," the ambassador says understatedly.

"This is a venue for British and American events, fundraisers." This grand residence, built in 1928 and designed by Britain's renowned architect Sir Edwin Lutyens, welcomes 15,000 visitors a year. It was originally designed to be both home and office for the British, but in the late 1950s, the offices were transferred to a new modern brick building next door, where 500 staffers work today, making it the largest embassy in Washington. Britain was the first foreign country to build, rather than buy, a residence and the first to build "way out" on Massachusetts Avenue.

However, for more than one hundred years, as their official press release reminds, "Great Britain did not consider her former American colonies worthy of more than a legation."

Today, the Brits own 71 houses and apartments and rent 34 others in and around Washington for their top diplomats and military officers. Accommodation officer Ruth Vitrikas, her assistant and a "technical works group" numbering about twenty do everything from redecorating and furnishing to painting and mowing the lawns. Senior diplomats may bring along a favorite piece of furniture or their own artwork, but otherwise they have the luxury of traveling with only their suitcases to this prestigious post.

The Embassy of the United Kingdom of Great Britain and Northern Ireland, as it is officially called, has its own theater group, store, fitness club, pub with dart board and bar, soccer and softball teams and tennis tournament on the ambassador's private court.

Around Washington, it often has been said that many diplomats don't take advantage of being in America and instead insulate and isolate themselves by working and socializing only within their own embassy. The bigger the embassy, the easier it is to do just that. Of course, in this embassy they at least joke about the differences amongst themselves. For instance, the ambassador is a Scot, Lady Kerr is Irish and the gardener is a "Kiwi" from New Zealand.

Without a doubt, the most coveted invitation in Washington diplomatic circles is the Queen's Birthday Party, now held not every year but usually once during each ambassador's tenure. This expensive June garden party (some say it costs $50,000) has become the elegant swan song for the departing British ambassador. For ladies, it's a great excuse to buy a fancy summer hat.

But when the guests are gone, be they royal or commoner, what happens here in these ceremonial corridors under the watchful eyes of King George III and Queen Mary? Surprisingly, it's not too different a private family scene than next door at the vice president's house.

"When the twins are here," Lady Kerr begins, "we have twenty year olds pouring in and out. Alison and Felicity are now studying abroad at Oxford and St. Andrews but went to Annunciation, a private Catholic high school here, when the ambassador served as head of chancery and politico-military counselor from 1984 to '87. Having the twins visit puts us back in touch with all their old friends and their parents, our PTA friends. It's a small circle of friends that are no way official." Two of their other three children live in London. David is married and teaches history at London University and Catherine is an English teacher. James, the eldest, is a solicitor (lawyer) who lives with his French wife in Brussels.

Lady Kerr says she "felt embarrassed" because they kept the house staff so busy when they were in Geneva and all five children were there with all their friends. But with the current "empty nest," she says, "our favorite thing to do is to not make a plan, not dress up and maybe sneak out to a movie or dinner alone." "We don't even take the driver," pipes in the ambassador. "I drive."

"We love the big screen and we're suckers for American movies, especially Hitchcock and Woody Allen." I ask him if that means the British ambassador can hide in the dark of an American movie theater wearing jeans. "Oh, no, an ambassador can't wear jeans," he retorts. "I just wear an old pair of soft cords."

Throughout this afternoon interview, I am struck by how friendly and funny they are and how much they make me feel at home. So, I ask how they met.

"In a library," she starts.

"I thought she looked nice and we just smiled," he adds. "Two years later I met her again at the foreign office. Cautious, we Brits," he whispers jokingly.

"He was still in university writing his doctorate and when we married, I got canned," she remembers, explaining how back then both husband and wife couldn't work for the foreign office.

For exercise, he's a "compulsive golfer" who wants "to play the next day again if all goes well." But he is too busy to play here and after all, "As a Scotsman, I prefer St. Andrews. I grew up playing that course." So here, he plays tennis on their private court and they both love their "healthy walks" in Rock Creek Park.

I ask if they feel safe walking around Washington. "We love to wander about, we feel at home here," she says. They seem safer here than in Brussels where they were tightly guarded. "My bodyguard in Brussels shot himself in the foot," Sir John says, making a funny face.

The ambassador graciously excuses himself to go back to work and, even though the butler reappears with my coat, Lady Kerr remembers that I requested a tour and a chance to see the rooms decorated by the late and well-known English designer, Laura Ashley.

As we walk down the striking black-and-white marble hall, the butler places himself just out of sight, tailing us a little like a good private eye. Lady Kerr first shows me how she arranges the ornate but airy ballroom to be "cozier for teas" but has the sofas moved and the mammoth oriental rug rolled up to create a dance floor for their more elaborate dinner parties.

"We love to entertain," she explains, laughing and shrugging her shoulders as she admits that the embassy's 82-year-old comptroller is correct when he says, "the Kerrs have gone overbudget with their dinners and dancing."

(She decides on the menus with the Scottish chef, Japanese sou-chef and the kindly comptroller, who regularly suggests fish instead of meat and lunches instead of dinners to keep costs down.)

Next, she shows me the charming breakfast room where they can watch the birds over breakfast or dine by candlelight together. Across the hall, the long, formal dining room is breathtaking. The 34 dusty-rose leather chairs, each with the "E II R" royal cipher in gold, make the sparkling chandeliers, huge marble fireplace, long line of elaborate candlesticks and famous flora wall prints seem even more regal.

Overlooking the gardens is the comfortable and expansive drawing room with sofas and chairs arranged "just so" in planned sitting areas. When I mention that this is the room I thought Laura Ashley decorated, the butler comes closer with my coat. I get ready to thank Lady Kerr for the private tour and say good-bye.

But Lady Kerr sends the butler away, again, to my amazement and his disapproval. (The butler shakes his head as he gives up and leaves my coat over a chair.) We head up the spiral staircase to their private quarters. There, where the carpets are thick and the drapes descend into dramatic puddles, she takes me through their elaborately decorated blue-and-white bedroom suite, which Laura Ashley *did* decorate, and which Lady Kerr thinks is "a little too fussy for my husband."

I realize I'm feeling embarrassed to be in the room with the ambassador's slippers and robe, reading glasses and bedtime book (I couldn't read the cover). But she is Lady Kerr, the wife of the British ambassador and she, of all people, knows what's proper! After all, I did ask to see the rooms Laura Ashley decorated.

Anyway, I was delighted with Lady Kerr's openness and straightforward approach. Of all the embassies in Washington, the British embassy is the last place I ever imagined having such an intimate glimpse into the ambassador's private quarters.

Lady Kerr talks about how different it is being in Washington "this" time. "Before, I had no staff and lots of dinner guests so I spent a lot of time cooking and grocery shopping." (One of the last things she did before leaving the embassy was to say good-bye to her favorite butchers at the local Giant and Safeway grocery stores.)

As we cross the hall upstairs, Zouzou, the eldest of their four cats (the other three are back in London) watches me carefully. Like the butler downstairs, she too isn't so sure I should be snooping around. Lady Kerr shows me the comfortable suite where Prince Andrew stays and the other formal bedroom suites named after former British ambassadors.

When it comes to her children's bedrooms, I detect wistfulness in this mother of five, whose nest is empty for the first time in decades. As mothers, we chat about not affairs of state but the state of affairs in which our children leave their rooms. The twin girls, away at college, left the typical telltale signs of real life. A stuffed Snoopy, odd pens and pencils and papers on their desks, and in their closets, abandoned paintbrushes and paint boxes amid other leftovers. The funny thing is that Lady Kerr was so warm and down-to-earth that I almost forgot I was upstairs in Britain's imposing diplomatic palace.

As we return to the official reception rooms, we pass by an 1837 coronation portrait of 18-year-old Queen Victoria and then the antique banner of William IV (1830–1837). But of all the impressive portraits and pictures I see throughout the afternoon, one snapshot means the most to me: daughter Alison, dressed in jeans, playing the baby grand piano in her barefeet—the epitome of what it's really like to live with teenagers in an embassy.

The butler reappears, and as Lady Kerr and I say good-bye, I descend the grand staircase feeling like I've just visited a good friend, hoping I haven't overstayed my welcome and having enjoyed every moment.

* * *

The next time I return to the British residence, the butler and Amanda are still there but the ambassador and his wife are not only new, they are *newly* wed and absolutely the "hottest" diplomatic couple in town.

The Meyers met in Germany when he was ambassador there, married six months later in the hip section of Chelsea in London, and arrived in Washington the very next day as the honeymoon couple: Sir Christopher Meyer, KCMG, and Lady Meyer. "It could have been a disaster," she leans over and whispers to me confidentially. "We have two strong personalities."

The Washington Post immediately gave these young Brits all the credit for making "boring old embassy parties sexy again" and the November 1998 issue of *Vogue* magazine annointed them just plain "sexy" in their feature story. It is not hard to see why.

He always wears bright red socks with his tuxedo, often escapes the British compound wearing jeans in search of juicy American hamburgers and doesn't mind showing Washington how much fun a modern Brit can be.

At 55, this father of three boys "read history" at Cambridge and spent a year at the Johns Hopkins Nitze School of Advanced International Studies in Bologna, Italy, and a sabbatical year as a visiting fellow at Harvard's Center for International Affairs. A career diplomat like his predecessor, Sir John Kerr, Sir Christopher has served in Her Majesty's foreign service in Moscow, Madrid,

Brussels, Washington (as deputy chief of mission) and Bonn. In between posts, he worked in London as the head of the Soviet section, was a speechwriter to three foreign secretaries and, more recently, government spokesman and press secretary to former British Prime Minister John Major.

Lady Meyer wears short skirts and high heels, has an irresistible effervescence and doesn't blink about rearranging the residence's furniture or flowers if they don't suit. "You know," she says, "I have French blood and maybe this is why I am so conscious of presentation."

Carrying both British and French passports, Lady Meyer was educated in London at the French Lycee, speaks five languages and has a B.A. from the School of Slavonic and East European Studies. She has financial expertise as a former top account executive with Merrill Lynch, E. F. Hutton and San Paulo Bank in London.

Obviously, neither of them is all fashion and frolic. Lady Meyer, mother of two young teenage boys now aged 11 and 13, is engaged in the battle of her life to gain access to her sons following their abduction by their German father, a physician, in July 1994. The Meyers' storybook romance started in April 1997 when she went to Sir Christopher, then Britain's ambassador to Germany, to seek his help in this heartbreaking situation.

My interview was to be with both of them, but ever-efficient and gracious Amanda called ahead to say the ambassador may not be able to make it but still to come anyway. I am escorted out onto the spacious terrace, which is really the front of the house and overlooks the vast garden. Lady Meyer appears looking casually chic in tight pants and a black turtleneck, but with a limp. Her ankle is wrapped. It seems she got hurt at the embassy's own tennis tounament.

I tell her I find it hard to talk about anything else until we discuss her continuing battle for her sons. She agrees and lights the first of several cigarettes. "It is outrageous," says this mother caught in an agonizing situation. "I have had almost no normal contact with my sons since they were abducted four and a half years ago. Two hours one time was the longest. I have seen them a total of eleven hours altogether, and these visits were always in the presence of a third party. For two years, I didn't see them at all."

She has exhausted every option and has spent over $200,000 in the process. The birthday and holiday presents she sends probably never reaches them. "When I call, his [her ex-husband's] girlfriend answers the phone and says they are not there." The few times she has been able to talk to her sons, "they were tense, sounded terrified and would answer only 'Yes' or 'No.' Alexander [the older one] always tells me to speak German with him."

"I still have nightmares," says this mother, admitting that she can't decide if it's worse if she dreams they are all together again, only to wake up and

Newlyweds British Ambassador Sir Christopher Meyer and Lady Meyer on their wedding day. Photo courtesy of Lady Meyer.

find out her boys are not there or if she has nightmares of what her sons are going through without her, not understanding why she is not there.

"A year before I met Christopher all of my friends started gathering together and said, 'Catherine, you know you have to start living again. Otherwise, you will destroy yourself and when your children finally get to see you, you will want to be strong and healthy for them.' I think I sort of made an effort and maybe I was already a tiny bit ready to start living. But meeting Christopher was the last thing I expected and I certainly never thought I would remarry."

I ask how she handles having this happy new life of social prominence and luxury in contrast to the excruciating memory of her boys being so far away and not knowing if she will ever see them again. "It helps me to be busy, because it forces me to take my mind off the case," she says, gesturing out at the garden and back around to the new home. "I would say that for years the only thing I did was fight for my children by writing letters, sending faxes, lobbying and writing a book [*Two Children Behind a Wall: The True Story of a Family Torn Apart,* by Catherine Laylle]. The first three [years] were one hundred percent consumed with this. I did nothing else: I wouldn't go out in the evening and if I did I went out [only] with friends who knew about my story and we would be talking about my case."

As upset and sad as she can get, today Lady Meyer is hopeful at least that other children might be spared the traumatic experience of being separated from one of their parents in such a cruel way. "Four years ago nobody knew about child abduction. Now, the issue is more widely known and there is a certain awareness at the government level," says this mother, who just testified before the U.S. Congress about international abductions of children.

I ask her if being the wife of the British ambassador gives her added access to power, greater publicity for her plight, and helpful visibility for the issue in general. "Yes and no," she begins. "It works two ways. It is a two-edged situation: on one hand, it opens doors for me and the fact that I'm the British ambassador's wife obviously helps me to raise public awareness on this issue. For example, the National Center for Missing and Exploited Children approached me several months ago, and we are working together.

"But, on the other hand, you also have many more restrictions. For instance, two years ago, I was demonstrating with other French parents in front of the German Embassy because France has the biggest problem with Germany because it is its border country."

"Of course, I can't do those things today," she adds. "So I would say that being married to an ambassador has helped me with regards to the issue but definitely not to my personal case."

I ask her what happens when she sees German Ambassador Juergen Chrobog and his wife. "As wife of another ambassador I feel it would be wrong for me to bring up the issue. But, of course, if they do first, I would appreciate the opportunity to discuss it. So far, that hasn't happened.

"England has the best record," she says proudly, in returning children to their country of habitual residence, and she wishes all countries would comply with The Hague Convention. "In Britain the system works well. Parents get legal aid; cases are heard at the High Court, where only seventeen judges have been especially trained to handle these international cases."

In addition, Lady Meyer is happy that her book is being updated and reprinted (retitled *They Are My Children, Too: A Mother's Struggle for Her Sons,* by Catherine Meyer, foreword by Sally Quinn [New York: Public Affairs, 1999]) because she hopes more and more people will realize how unprotected children are *and* how unprotected parents are. "For instance, when I married a German national, I had no idea that German family law would be so different from the U.S., the English and the French."

Finally, we both agree to change the subject, and I ask her what she finds different between the English and the Americans. "Our humor I suppose," she says, laughing and throwing her head back like a carefree colt. I am impressed that she can still laugh so easily. "The first time in New York together, my husband made a speech in front of fifty men when I was present. He started the speech by making fun of me but only one person laughed—me! They didn't realize he was just teasing me."

As far as work, "People here work constantly, they don't seem to take weekends off, they have less time to themselves. In England and in Europe, weekends are still sacred. But then, this is why maybe your economy is doing so well."

Before arriving here, Lady Meyer "rang up" Amanda and asked her what to bring. "She told me to bring long gowns, but I only had one, it's green, and that's all I brought." As for the rest of it, "I've learned to be myself. I love sitting next to interesting people and in this job we meet so many fascinating people. At first, I was shy but if I have an opinion, now I say it.

"Here, perceptions of the British can sometimes be old fashioned," she adds. "Some think of Britain as a land of beefeaters and tea at four. But we also are leading in pharmaceuticals, software, aerospace and research. We're outgoing and lots of people in power are younger than me," she says. "Tony Blair's just forty-five."

As we stand to part, I thank her for her time and ask if she will continue to wear the short skirts for which she is already famous in Washington. Kicking her leg up, forgetting for a moment that she's supposed to be nursing that ankle, she replies, "I like them and I might as well wear them short as long as I can."

* * *

Several days later, I have an appointment with Sir Christopher. I'm instructed to park next to a back door of the chancery marked specifically for the ambassador's guests. A staffer appears and lets me in the back way, taking me on a very unceremonial route to the ambassador's office. Sir Christopher greets me warmly, in his shirtsleeves and wearing his security ID tag around his neck. (He was the only ambassador I met who wore his badge like all the other embassy staffers.) I decide to break the ice by asking what color socks he had on and if the colors were a kind of "signal" like Secretary Albright's broaches. We laugh together as I jot down, "No signal, yellow tie and yellow socks" and sit down in his spacious but unpretentious office where artwork from his sons mixes with the formal pictures of famous Brits and Yankees standing side by side.

I ask him what it was like to arrive in Washington with a new post *and* a new wife. "Like standing on the top of a high dive, closing your eyes, holding your nose and you *leap* out into space and you crash into the water and you sink or swim," he says, laughing. "We had no big doubts, but every once in a while we look back and think, 'My God, we must have been crazy!'"

Already I know this is not going to be a boring interview with this career diplomat, who was a "foot soldier" in Britain's Moscow embassy with his Washington predecessor, Sir John Kerr.

"Over the last 32 years in the foreign office I've seen a lot of changes in style and substance. Everything is much less formal and rigid than it used to be, but you have to adjust to your post."

I ask what differences he sees between being an ambassador in Germany, his last post for just seven months before the foreign office asked him to repack his bags for the United States. "Germany was more formal, certainly in Bonn you found an older style. Berlin will change things radically."

"But I've always had my own style, always liked a public style and enjoyed speaking and dealing with the media," admits this former press secretary. "Catherine is my best critic." He explains how much she helped during their first nine-month "road show," a 14-city public diplomacy campaign. "She tells me if I'm talking too long or scratching my head too much."

Obviously, he loves talking about his new partner. "On a personal level, I depend on her. We pool information together between us and operate as a partnership. Professionally, the job is so demanding that two doing it is a damn sight easier than one. And thirdly, precisely because she has never been a foreign service wife, she brings new insights and new experiences that I find her advice and intuition invaluable.

"Every Monday I have a big staff meeting with every section of the embassy, maybe twenty to thirty people. I brought her to the first meeting I chaired; I wanted to make a very clear statement that she was my equal and was to be treated that way—it was the first time it had ever been done."

Sir Christopher, who admits that his wife handles all their personal finances because "I haven't a clue!" also says her financial experience is "helpful" to him at the office. He boasts that whether or not Britain later decides to join the EMU, as many of its "continental cousins" already have, "the City of London will remain the greatest center of the Euro market."

As for Britian's "devolution," making Northern Ireland, Scotland and Wales more autonomous, "We've got a new frontier before us—we are changing the balance of the British constitution in a way that hasn't been changed in several hundred years, by pushing power and responsibility down to the regions. … These reforms and changes take us into uncharted waters but the effect should be overwhelmingly positive. It's going to rejuvenate the democratic spirit of the regions and we shouldn't be afraid of this."

He calls the latest peace in Northern Ireland "an inspiration" to others around the world who have been "laboring for decades" to find an end to bloodshed and terror. "Sustained, concentrated effort at the very highest level—

British prime minister, American president, Irish prime minister—can deliver and that it's worth taking risks for peace.

"Fundamental things can change at the grassroots, which makes political solutions easier to arrive at," Sir Christopher explains. He lists two important ingredients for the Irish peace: "People were sick to death of the violence" and "the enormous rise in the prosperity in the Republic of Ireland."

I ask this father of three boys (from a former marriage) about Lady Meyer's continuing battle for her children. "It was her problem which brought us together. So I went into this marriage with my eyes wide open. It is incredibly frustrating that in this time we've been married, we don't really seem to make any progress at all [with the access issue]. In some ways, that fact that she's married to the British ambassador, not just an ordinary British citizen, may well have made the thing harder, not easier to resolve. Because I think that at the other end, in Germany, this has probably set up a kind of resistance even greater than before to do the decent thing.

"I think Catherine does have to be careful what she says. … I think she has to choose the right moment when to go public and when to stay quiet, and I have to as well. At the end of the day when you cut away all the diplomatic niceities, and you get down to the heart of the issue: four and a half years after her children were abducted, she has never been allowed to be alone with them. No judicial system in the world can claim that is a delivery of justice, and I feel very strongly about it."

Sir Christopher says that his wife has always been told, "This is a matter for the courts, and the government can't interfere with the courts. And I don't particularly want to engage the German ambassador and be told that again."

To conclude, Sir Christopher and I review the *diplomatic dance* on the verge of the new millennium. "The music has changed enormously," he begins. "Although we, the United Kingdom, have a wonderfully close relationship with the United States, which is sometimes called 'a special relationship,' I say to my staff: 'Don't use that phrase too much, because it suggests that we don't have to work on the relationship.' There are many, many people operating in the U.S. market, and we have to work like everyone else.'"

I ask this veteran diplomat what changes he has personally witnessed in diplomacy, in this capital city and his other recent posts. "In Washington, you're not so much a diplomat, you're a lobbyist."

To Sir Christopher there are "three things that have transformed the profession. First, it's very hard now to draw the line now between what is foreign policy and what is domestic policy. Second, it is very hard to draw the line between what is political and what is economic, and, in fact, you shouldn't try to do it. And, thirdly, the enormous exponential increase in multilateral diplomacy alongside bilateral diplomacy.

"Plus," he adds, "the fact is that the media—the public searchlight—is brighter than it's ever been before. We should not be afraid of it. We should use it to our advantage."

According to this top diplomat whose wife often travels with her laptop, the future of diplomacy will change even more with the use of more and more communication technology. "We're babies in the proper use of information technology."

* * *

Sir John Kerr is currently permanent under-secretary, Foreign and Commonwealth Office. He and Lady Kerr are enjoying being back in London.

2

Brazil: Not Just Soccer and Samba

The first time I met Brazilian Ambassador Paulo-Tarso Flecha de Lima and his wife, Lucia Flecha de Lima, it was June 17, 1997, at the high-profile American Red Cross fundraiser for land mines victims. Princess Diana, looking radiant in a long red beaded dress, was the featured speaker and everyone was thrilled to be in her presence.

The Flecha de Limas were sitting with Princess Diana at the circular head table in the midst of the glittering black-tie gala. The princess had come to Washington hoping, along with then American Red Cross President Elizabeth Dole, to embarrass President Clinton into signing the International Land Mines Accord, which Canada had already convinced more than 75 countries to sign.

During her stay in Washington, however, Princess Diana was not staying at the stately British residence. Instead, she was visiting her "best friend" in Washington, Lucia Flecha de Lima, wife of the Brazilian ambassador, just two doors down Massachusetts Avenue at their handsome home.

Sir John Kerr, the British Ambassador and Princess Diana's official escort for the evening, graciously introduced me to the princess. We chatted about the handsome, engraved silver jewelry box that she had brought from London to be auctioned off that night. The enthusiastic princess asked me to keep her posted on the bids. The heavy, velvet-lined box, handmade and stamped by the queen's jeweler, was engraved on the domed top in the princess's own script, "With my love, Diana, June 1997."

Before I left their table, I met Ambassador and Mrs. Flecha de Lima and we talked about my book and doing an interview together. I told them that I wanted Brazil, the largest Latin American country, to have its own chapter and that I had heard their story was especially interesting. I was to call for an appointment soon after they returned from Brazil at the end of the summer.

But on August 30, two and a half months after we were all together in Washington, everything changed. Princess Diana, the People's Princess, beloved by the British and literally millions, perhaps even billions, of people around the world, was killed in a horrific car accident in a Paris tunnel along with her friend Dodi Fayed, and their driver that night, Henri Paul.

I learned the news late that night when my mother called from Florida and told me to turn on CNN because something unbelievable had happened to the princess. Like everyone else who watched the late-breaking news that Friday night and throughout the weekend, I saw pictures of Mrs. Flecha de Lima, with a scarf covering her head and dark sunglasses covering her eyes, rushing to catch a plane to Paris. She left immediately after learning of her dear friend's death. Understandably shaken, she was devastated by the sudden loss of her young friend.

And still to this day, Mrs. Flecha de Lima, Princess Diana's loyal friend in Washington, does not grant interviews and no longer speaks to the media. Since Princess Diana's death, the Brazilian Embassy has been inundated with hundreds of interview requests but the embassy staff knows the answer—"No." Only once has Lucia Flecha de Lima granted an interview since Princess Diana's death. She agreed to be part of *Diana: The True Story,* a major commemorative television program orchestrated by Sir Richard Attenborough, which aired on PBS the eve of the first anniversary of the princess's death.

Because I had heard the stories about Mrs. Flecha de Lima's inaccessibility, I asked her husband, the ambassador, to intervene for me. He said he would. But finally, months later, after asking her several times, he said even he could not change her mind.

In Brazil, however, she still does interviews. Ironically, just a few days before the princess's tragic accident, Mrs. Flecha de Lima explained their friendship on a Brazilian television show. "I think that it [the friendship with Princess Diana] is very natural. The necessity that she have a family, and the fact that I am a foreigner and not a subject of the queen, facilitates my understanding her reasoning."

Ana Paula Silva, the ambassador's 32-year-old executive assistant, who was personally chosen by the Flecha de Limas to be close to the ambassador and close to the family, was, in this case, selected to gently give me the final "No." When I tell Ana Paula that I will never stop hoping to talk with Mrs. Flecha de Lima she says, only half-jokingly, "What do you want me to do, start packing my bags to go home?" It seems Lucia Flecha de Lima doesn't take orders from anyone, including her husband. "I think a woman is always in charge," says diplomatic Ana Paula, who wants to stay out of trouble. Even the ambassador, when asked by an interviewer once which one of them makes the decisions, answered, "I'm not silly to disagree with her!"

After more than 40 years of marriage, Ambassador and Mrs. Flecha de Lima have five children and four grandchildren living in London, Rome and Brazil. Their oldest daughter, Isabel, is married to a Brazilian diplomat.

Prior to Washington, from 1990 to 1993, the ambassador represented Brazil to the Court of St. James in London. It was during that time that his wife became such good friends with Diana and had ever since offered the princess privacy and a safe haven.

According to Ana Paula, even as important as the ambassador is to Brazil's presence in Washington, she says that it is his wife who makes all the difference. "He would not be where he is without her," she says. "She's his full support."

At 66, the ambassador has already officially retired from Brazil's foreign service and has been by presidential appointment since November 1993. To show how irreplaceable he is to his country, this quintessential diplomat has remained in Washington even though he suffered a brain hemorrhage on August 25, 1995. Two surgeries later, he still has three physical therapy sessions a week and has to work hard to get around and make his words understood. But I don't know another ambassador in Washington who is as well-respected and loved by his staff as Ambassador Flecha de Lima.

For his courage, good humor and relentless determination toward his own "amazing rehabilitation," in December 1996 Ambassador Flecha de Lima won "The Victory Award" from nearby National Rehabilitation Hospital. In accepting the award, he thanked his staff for their "permanent support [which] made it possible for me to continue my work as usual." His staff remembers coming to his bedside while he continued to work, even in the hospital.

He is extremely matter-of-fact about his physical handicap. "I am a disabled person so I have to do twice the effort. I am a determined person. But access [for the handicapped] is easier here—in Washington, Providence, Boston, Atlanta. My country is not very used to this," he says. And he doesn't expect or get preferential treatment. "Not at all. I have to fight from the ground floor."

According to his close aide, Ana Paula, "He is still a workaholic" who remains "very curious about everything. If someone comes to see him about biotechnology he says, 'Have a seat and let's discuss that.'" She says that "his agenda is on the computer in his own system and he teaches me the computer. He loves office gadgets. We call them his 'toys.'"

When I arrive for my interview with the ambassador, I'm anxious to see what it's like inside Brazil's distinctive dark-gray glass box. This three-floor contemporary office building has always been one of my favorites, adding style and variety to Embassy Row. When it was dedicated on October 1, 1971, *The Washington Post* said, "All taken together, the fresh-as-Brasilia chancery gives the impression—as it was no doubt designed to do—of a dynamic, self-confident country on its way to becoming a world power but still aware of its ties with the past."

In contrast, on a point of land next door, is "Villa McCormick," the Brazilian residence that is patterned after a fifteenth-century Roman palace. This formal residence where Princess Diana often visited was designed in the early 1900s by a famous American architect, John Russel Pope, for U.S. Ambassador Robert S. McCormick. Pope's other works include the graceful Jefferson Memorial, the almost windowless National Gallery of Art, the National Archives and the two homes at the Meridian International Center.

As I wait on the wood-paneled third floor of the chancery, I find myself amid huge trophies, testimony to the embassy's formidable soccer team, which the ambassador passionately supports.

I review my questions and remember all the things Brazil and the United States have in common. First, the United States was the first country to recognize Brazil's independence from Portugal in 1824. These two huge nations of about the same geographic size are the Western Hemisphere's largest economies and most populous countries. Both have long Atlantic coastlines and each possesses one of the three longest rivers in the world, the Amazon and the Mississippi. (The Nile is the longest.)

The ambassador's expansive office stretches across almost the width of the chancery, with floor-to-ceiling window walls overlooking busy Massachusetts Avenue. As I am ushered in, I notice that the ambassador, a big man, is sitting in a chair with a specially designed left armrest with lots of buttons. His office has been organized to help him be as efficient and self-sufficient as possible.

Of course, that's what Brazil wants to be as a nation: efficient and self-sufficient, especially during these tough times of global financial troubles. Soon after we start talking he delivers his main diplomatic punch. "We think the American public should know that we are not after aid or help. We are a good, cooperative trading partner."

Emphasizing that Brazil is the largest country in the hemisphere and accounts for more than 40 percent of Latin America, he adds, "We are very loyal and good trading partners for the United States and politically we are very cooperative as well. … Brazil is very prominent in the fight against drugs and very active in space, being members of the International Space Station. We are a very good market for American products and for U.S. surpluses."

Brazilian Ambassador Paulo-Tarso Flecha de Lima (center, holding trophy), with team coach Aluisio Lima-Campos and "BEST" (the Brazilian Embassy Soccer Team). Photo courtesy of Ambassador Flecha de Lima.

That was before the global financial crisis had made its way to Brazil and before there were daily news reports of Brazil buckling under. Since then, Ambassador Flecha de Lima is still praising Brazil's economic potential. "We are an active international player," he says. "In five years, it will be a totally different country. We will have managed the current illnesses," proving that Brazil under President Fernando Cardoso is ready and able to take care of itself.

In a letter to the editor of *The Wall Street Journal* printed October 29, 1997, the ambassador confronted that popular financial daily on its October 16, 1998, story titled "While Brazil Agonizes, the U.S Makes a Move": "The economic situation in which we now find ourselves—not only Brazil, but all of Latin America—is due to foreign investors' lack of confidence in emerging markets, with insufficient attention to distinguishing among countries and regions." He suggested that "the consequent uncertainty we are experiencing was imported from foreign markets, and did not arise within our own borders." In closing, he reminded everyone, "It is not Brazil that is 'agonizing'" but economists and market analysts "whose unfounded speculations add more anxiety and tension to the already turbulent international financial markets."

Maria Stela Frota, the embassy's minister-counselor of economic affairs and a former minister of foreign affairs for Brazil, later mentions to me how "the turmoil had already started in American companies—out of the top *Fortune* magazine 500 companies, 405 have subsidiaries in Brazil." She says, "The U.S. is the biggest direct investor" in Brazil.

"We will have to do internally as you did" to react correctly to the crisis. In the first and second round of Brazil's belt-tightening under President Cardoso there is a "sharp cut in spending, tax raising to juggle the money we have."

"With the Mercosul, our NAFTA, there is no tax in between the two countries," says the embassy's highest-ranking woman. "The more free trade the better. We are the ninth economy in the world and we [Brazil and the United States] are very much linked together—trade, investments, jobs here and there."

Besides the economy, the ambassador and I touch on many subjects: his concerns for the rain forest, Brazil's new ecotourism and legendary music, its Portuguese heritage and racial mix and even how Brazil wants Americans to use gasohol.

As expected, he is dramatic in his appeal to rescue the daily devastation of Brazil's rainforest. "The future of the [rain] forest is important for the future of mankind," he says firmly, citing it as a potential resource for pharmaceutical products among many others. "The whole notion of sustainable development rests exactly in this biodiversity: our ability to use the resources of forests without depleting them."

Then he gracefully says that Brazil and the United States share "a common agenda for the environment" and that exploring the forest's future "has been providing us a very good channel for understanding better our two governments." In other words, Brazil and the United States may not always agree, but they're figuring out who's who and how to get things done together.

When I ask him what he wishes more Americans knew about their big South American partner, he seizes the opportunity. "Americans get very surprised when they know that we speak Portuguese, not Spanish," he begins. "Europeans know Brazil better because of soccer," he says, suggesting that American schools do not teach the history and geography of the Americas.

I mention that I remember reading that Brazil and the United States have a common history: European colonization and emigration from Europe, Africa, the Middle East and Asia. And that many families emigrated to the New World, one branch settling in Brazil, another branch choosing the United States.

"We have a very interesting culture of Western, African and Indian," he begins. "We have a good case of racial harmony and a very open society where a lot of minorities are not treated as minorities and a lot of ethnic groups live together without problems."

"We are nice people, and we are not very aggressive," says this ambassador who had just told me how competitive he is. "Brazilians are romantic, congenial and we have happy music and wonderful beaches."

He thinks that Americans might want to take the eight-hour flight to his tropical country on the Equator especially for ecotourism. "There are a lot of new hotels in the Amazon forest." He especially hopes Americans look beyond the three big cities: Brasilia, the capital since 1961, Sao Paulo and Rio de Janeiro.

My questions about tourism and soccer both led me to Aluisio Lima-Campos, an economic advisor who has been at the embassy since 1981 and the head coach of "BEST," an acronym for the Brazilian Embassy Soccer Team. "In Brazil, the moment you start to walk you start to play soccer on the beach, in the streets or even at home in your room." Today, there are all-women's teams that prove that "the old macho society is no longer," says Lima-Campos, who is excited about the new soccer schools in Brazil that teach community and school teams from other countries how to play "like the best" in only one week.

As far as their team, "The ambassador is our number one supporter and fan. And what's so great about soccer is that everyone from the top to the bottom, drivers to diplomats, is equal on the field. I yell at everyone the same!"

This embassy veteran who has worked with five different Brazilian ambassadors during his tenure in Washington and also serves as the president of the International Cotton Advisory Committee, of which Brazil is a member, is also a big fan of Ambassador Flecha de Lima. "This ambassador is very good, very easy. His pragmatism—he works like a businessman and takes and decides each item immediately on its own merits—makes it a pleasure to work with him," says Lima-Campos. If you have a problem and a proposed solution and if it's okay, he will back you all the way. And if not, he'll let you know immediately. He's very transparent, direct, clear. It makes my work real easy. It's good to know I have someone behind me."

Obviously, Ana Paula isn't alone in her appreciation of this ambassador. "Personally, he is sweet and tender," she says. "He treats me—and everyone—as if they were a member of his family, but he expects more from us too," she says. "He calls me affectionately 'Ana' unless something is wrong. I know it right away; then it's 'Ana Paula.'

"The hardest thing is that I never know what is coming next." According to her, he's always deciding to attend a conference here when he's already scheduled to be speaking in Brazil. "Everyday, there're always surprises like two appointments for lunch! Sometimes it drives me crazy. I didn't relax for the first six months," says this energetic woman who struggles to keep up with her boss.

Since most Washington ambassadors are in and out all day, up on the Hill or in other American cities giving speeches, I wonder how much his daily schedule has changed since his stroke. "He travels less now because he knows so many people, he can just call them up," she reports. "But even when he goes home on vacation he may be a keynote speaker at four events and have many other speeches, spending only weekends on their farm," where they raise beef, cotton and soybeans.

She does admit that in Washington he is usually driven to the office from the residence next door. "He has slowed down on how long he stays at receptions" and often spends evenings at home watching the History Channel or movies, when he often invites other movie buffs on his staff to join them. Some of his favorites are *Pretty Woman* and *My Best Friend's Wedding.*

But while he is at the office "he leaves his door open. It's as if he doesn't have a wall. Even if it's a clerk or his driver, he says, 'Just call me.' He gets his ideas from colleagues," Ana Paula says, and "often will say, 'Let's go for a walk,' and he goes around the embassy to see everyone. He loves young people and wants to know what they like, dislike." He still considers himself a mentor to Brazil's different generations of diplomats and remains an inspiration to his staff and Brazilian business leaders as a veteran promoter of Brazilian products worldwide.

But what this young foreign service officer admires most about her boss is his ability to be positive and talk with anyone about anything. "He is very realistic about his disability but he never complains. He considers himself lucky and blessed by God because he is still alive and well and enjoying life," she says.

"It's amazing how quick he can become the friend of the guy who just a little bit ago was his opponent," she says. "I open all his mail and I know the letters he gets from people thanking him for helping them. There was this woman who was a U.S. trade representative, Carla Hills, and they used to have terrible fights—about cars, computers, everything. Now, they are such close friends. In fact, it happened the same way again with the current USTR Charles Brashewsky. The ambassador is a tough negotiator but gentle and friendly at the same time."

"He is 100 percent Brazilian," she says. "I can't say where diplomacy stops and the human being starts." Even with this physical handicap, "He's the best we have," says Ana Paula, who can't believe her "incredible opportunity" to work for him in Washington on her very first foreign post. "He's famous at home, a big deal. I'm honored to work with him."

3

Canada: The Outspoken Neighbor

Everything about Canada is big: the country, the embassy, the ambassador, the diplomatic and economic involvement.

Canada, the second biggest country in the world—if you count the tundra—has almost twice as much land as the United States but only one-tenth the population. The two countries share a 3,000-mile unfortified border—the longest stretch of land anywhere between any two nations.

Canada's big, striking white-marble embassy, often mistaken for an American monument, could not have a larger presence in Washington. It is the only embassy between the U.S. Capitol and the White House and sits right on Pennsylvania Avenue, our national inaugural parade route, across from the National Gallery of Art. Its award-winning Canadian architect, Arthur Erickson, calls it "a House of Friendship" that exhibits "Canadian reserve and good manners."

Even Canada's ambassador is big with a big, booming voice and big, sweeping gestures. As the nephew of Canada's Prime Minister Jean Chretien, Ambassador Raymond Chretien—himself a distinguished career diplomat who's not afraid to speak out—casts one of Washington's biggest ambassadorial shadows.

"You don't pay as much attention to us as we do to you—and we are occasionally taken for granted [by the United States]," he says honestly. "But, then again, this is understandable—it is probably inevitable that we would pay more attention to a country that has massive importance to us. Though the reverse is also true."

According to the ambassador, these two NAFTA partners exchange more than one billion U.S. dollars of goods, services and income per day in what is

Exterior of the Canadian Embassy. Photo by Brien St. Jacques.

the world's largest trading relationship. Since 1989 and the first free trade agreements, U.S.-Canadian trade has doubled. Eighty-five percent of all Canadian exports go to the United States while almost one-fourth of all American exports go to Canada. In fact, for the past half century more American goods have gone to Canada than to any other country—even more than the combined U.S. exports to the 15 member countries of the European Union.

"This is a business post more than anything else," says Ambassador Chretien. "The most important trade partner for the U.S. is Canada; the second most important trading partner is the province of Ontario; the third is Mexico; the fourth is Japan. One of the ten provinces is a more important global trading partner than Mexico or Japan. This is revealing."

But even this impressive economic involvement between the two countries doesn't tell the whole story: There are many other important mutual concerns. Together, Canada and the United States are "joint stewards" of 40 percent of the world's water and share many ecological worries. The countries are longtime military allies and defenders of North America who politely police more than 200 million border crossings between them each year.

Canadians and Americans "are intermarried, people visit each other across the border. It means that somebody from Bismarck in North Dakota crosses the border to Saskatchewan to go and see a movie or vice versa," says Chretien, once Canada's ambassador to Mexico.

We are sitting in the ambassador's dramatic creme and grey "half-oval" office of wrap-around windows. Looking out from this penthouse executive suite you have a breathtaking view of the U.S. Capitol. It is hard to take your eyes away. The view itself is empowering and unique to Washington embassies.

In fact, Ambassador Chretien is so proud of his embassy, its coveted location and spectacular view that when I first arrive at his office, he immediately takes me out on the huge rooftop terrace. This is where Canadians and their lucky American guests have had front-row seats for Fourth of July fireworks since the new embassy opened in 1989. But, "This year, we're going to have only Canadians and our embassy staffers," he explains, giving up his perfect vantage point for entertaining Washington's most powerful people on their own national day.

"We use this building intensely," he says, agreeing that Canada has the prime diplomatic real estate in town. "This is probably the most beautiful of embassies—on the whole planet." His big smile, broader than ever.

"Public affairs is very important in this town," he says, defending the attention the Canadian embassy has received. "When I arrived here I was determined to be very active on the public affairs front—I think it is important for Canada to have a higher profile," says one of Washington's most outspoken foreign diplomats, who has been known to publicly lecture his American audiences and their elected leaders. He proudly refers me to several major speeches in which he reminds Canada's "colossal neighbor" to "fight the forces of global disengagement."

For example, speaking to the Carnegie Endowment for International Peace in January 1997, Ambassador Chretien told his audience, "I will speak through you today to President Clinton and the new Congress." Then he called for the immediate repeal of the controversial Helms-Burton Act because "it has angered your friends and will not be productive." He advised the Congress to pay its long-overdue bill to the United Nations and stop holding the international organization "hostage." Chretien also suggested that the United States "refresh its networks of consultation with key friends and partners" to handle post–Cold War problems like NATO enlargement and relations with Russia and China.

Plus, he urged the United States to continue its "usual generosity" in international humanitarian crises. "While it is true you cannot be the world's sole policeman or physician," he said, "you cannot be a disinterested bystander either. Genocide, famine or aggression literally anywhere in the world must be an alarm bell for American action."

"A lot of my colleagues [other ambassadors] would be very reticent to do this [speak out] because we are not trained to be like this," admits Ambassador Chretien. "But my point is that if you come to Washington and you don't do this, you will not have the same impact. You have to know what you are talking about, you have to say it right and you have to take some calculated risk," says this tireless lobbyist. "There is always a risk in this town."

"We have [official] positions, we have [official] policies," says Chretien, but "if you express them politely and with respect, here you can do so—even though they might be totally opposite your [U.S.] policies."

"This is a political job," vows this career diplomat who enjoys using the podiums of today's public diplomacy. "I have been an ambassador four times and never before have I been put in a post where I felt the need to be as public and political as I have been here. I like it. It is not usually done in other places in the world."

To push the UN dues issue even further, he invited UN General-Secretary Kofi Annan and top American news journalists to dine together and discuss the problem. Of course, he entertained these influential guests in his aerial diplomatic dining room overlooking the U.S. Congress, which has held up approval of payment.

"You are watched in this town. People make judgments. They watch you for a year or two and they say this guy is serious or he knows what he is talking about."

But sometimes, his outspokenness backfires, as it did on the Cuban issue. Once in an interview with *The Miami Herald,* Chretien angered the Cuban American National Foundation (CANF) when he counted, along with the Pope's 1998 visit and Cuba's growth in foreign trade and tourism, the recent death of a leading anti-Castro Cuban-American as a hopeful sign for a potential American policy change. But the deceased man, Cuban political refugee Jorge Mas Canosa, had founded CANF, so the organization's current chairman was quick to criticize Chretien.

"There is no way to describe this man's words other than vile," *The Miami Herald* quotes CANF Chairman Alberto Hernandez (in reference to Ambassador Chretien). "This is a diplomat? This is an ambassador?" Mr. Hernandez added, "They [Canada] don't care about freedom for Cuba—They care only about how good they think they look 'standing up' to the United States."

When I mention Cuba and Prime Minister Chretien's unprecedented trip to meet with Fidel Castro, openly opposing America's long-standing

Bill Reid's sculpture "Spirit Canoe," which honors Canada's aboriginal peoples, welcomes all visitors to Canada's spectacular home on Pennsylvania Avenue. Photo by Brien St. Jacques.

position of nonrecognition, the ambassador is ready. "We were moving towards a change of policy—and more and more Americans have questioned the [U.S.] policy. This is bound to open their eyes. We are losing a lot of business opportunities [with Cuba]." The anti-Castro lobby is "one of the most powerful lobbies in this country. But it is not unanimous."

"I made a speech down there," he says, remembering a trip to Miami. "People left the room and were upset. It was very difficult. It was probably the most tense crowd I had in the U.S." Finally, Miami's Cuban Americans agreed to disagree with this Canadian ambassador on what "democracy and market economy" means. "History will decide which strategy is the best."

Obviously this ambassador, a proud French-speaking native of Quebec, is not afraid of controversy—be it American or Canadian.

"I am from Quebec. I don't need any constitution to tell me that I am different. I know it. It's in my blood and in my bones. I am a Canadian and a Quebecer. I profoundly believe that it is in the interest of Quebec to belong to this greater entity called Canada." He understands that "the [Quebec] government would have liked to separate [from English-speaking Canada]" but they couldn't. "We are only 30 million that run the second largest country in the world; we needed to help one another."

Unlike the United States, "We could not have built our country on 'individualism.'" In Canada, "the importance is [what's good for] society."

We continue to talk about the subtle but important differences between these two countries: In Canada, the prime minister's cabinet must be members of parliament and here, the president appoints his secretaries of defense, state, and so forth. Chretien says Washington's most successful ambassadors quickly discover who has the power.

"It is a very interesting phenomenon for Canadians to watch a U.S. cabinet secretary [nominee] go to Congress and be forced to testify—with the questions coming from the senators. When I go to see a [U.S.] cabinet secretary, they check with the White House an awful lot of times," he says, flashing me a big grin.

Ambassador Chretien is one foreign ambassador who feels comfortable dealing directly with President Clinton and says he wouldn't hesitate to call him if the issue warranted it. However, more often, the Canadian deals directly with Vice President Gore on mutual environmental and natural resource issues. "Vice President is all business, serious, and always very well prepared. President Clinton is charming."

When I ask him if being the prime minister's nephew gives him easier access into the Oval Office, he admits he has an inside track that most Washington ambassadors don't have.

According to this Chretien, he and his uncle "have the same instincts. We come from a political family with a very direct style, open, transparent approach." The ambassador adds that they only talk "a couple of times a month" because the relationship is "so well managed" and that he sends "highly personalized reports" home.

But then Chretien explains how his father was the oldest child and his uncle was the 18th in that family of 19. "We almost grew up together. In blood terms, he's an uncle but in real terms, he's my brother—We would swim, water-ski in Lac-des-Piles, this small beautiful lake in Quebec, about two hours from Montreal." They even went to the same schools.

* * *

Several days later, in the handsome Canadian residence facing Rock Creek Park, I have the unusual opportunity to interview Madame Chretien for her very first interview since coming to Washington more than four years ago. She has turned down dozens of requests before. But Madame Chretien is anything but shy, so that's not why.

Sitting in the formal parlor, facing her husband and the embassy's director of public affairs, she explains why she seldom talks to the media. "He is the one doing the job," says this busy diplomatic wife and mother of two grown children who has always stayed behind the scenes. "When it is a public position like this, I think that you are there to support and that's my role. I haven't been given this job," she says emphatically. "I have been doing it like this for thirty-two years and that's the way it will probably be 'til the end. So there."

She laughs and we all follow. Now I understand why everyone at the embassy refers to her only as "Madame" Chretien.

"And they see only five percent of what they are invited to do," testifies gatekeeper Terry Colli, the embassy's longtime director of public affairs, who intercepts their nonstop invitations. "There is a massive filter," he says, pointing to himself. We all laugh again.

Even though it has ben a "basic tenet" of their marriage that she would stay home while he worked, this powerful ambassador admits that "countless times" it was his wife's new social connections here that made all the difference. "I remember my first two years in Washingon, many of the contacts I made were through her," he admits, saying that she would often already know the spouse of some important cabinet member or senator he wanted to include in a dinner party.

"It's hard to penetrate this city," he explains. "She could get to a high level before me." He praises her sharp wit, good knowledge of current events and ability to quickly diagnose personalities. Plus, "spouses can be more relaxed, can say things that principles don't say. They have more freedom."

She responds. "I would hate to say I haven't had a good time, but it has been work. It's definitely a job," says the formidable blond who is active in 18 different charities and cultural groups. She received an award for her participation in the Race for the Cure, chaired the AIDS Walk and worked out in the Washington community with Arena Stage and the D.C. Public Schools' Embassy Adoption program. "She doesn't miss a beat, she doesn't miss anything," says her proud husband.

When I ask her if she's surprised her husband became a diplomat, he interrupts, "She pushed me into diplomacy!" "It was my idea," she agrees. "He was studying for the bar and there was this contest for candidates for foreign service." Again, he can't resist. "She said to go for it." Again, she explains. "He got a scholarship for three years. It was wonderful for the children [to live abroad]."

I ask Madame Chretien how she managed to balance mothering with her official duties. "I have certain rules and the children know how far to go," she says firmly. "One day I will say to my grandkids, 'You can come on Sundays for tea,' so they are dressed, all prim and proper!" For now, Caroline, the Chretiens' 31-year-old daughter who was born on her mother's birthday, travels constantly as a senior advance officer in the prime minister's office. Their 28-

year-old son, Louis-Francois, is a law student at the University of Ottawa and often visits them in Washington.

"We spent a lot of time with our children," says this ambassador who prides himself on keeping "balance" in his life whether he is living here, Kinshasa, New York or Beirut, all former posts. In Washington, he often sneaks home to swim in their backyard pool, pausing before a busy social evening. And when they do have a night off, they love to listen to jazz and read. "I will never retire. Maybe I'll teach, keeping busy intellectually and physically."

Comparing the two cultures at the family level, Madame Chretien thinks that in Canada, "the family is under pressure" but adds, "here, the family is falling apart. Everything that happens here also happens there [in Canada] eventually."

However, her husband thinks that Canada is "much more socially tolerant—not as polarized." He points out that Canadian tax law is based on a common law partnership with gay rights much like France, Holland, Scandinavia.

When I ask what Canadians think of President Clinton and the White House sex scandal he doesn't hesitate to answer. "Clinton is very popular. The state has no business in the bedrooms of the leader."

He tells me how important it is for diplomats and their families to "keep their feet on the ground. I think we are both very practical so [we decided] we mustn't get starry-eyed. There is a very artificial side to these positions and you should never forget that it's not really you. We have been doing this for so long, this is our seventh posting. So, we can say, 'This too shall pass,' and take advantage of it as much as we can."

Before Madame Chretien has to leave, I ask them how they met and they both roll their eyes. She begins, "Oh, we met a long, long time ago. Both of our parents had summer cottages by the lake. He was 16 and I was 17. It was innocent." And, the subject is closed, for the moment.

But later, after she's off to her appointment, the ambassador tells his version of that day on the lake. "I was in this little boat, a put-put, and the two and one-half horsepower motor died," he says making a face. He didn't know what to do until he saw her, off in the distance, and flagged her to come help tow him in.

"It was a long, long trip and my heart was going, 'Boom, Boom, Boom,'" he says, pounding his chest dramatically while his embassy aide winces. "While she's pulling me, about 20 minutes, I kept thinking what can I say, how can I see her again. Then, I thought of asking her for a date to play badminton."

I am struck by how open and even boyish this big, powerful man lets himself be in front of a reporter. How charming and disarming.

4

Russia: Secret Hideaway

The first thing I notice is his voice—a big part of his charm. There is no accent. Just his melodious answer to my interview request, "Yes, yes, Ms. Scott, we must talk!"—and his big smile followed by an endearing wink. I think, this ambassador could be Italian or French or from some fun-loving, sunny Latin American country.

But he is Russian, and I am *flabbergasted.* I am sure that Albert, the ever-present diplomatic photographer, caught my surprise with his camera.

For all my years reporting in Washington, I feel like a naïve, little American schoolgirl who has been fed too much Cold War porridge. What did I expect? Some grumpy old grandpa with such a heavy accent we could only nod hello to each other?

I am right, but only about the "grandpa" part. This charming and warm ambassador is Yuli Mikhailovich Vorontsov, a "seasoned warrior" of the Soviet Union, now ambassador of the Russian Federation and the protégé of Anatoly Dobrynin. And, he has just taught one more American that stereotypes don't always hold in diplomacy, a field where you expect each ambassador to personify their own country.

Months later, I arrive for our interview. In the far end of a large formal reception hall with elegantly draped walls of aqua silk, Czech chandaliers above and intricately designed parquet floors, Press Counselor Mikhail Shurgalin and I are sitting on delicate silk upholstered furniture. In front of me, I recognize the Pepperidge Farms cookie assortment while we await the ambassador's entrance. Tea and coffee are ordered on cue as the spry ambassador crosses the huge hall. As we greet each other there is a small but unnerving echo. I admit how disarming it was for me that he spoke English without any Russian accent. "That's good," he replies smiling. "That helps."

Then he reminds me that he's had more than two decades to practice his English here. Since 1966, he has represented the old Soviet Union and now the Russian Federation on and off either in Washington or in New York: first as counselor, then minister-counselor and deputy chief of mission here. Then at the United Nations, he was permanent representative with the rank of deputy foreign minister of the USSR and most recently he filled Russia's seat on the UN's Security Council.

"When I was ambassador to France and went to present my credentials to President Mitterand … his smile got broader and broader. I told him I was sorry to be 'torturing your wonderful language.' He told me I was the first Soviet ambassador to France to speak French with an American accent and that was funny!"

Cold War child that I am, again I remember my old CIA buddy telling me that any Russian without an accent is an automatic suspect of KGB training. And, even though I have my questions carefully crafted and written down, somehow I feel unprepared for this interview.

He smiles and nods when I tell him that *Diplomatic Dance* will be the name of my book. On the spot he invites me to their next dance, adding, "We have the facilities for that," proudly gesturing toward the adjoining grand ballroom. Then he agrees that it is an apt title for the current state of diplomatic affairs. "Of course," he laughs, "some [countries] are doing a tap dance."

"Since America is involved everywhere, the whole world picture is more visible here and the whole dance, by the way, the diplomatic dance, is more visible here. So it [Washington] is very interesting, very real. I would say fascinating."

I mention his particular, much discussed vantage point, the fenced 12-acre Russian compound, high on Wisconsin Avenue overlooking much of the city. "It's a very good observation post. You can see the whole world from here. We have been criticized in Congress for that." Their premier hilltop, Mount Alto, gave the Soviets a serious communications advantage during the Cold War.

We start talking about how different it was when he was here in the 1960s.

"One of the differences is that I'm not being awakened during the middle of the night and expecting a major crisis in the Soviet Union and the United States. Now is much easier."

"I was awakened … in the past years during the Cold War period with invitations at two, three, four in the morning to come immediately to the White House and that was not a very pleasant drive, 15 to 20 minutes, wondering what happened.

"Nixon was knowledgeable in international affairs. He was in difficulty at that time because of the Vietnam War and somehow he decided that the key or the solution was in Moscow," he says with a surprising little chuckle. "That was not completely so, the key was in Peking as well, Beijing or whatever the name is, and in Hanoi because they had been very independently minded in trying to reunify their country by military ways. But Nixon somehow felt it was very important to deal with the Soviet Union."

I asked him if he had a red phone then with a direct line to the White House. "Just a black phone but it was very red when [we were] talking."

During the Cold War, Vorontsov says, "It was impossible to escape" these calls even at his much-beloved American dacha on the Chesapeake Bay. More than once they radioed him while he was speeding along in his motor boat, his one big passion. "Then, we were able to hide only in Moscow!

"That was tense," this ambassador admits. "We were nervous. Really, I think we were lucky that we avoided at that time a military clash. Previously, we had the Cuban Missile Crisis. Later on, all the crises in the world like the Middle East Wars. All the time we have been very close, very, very close."

He refers to President Eisenhower's published letters to a friend, which were reprinted in *The New York Times,* when "twice he got recommendations from the Joint Chiefs of Staff to drop nuclear bombs on the Soviet Union—twice. First time, it was the Korean War and the [second] time, development of hydrogen bombs in Russia. He [Eisenhower] got recommendations to bomb that facility. That was close, that was very close. Cuban Missile Crisis came later, which was also very close."

During most of these "skirmishes," the ambassador jokes, "[then-] Ambassador Anatoly Dobrynin was out of the country and [I] was sitting there," and as deputy chief of mission in charge. "Something [always] happened because Dobrynin was not there. I think Kissinger was arranging it. He [Kissinger] kept telling everybody, 'When Vorontsov is alone, something is happening.'" The ambassador enjoys a hearty laugh.

Ironically, on the day we meet, Dobrynin is in Washington visiting his protégé. Vorontsov calls him "my guru" in diplomacy and in chess. "Dobrynin beats me all the time in chess."

Later this senior diplomat would tell me that Americans have "two sins. The main sin is that they don't want to know more. ... They are satisfied with the knowledge they got during their school days and then university days and period. They stop like that. They are not interested in more. That is wrong!" he says emphatically, snapping his fingers.

"The second thing, Americans don't play chess. In chess, you don't have to make only one move. You have to think about the second, third, and fourth move that you're going to do after your first. That is the chess player."

Russian Bear at the Russian Dacha on the Chesapeake Bay. Photo by Gail Scott.

"I play chess but Dobrynin was … a master. You don't make the first move without thinking about all the elements ahead. I'll move this," he says moving an imaginary pawn, "and they'll move this, then I'll do this, then he'll do this. Then, I'll crush them there." I recoil as he jabs toward the floor.

"You," he continues comparing the two former enemies, "play checkers." And I ask him who plays dominoes, encouraging him, but he sidesteps.

"Our pensioners in Moscow, they play dominoes in all the squares in the summertime, even in wintertime." He admits he doesn't usually play anything in America because "foreign policy is practice for me here."

I mention that speaking of "checkers" reminds me of Nixon's dog, Checkers, and Nixon's famous "Checkers Speech" when the president refused to give up the family pet in response to questions about his campaign gifts. Vorontsov takes my cue.

"Nixon was more experienced but Clinton is good. Of course, Nixon was vice-president too, the 'back seat of the foreign policy car,' but he was watching. Clinton is doing fine. The White House teaches him. Now he is knowledgeable and thoughtful and does it without cue cards."

In further comparing the two very different administrations in very different times, he adds, "Today, the team is larger. … Kissinger was the one and only. Surrounding the president from all sides. Here, they have more brain power," he says judging the Clinton foreign policy team of "Madeleine Albright, Strobe Talbott [former deputy secretary of state and now U.S. Ambassador to Greece] and Sandy Berger [White House national security advisor]." Vorontsov says he thinks larger is "better" and "safer."

To this major player in foreign policy, Kissinger and Albright have a lot in common. "They are different people altogether though they are from the same background." I ask him if he means that they are both of Jewish heritage.

"No, they come from the same European origin that makes them a little bit more knowledgeable and more understanding of world situations than some of the domestic secretaries of state. Both European, they have broader thinking. The American thinking is rather narrow. Europeans are able to consider many factors at the same time."

Ambassador Vorontsov still leaves Washington three or four times a month to speak at universities, foreign relations councils and business groups even though his wife, Faina, has suffered a stroke and is confined to the residence.

"I like to feel the people. Of course, Washington is very, very seriously charged political center. But sometimes there are different views between the people out there and [those in] Washington. What people are thinking and their attitudes toward world affairs and my country is very interesting." I'm thinking, *he's out taking his own personal poll.*

"My job is explaining American policy in Moscow and explaining Russian policy in Washington," he concludes, giving one of the best answers I've heard for, "What does a modern ambassador do?" He uses the current controversy over NATO membership as an example. "We don't understand why you want the enlargement of NATO. We are fearful it will create difficulties later on … spoil our [Russia-U.S relations]."

"And we don't like U.S. demands that Russia stop doing something. We hear, 'Don't do this, don't do that.' We've got our Independence Avenue in Moscow as well; it's not only in Washington! This is not the way to talk between partners," says Vorontsov, who claims that the current "good relations" between the United States and "democratic Russia" should be "cherished."

The United States as sole superpower is a "wrong notion," he claims. "What has the United States gained now that they haven't had before during the Soviet Union period? We don't know what Russia has lost now that we had before."

He continues describing a "superpower" solely by nuclear might, not taking into consideration the obvious political changes with the dissolution of the Soviet Union, Russia's economic decline and their weakened global status since the end of the Cold War.

"The superpower title was given to both countries for their terrible capability to destroy the world by nuclear weapons and that remains," Vorontsov says. "We still have tens of thousands of warheads in Russia and you have tens of thousands of warheads. Before we didn't have money. You had all the money. So, in this case, nothing has changed. You can be destroyed in 15 minutes same as we can be destroyed in 15 minutes."

I ask him how he feels about Hungarian-born American philanthropist George Soros donating hundreds of millions in Eastern Europe and the former Soviet Union. "I think it is a wonderful gesture," but he is a "controversial figure," the ambassador admits, because "they think he is buying the brains" of Russia. "He supports various scientists for this or that project and that looks suspicious."

I wonder aloud what he wishes Americans knew about Russians. "I'd like them to know what actually happens in Russia and not to invent our way of thinking ... but to go to Russia and understand. ... Sit down and talk with us instead of sitting here in Washington and inventing. It's not the Cold War period behind all sorts of curtains, Iron Ocean or whatever. ... That's my appeal, especially to the people in Congress. ... But they still proclaim and put resolutions and warnings and threats to Russia while they are sitting in Washington without leaving their cozy places on Capitol Hill. That's wrong.

"You have a very young Congress ... and the people who don't remember the Cold War but they do remember something that Russia was the enemy, they got it from school," Vorontsov says.

Ironically, he thinks Russians are freer to think for themselves. "We had less notion of the United States as an enemy. It was the dictate. But people didn't like dictates in Russia. They were saying, 'Yeah, yeah, they're the enemy' ... but they helped us tremendously in the Second World War"

Vorontsov, a grandfather himself, thinks Americans can learn from Russia's closely knit families. "Grandmas and grandpas are sitting with their grandsons and granddaughters and the younger people go to work. But the grandpas and grandmas are tending the children. ... In your case, the man goes to university in faraway place. I don't know why they choose, living in Washington, that he goes to California or Texas to university. You have three universities here. In our case, they always stay home. Very rarely, unless they live in a small village, do they not study in area where they are.

"Respect and understanding and willingness to learn. To have open eyes and ears, not to have preconceptions, that's what I'm *peddling* here." He's delighted with my reaction, acknowledging his glib use of American slang.

With all this talk about grandparents, I ask him to tell me about his family. "I have three 'children.' My son-in-law in the Secretariat at the UN, my 45-year-old daughter Olga who has been in the diplomatic service, and my grandson Anton who is 23 and graduated from NYU in political science." Surprisingly, he says his daughter "wanted to work. But somehow she cannot find a job in New York."

His wife, Faina, formerly a researcher specializing in history of the French Republic, has not been able to speak since her recent stroke. But each evening when he returns to the historic residence on 16th Street he still talks to her about his day and he says she understands. They enjoy going to the dacha together every chance they get.

"I like to cruise around Chestertown," he admits, now smiling broadly. I told him I heard he speeds in his motorboat. He shrugs his shoulders in an impish way and then invites me to tour the residence and his coveted hideaway on the Chesapeake Bay. I'm delighted.

* * *

Surprisingly, the official Washington residence is not only within walking distance of the White House but is the backyard neighbor of *The Washington Post* offices—with only a narrow alley and a brick wall topped with barbed wire and those old-fashioned prison lights dividing them.

Mikhail Shurgalin, again my tour guide, had already parked his plum-colored Lumina on 16th Street and was waiting for me outside the gates, his chance to light up another Marlboro.

As we entered through the handsome old iron gates, the vintage security cameras welcomed us to the Pullman house, built in 1909 for Congressman Frank O. Lowden of Illinois by his wealthy mother-in-law, Mrs. George M. Pullman of Chicago. Her husband originated the Pullman sleeping cars on the railroad. The opulent home changed hands and was sold to the Imperial Russian Government for $350,000 in 1913. The following year the Russians bought the land next door and soon began construction of a chancery wing.

After the fall of the Imperial government and the Kerensky provisional government in 1917, the house was occupied only by a caretaker and fell into disrepair. When the United States recognized the Soviet government in 1933, the old embassy was refurbished; in 1937 the Soviets purchased the small house next door.

In 1994 the Russian Consulate was moved to a brand-new, albeit ordinary-looking, high-rise office building right in the middle of the spacious but secure Mt. Alto compound. The embassy staff and their families had already been living in this residential block on upper Wisconsin Avenue since 1979. Today the facilities include apartment houses, a school, a kindergarten and outdoor playground, a pool and indoor sports facility and a commissary and social hall. More than 200 diplomats and technical staffers and their families live and work within the compound. Oddly, their apartment windows often look directly into neighboring D.C. apartment buildings only feet away, but down on the ground the high fence still separates the Russians from their neighbors, just like it did during the Cold War.

When I asked Mikhail if he has to ask permission to go beyond the compound's gates onto Wisconsin Avenue, he said, "No, but the other night I almost got locked out when I went out to walk the dog." It seems security closes the big front gates whenever they want whether all the Russians are back in or not. That's when he discovered the back gate for latecomers.

The Pullman house is now solely the ambassador's residence, used infrequently for small receptions, visiting dignitaries and news breakfasts with the Russian press corps posted in Washington. (The massive reception hall on the main Wisconsin Avenue compound where we did our interview is where most functions take place.)

When we enter the old residence, it's dark and musty, but as we ascend the grand staircase, elements of past grandeur are everywhere. Resident manager Nikolai Pulin turns on the chandeliers, showing us the formal Gold Room with its impressive matching marble and mirrored fireplaces decorating each end, the red-silk reception room and the dark-paneled dining room.

As I reach to open one of the five little square doors cut into the elaborate wooden panels of the dining room, staring back at me is a huge camera lens. The next door exposes another lens, only bigger. Spooky. Mikhail sees me flinch and nonchalantly pulls back the dusty old gold drape on the far wall hiding a mammoth movie screen. We laugh, nervously. Just as I was beginning to feel comfortable with these Russians, a flash of Cold War distrust sweeps through me and it seems that Mikhail suspects it.

My imagination flies into overdrive with visions of top secret diagrams and battle plans flashing bigger than life in black and white. Big Soviets on the big screen. Or maybe, secretly taped conversations of unsuspecting American leaders or even lip-reading. Never *Casablanca* nor *Mary Poppins.*

Mikhail says he doesn't think the Russian viewing room is used anymore. But still, my mind imagines the projector's lights crisscrossing the room, the smoke swirling up from *big* Cuban cigars held by *big* Communists leaning back in their *big* chairs after a *big* dinner of meat and potatoes and vodka, lots of vodka. The Cold War kid. I laugh at myself but am too embarrassed to tell Mikhail why.

Although original oils by famous nineteenth-century Russian painters like Scherbakov and Aivazovsky, cobalt blue and white Gzhel china, and marble and gold leaf abound, the once grand residence is compromised by low-budget, modern repairs. I retreat to the powder room only to find more incongruities of style with mismatched colors and mock marble. Not good enough for the czar yet still much too fancy for today's Russian in the middle of their own economic crisis.

* * *

We drive to the dacha on a sparkling early winter day. Crossing the Chesapeake Bay Bridge I think how lucky I am to be on this "foreign" adventure. I tell Mikhail about John Barth's *Sabbatical,* a mystery about CIA "safe houses" on the Chesapeake, and how often I have wondered where this secret Russian dacha is while I am sailing on this wide bay and anchoring in yet another private cove.

As Mikhail and I continue on Route 50, I also mention that my mother and I have just learned that my father's family may have been Russian, not Czech. He smiles and I tell him what I know.

As young teenagers, without their parents, my paternal grandparents had fled in the night and sailed to America: my grandma with her sister and my grandpa with his brother. They would never see their families again.

But I heard stories how my grandma answered the cry for help from her "little brother" during World War II. She sent this young soldier, my great uncle, my father's old clothes with letters and American dollars she had sewn into the linings. The clothes came back all tangled and ripped, the letters and money gone. A note scolding her was enclosed. It read, "These people are now being taken care of by the Soviet government and they don't need your help. Don't do this again."

As we drive along together, Mikhail and I, I'm thinking how much has changed in my lifetime. Now we leave Route 301 and I start writing down the turns. I wonder why and if he minds. I have a camera stuffed in my bag, too, just in case. We pass the historic signpost that reads: "This is the birthplace of Charles Wilson Peale." Expensive horses dot the fields. Ironically, we turn onto "Spider Web Lane," then Corsica Neck and Cove Point until we finally start down Town Point Lane.

Through the security gates, I feel a little like I am back at Mt. Lake Camp. There are the tennis and the volleyball courts, the soccer fields, the rowboats and the cabins. Down the tree-lined lane are new equally spaced benches and matching trash cans with their black plastic liners showing. Two big red brick buildings on the right come with the 58-acre country estate that Vorontsov had found and convinced the Soviets to buy in 1972 when he was deputy chief of mission. We pull into the horseshoe driveway at the ambassador's beloved getaway. Under the ivy by the front steps I discover an old plaque, "Hartefeld House."

Supervisor Yuri Nikolayevich Zhurba is there to show us around and, as I later found out, keep us from going upstairs to the private quarters. After touring the main floor dining room full of Mrs. Dobrynin's figurines, the living room with its gigantic Mitsubishi big screen and the dusty library with its curious book collection (from *Moody's Industrials* and *Lorna Doone* to Elie Abel's *The Missile Crisis* and *One Hundred Years of the Monroe Doctrine*), we meander down through the giant, unruly boxwoods to the pool and gaze out on the Chester River.

No wonder the ambassador likes to come here, especially now in the winter. It's peaceful. We grab our coats and walk through the orchard to visit an unoccupied cabin. Lace curtains hanging in the doorway remind me of my grandmother's house in Connecticut.

In the summer, explains Mikhail, "We have sign-up lists on Wednesdays at the embassy, and we bring our own bedsheets and towels. It's three dollars for the weekend, first come, first served"—except, "It's by rank." Yuri adds, "It's quite noisy in the summer." I learn that there are several shifts of summer camp for the embassy children. That's when the pool and disco hall are the most popular spots. The other brick house is the dorm and dining room for the campers.

By the time we get to the boathouse the sun is warm and I just want to stop talking and drink in the winter light. I can imagine summertime with Russians barbecuing over on that bank, while others fish here on the dock, just able to hear those playing tennis and volleyball yell out their scores—in Russian. In the meantime, the ambassador, an old naval grad, has escaped this crowded, noisy scene by boat. "He goes alone with no formal body guard," confides Yuri.

Before we leave to return to Washington, I can't resist taking a picture of the ceramic baby bear Vorontsov put in front of his American dacha. Amidst ivy and a basket of pinecones, this Russian bear looks skyward as the Canada geese fly by. He has such a sweet face, I want to take him home.

* * *

Ambassador Vorontsov has retired from Russia's foreign service and returned to Moscow with his wife. However, he continues to be involved in Russian-American affairs and has accepted an unofficial, unpaid consulting assignment with UN's Secretary-General Kofi Annan.

5

Uzbekistan: The Old Silk Route

They are highly educated, warm and friendly, and this ambassador and his wife want Americans to know that their land, Uzbekistan—albeit a former Soviet state—has an ancient cultural heritage, remarkable religious tolerance and a new government that is worthy of American trust and respect.

"We supply our uranium only to the U.S., which is understandable because it is a very strategic raw material," says Dr. Sodyq Safaev, ambassador of the Republic of Uzbekistan, hoping to quickly establish Uzbek political loyalties in its new market economy. Representing the most populated country of the five landlocked Central Asian States (all once part of the Soviet Union), this former economics professor is quick to defend Uzbekistan's independence from Mother Russia.

"First of all, I'd like to argue the statement that Russia is the 'mother country.' My country used to be part of the Russian Empire for almost one hundred years. But, in [the] course of the history of mankind, this is an eyeblink," the former visiting scholar at Harvard's Institute for International Development (HIID) begins my tutorial. "From this fact you cannot draw the conclusion that Uzbekistan is child to Russia. Quite the contrary.

"The Central Asian civilization [today divided into Uzbekistan, Kazakhstan, Kyrgyzstan, Tajikistan and Turkmenistan] is one of the oldest in the world—and a unique contributor to the history of mankind," he says, enumerating the "many important spheres of knowledge influenced by Central Asians: mathematics, medicine, astronomy, physics, chemistry, architecture, poetry." In fact, this fascinating melange of the Far East and Europe, once the crossroads of the Great Silk Route, "absorbed the influences of Iranian, Arabic, Indian and to some extent, Chinese civilizations."

This mixed heritage is evident in Ambassador Safaev's handsome face. His accent and his English are charming but make note-taking tedious. I regret that I have to rely on my tape recorder so much.

We are sitting in the consulate's elaborately decorated Bukhara Room, named for the ancient Uzbek city famous for hand-cut plaster design, or "ganch." The brilliant robin's egg "Uzbek blue" walls are reflected in the bits of mirror peeking through the opposite wall of this delicate white latticework. In front of me is a silver server of pistachios, raisins, apricots and other sweets. As this handsome ambassador enters and shakes my hand, I realize that I have been transported halfway around the world to this exotic country of ancient cities, great universities and endless passing caravans.

Ambassador Safaev, a much-published economist, is here to draw such an updated and inviting picture of his historic homeland that Americans will consider Uzbekistan for business and for pleasure. As an economist, he can discuss Uzbekistan's new market economy; large, educated, skilled and hardworking workforce; legendary cotton and silk; and rich reserves of natural gas, gold and uranium. As a scholar, he can expound on Uzbekistan's rich cultural and religious heritage, its famous early thinkers and its unique place in world history. As a civil servant, he has served his country in various governmental agencies dealing with science, education and interethnic relations. And most recently, he was ambassador to Germany and counselor of state to Uzbekistan's President Islam Karimov. This ambassador and his wife, Rahima, also a former professor, epitomize the well-educated, passionate Uzbeks who want the Western world to know more about their world, which was hidden behind the Soviet's Iron Curtain for three generations.

Uzbekistan, which gained its independence from the Soviets in 1991, is a Muslim cultural treasure that proves Muslims can be friendly to the West. Students of world history know that Uzbekistan has been the home to successive civilizations and multiple cultures, resulting in extraordinary ancient architecture, intricate art and handicrafts and legendary centers of learning.

These lands, inhabited since prehistoric times, were once part of the many Persian-based empires. Uzbek cities Bukhara and Samarkand were already important trade centers when Alexander the Great marched into Central Asia, 300 years before Christ. Following the Arab-Muslim conquest in the seventh century, the people converted to Islam. Today, the Uzbeks speak a Turkic language and are mostly Muslim, although church and state are officially separate. Contemporary Uzbeks are descendents of the sedentary people, mostly farmers, ruled by Cyrus the Great, Alexander the Great, Attila, Genghis Khan and Timur, better known as Tamerlane in the West.

The ambassador reminds me that "Uzbekistan is the natural hub and heart of the region" with one-half of Central Asia's population living there, mostly in Tashkent, its capital of two million people. Yet, Kazakhstan has the most land with a 3,000-mile Russian border, and Turkmenistan has the most oil and the world's fourth largest gas reserves. Because all five Central Asian states are landlocked, they have been forced to work together to secure their full independence from Russia and efficient trade routes to the outside world. In fact, it was the Transcaucasian Railway, built by the Russians in the late 1800s to connect Central Asian cities to the rest of the Russian Empire, that sealed Russia's hold on this region.

The four Central Asian ambassadors in Washington (Tajikistan's only U.S. representation is at the United Nations) get together "to exchange views—support each other—but we already have very good and healthy relationship," says the ambassador.

When I ask if Americans in general, or American officials in particular, get these Central Asian countries mixed up, he says dramatically, "No, absolutely not! The State Department, the Congress, of course they differentiate and have different approaches to each country. But at the same time, we appreciate more and more using the term 'Central Asian Caucus.'"

However, he is quick to point out that Uzbek spirit is special, even amongst neighbor states. "As Uzbeks we are the inheritors of an old civilization." The ambassador gives me an impressive list of scholars who studied and lived in Bukhara or Samarkand. They include Musa Khwarezmi, ninth-century mathematician who "laid down the beginnings of algebra"; Avicenna, philosopher, author of *The Canon of Medicine* and "the father of modern medicine"; Abu Reikhan al-Biruni, 10th-century intellectual with major work on astronomy, physics and geography; Ulugh Beg, grandson of Asian conqueror Timur, who made Samarkand a Muslim cultural center and built the famous observatory there; and late-fifteenth-century poet Ali Shir Nava'I.

"So, we have a rich scientific legacy and a rich spiritual legacy and we're very proud of this. Uzbekistan is a very important part of the Islamic world."

I ask him if that religious orientation makes it harder for Americans and other Westerners to accept or trust Uzbekistan and its people. "No, Uzbekistan never has the propensity to the fundamentalist Islam or the extreme, never evidence of prejudice against the West." Later he added, "We are in the Islamic world but at the same time not antagonistic, not anti-Semitic. There is no prejudice. During World War II, 200,000 Jews found shelter in Tashkent. I grew up in a Jewish neighborhood," says this Sunni Muslim. "And I know there are very sincere sentiments toward the Uzbeks [by Jews].

Uzbekistan Ambassador Sodyq Safaev. Photo by Valentine Wilber.

"For example, look to the history of the Jewish population in Uzbekistan, which is the oldest outside of Palestine. For 2,500 years there has been a Jewish community living in Uzbekistan. I had the honor to accompany the First Lady, Hillary Clinton, to a 500-year-old synagogue. It was a beautiful experience to show how people of different faiths can live together in peace. I remember vividly how she especially encouraged the old people 'to go for' democracy and a 'civil society.'"

In fact, during her official visit in November 1997 "to see the old and the new Uzbekistan," Mrs. Clinton praised how President Karimov, ironically once himself aligned with the Communist Party, "restored religious freedom and encouraged religious and cultural tolerance." During those seven Soviet decades the goal was "to stifle difference and erase culture and religion." She marveled at "the beauty of your places of worship" but said that her "sharpest impression" was how, for centuries, Muslims, Christians and Jews had peacefully worshipped in such close proximity to one another.

America's First Lady reasoned that "strength in your diversity" probably came when "travelers from China, Europe, India, Byzantium and the Arab world would sit and talk and drink tea together in the caravansary—an experience which could only deepen the bonds between individuals." Then she reminded her hosts, whose ancestors were some of the world's most famous traders, "To trade, you must live in an open society, free from walls and barriers." Also, as a highly educated American mother, she congratulated "this country that invented algebra" for their current "strong system of education for girls as well as boys," a somewhat unusual policy in this part of the world.

Ambassador Safaev is understandably proud of Uzbekistan's record on women's rights. Forty-eight percent of the labor force is female, with women holding many academic and political positions: one-third of the seats in Parliament, a vice speaker of Parliament, and vice prime minister.

"Our organization called Women for Democracy has revived a Marxist philosophical legacy that still holds true, even in a democracy. It says that the situation of women is a real gauge in assessing the development of a society," says the ambassador, who sees this social progress as another reason for respect and partnership with the countries of North America and Europe.

Because Uzbekistan is at the center of trade and cultural interaction, the Uzbeks are probably the most cosmopolitan people dwelling in Central Asia. "We are 100 percent literate," the ambassador says. "We have 52 universities and institutions of higher learning and many are very distinguished. Thousands of people come from around the world to study in Uzbek universities.

"Now we are working hard to set up with Harvard an American university in Tashkent not only as an educational institution which will provide knowledge but an institution which will bring values, ideas and which will bring to Tashkent, to the heart of Central Asia, what does [it] mean, the American way of life."

He isn't finished yet. "In Uzbek, people—they are more skillful, more industrialized, more urbanized" [than the rest of Central Asia]. Ironically, some of the credit for that goes to the Soviets, who modernized agriculture and introduced industry to Uzbekistan in order to keep essential production safe and tucked away from any enemy attack. Plus, 80 percent of the population is under 30 and of that, 50 percent is under 18. That's half a million new workers entering the labor force each year. "That's why attracting investment is our primary focus," says Ambassador Safaev.

When I try to apologize for not knowing more about his homeland, he stops me. "I think it is one of my duties to provide the American audience with information about my country. I have no reason to complain. It is reality of the past century when the region was closed to the outside world." (Imperial Russia conquered the area 30 years before Soviet rule.)

"We are the only country in the region with common borders with all other [Central Asian] countries." Thus, surrounded by the four landlocked former Soviet states, Uzbekistan is the sole double landlocked country in the world. For that reason alone, the Uzbeks must remain good friends with their neighbors.

"First of all, competition is a positive thing [among the five countries], of course. We must compete with each other to attract more investments, trade [to the region]. And, competition is good. As long as there is competition there will be an impetus for improving the internal situation.

"Our countries [Central Asian] can survive only together," he says. "From time immemorial, Central Asia used to be a single space without any borders. Uzbekistan and the other four republics were once known as Turkestan. It was a cultural entity—so I don't see any reason why now, at the threshold of the 21st century, that new obstacles for trade, for contact between the people should be created." Uzbekistan does have a free-trade agreement with all the other Central Asian states.

"At the same time, the countries can only benefit from economic integration and cooperation" in dealing with "diminishing the cost of trade and ecological disasters." Uzbekistan, a bit bigger than California, is two-thirds desert or semidesert and faces the drying up of its rivers and the Aral Sea and the salinization of its land, half of which is permanent pasture. When irrigated, its fertile valleys produce a fourth of the world's cotton, incredible fruits and vegetables and ample grain. Later, he says the countries must also work together to combat narcotic traffic and keep Central Asia nuclear free.

I can't resist asking him what kind of relationship he had with former Russian Ambassador Yuli Vorontsov. "We have a very important relationship. The Russian ambassador is one of the most prominent in diplomacy in the world. I have deep respect [for] him and his way of doing his duty, and excellent example of how an ambassador must behave." I remind him that we first met in the silk-draped reception hall of the Russian Embassy during a celebration for the 300 years of the Russian navy. He counters, "From time to time, I met him at such diplomatic events but I do not call on him to help."

When I ask him if he's angry about Uzbekistan disappearing from the world stage during the century of Russian and Soviet domination, he shakes his head. "You must separate attitudes of personal feelings toward individual Russians and the Russian people from the policies of the Soviet government. Their policy was oriented to split us from our spiritual heritage and Uzbekistan from its glorious past." Today, the diplomatic dance for Uzbekistan is still to dance with Moscow but only as equal partners and to find new partners independently for Uzbekistan.

Now is the perfect time to talk politics and security for Uzbekistan, a NATO hopeful. "I'm convinced that the most fragile stage of our development is over. Now, Uzbekistan is committed and firm on this other way. But at the same time the problem of national security is never over [for] any country," he says, adding that "to strengthen national security and strengthen independence is one of the main tasks of any state."

NATO's boot camp, the Partnership for Peace, "is not only a piece of paper, it's a program which works," says the ambassador. "In case of need, the international community can come and participate in peacekeeping, rescue operations. It is a signal to the north and the south of Uzbekistan that it is part of the international system of security." He's proud that during last year's military maneuvers in Central Asia, the American military flew directly from North Carolina to Uzbekistan, which "showed the world changed, there is no forgotten corner of the world anymore."

And that kind of global interconnection is exactly why the Asian financial crisis has been spreading like the flu. But though some of Uzbekistan's biggest investors are South Korea and Japan, and though Russia, Malaysia, Indonesia and Thailand are trading partners, the Uzbek economy has "held its own," according to this economist. "It's because we pursued a diversified economy and so far it hasn't affected us significantly. We have confidence for the future." The United States, Germany and Turkey are new, nontraditional trading partners for Uzbekistan.

"The lesson [for] any new independent country is what's behind the Asian financial crisis and how to avoid this possible scenario in the future," he says. "A market economy is a comprehensive system and each part of that system must be coherently tied with other parts. The lesson to be learned is to consider the financial system as an organic part of the market economy, as a whole of the global picture. Not closed. We need integration or at least regional coordination of financial markets." And the "transparency" or obvious track of money must be made "available to the public and must be taken into account for a new independent country like Uzbekistan."

As we talk more and more about economics, I ask this economist how much of his time is spent on commercial diplomacy. "I am convinced in the contemporary world, the economic diplomacy, the commercial diplomacy is important and as a whole is increasing. The time of diplomacy of protocol, diplomacy of the ceremony is over," he says, adding that governments can no longer "monopolize" diplomacy in our global village. Today, international businesses and nongovernmental organizations need to their own diplomats.

"Diplomacy must be pragmatically serving the national interest of the country to facilitate more trade, more exchange of information, creating more opportunities and more choices. The understanding of modern diplomacy by my government, my president, is that it must be concentrated in pushing trade, and when there is trade, political interest will come eventually. They are interconnected." This is important for "newly independent countries, especially those which just emerged after the collapse of the Soviet Union," he says.

"Unlike Germany, unlike Switzerland where they have the infrastructure, the experience and the skills to take care of themselves, we have an immature private sector. In my country, we unfortunately don't have any of these dimensions. The embassy should not hesitate to promote the interest here of American business in my country and vice versa, to my countrymen, about opportunities here."

* * *

Along with uranium, Uzbekistan's main exports to the United States include gold and cotton. The government-controlled mining consortium in a joint venture with Newmont Mining of Denver, Colorado, exported 25 tons of gold last year and Uzbekistan is the world's fourth largest cotton producer and the second largest exporter after the United States. Major oil companies, several of them American, are exploring how to convert Uzbekistan's abundance of natural gas, and more importantly, how to get it to market from the double landlocked Uzbekistan.

At Uzbekistan's national day on September 1, I met several businesspeople who were obviously courting this country. I learned from Molly Curtain, an environmental planner who designed the irrigation system in Uzbekistan for four years, that "Uzbeks are a very proud people. They have a sense of superiority but everyone is aware that Uzbeks will lead the economy and the tone for the region." But as a young woman just out of grad school, she found that "everyone is suspicious of the West and especially of Americans. After all those years of Soviet rule and the KGB they assumed that if I was doing water, I was CIA!"

Geophysicist Werner Johnson, a commercial advisor for Mobil Oil, made more than a half dozen trips in 1996 and 1997 "to evaluate the commercial viability to monetize gas. We never had an office there; I was just scoping the opportunities." But, according to Johnson, Mobil decided "not to pursue anything right now but leave the door open" mainly because of "the market aspect. With the conversion of natural gas into a liquid, which is what Uzbekistan has, the transportation makes it most difficult." Mobil does have an office in both Turkmenistan and Kazakhstan, where their "upstream" operations are already exploring and producing oil and gas.

Johnson reports that "Russian is the primary language for business in Tashkent," and he always had an interpreter by his side. He also found the mood to be very upbeat for business with "Germans and Koreans in the forefront for everything from telecommunications to making automobiles." Although he experienced one and a half inches of snow one January, it is often very hot, 110 degrees, which makes the business suits expected in Tashkent very uncomfortable. "It is very cosmopolitan, European-type business."

"I really got to know my Uzbek colleagues and found them very hospitable, open, friendly. We'd socialize, they'd take me home for dinner," says this American. "The food was outstanding." Furthermore, "They are really progressing; I saw a big difference between my first and last trip." For example, he says, "The entrepreneurs: some local guys opened a pizza place and it was excellent—some of the best pizza I've had anywhere in the world!"

This businessman says the Uzbek government tries "to keep control to protect the average person from the volatility and hardship of plunging into market reform. But, they will have a full, open market economy," says Johnson, who brought daggers, traditional Uzbek caps, brasswork and other artwork home as souvenirs.

* * *

Rahima Safaev is a small woman with big energy. Shortly after the ambassador leaves, she enters the Bukhara Room and takes his seat, tucking her mobile phone close to her and nodding that she is ready.

When I ask if she misses teaching, this diplomatic wife says, "Oh, yes. For ten years I taught but then I became the wife of an ambassador six years ago and already I do not think as a political scientist anymore." She is an academic who followed her husband to Bonn with their two-and-a-half-year-old son, leaving two college-age daughters back home. "I am dreaming to go to the Library of Congress to start my research and read a little bit," says this bright-eyed woman who already has two advanced degrees.

"I would like to do some kind of research in civil society here to see how democratic organizations are based. Without understanding it we can't create something similar," she explains. "I was not allowed to do that, being in the Soviet Union. I would like to do more and research about our nationality, our mentality, our culture because it is very important for the future. Without researching what happened in the past, we cannot think and prognosticate the future.

"I would love to go back to teach, I'm dreaming of teaching," she says, rolling her big black eyes. "This last six years has been a big experience. We came the first time to Europe and I didn't know how should I talk, how should I dress, how should I set out the table for the protocol. We never thought that we will be able to be a diplomat or to represent the country.

"The first week after arriving in America I was contacted by Marjory Shanklyn, then president of T.H.I.S., The Hospitality and Information Service of Meridian International Center. For me, it was the best group I ever met, that was the best way to make friends here with diplomats' wives and volunteers together. We meet twice a month for morning tea or lunch in someone's house or at an embassy to practice our English and discuss all sorts of topics.

"This is a completely different world for us, the people from the former Soviet Union countries. It's a different mentality." I ask her for an example. "If you ask me, 'How are you?'" she explains, "I'm supposed to say, 'Not bad.' If I say [like Americans do], 'Oh, Excellent,' 'Perfect,' how could you be perfect in this life? Because we have to think about the society, about the problems, and only then, about ourselves."

I wonder aloud if it was harder or easier for her to make the transition in Germany. There, "it was more difficult to learn because it was more protocol, it was more official. Here in America, I can be more normal, but it was good for me to go to Germany because I learned to be strict."

Speaking of being strict, I ask her how hard it is to rear her son in foreign countries. "My son, Jon [whose Uzbek name is Johongir] likes the freedom [of America] because he likes to be independent. He can speak with everybody and feel like a citizen of society. At home, it is more complex, more limited in everything. Even in first grade they say sit like this," she says, crossing her arms. "And if you need something and ask the teacher, they say, 'Don't do this, don't do that, don't go there, don't say this.'"

Her daughters are both married and living in Tashkent. Twenty-five-year-old Kamola is a research endocrinologist and the mother of their only grandchild, Ibrahim. Saida, who is 21, is studying dentistry. "They graduated from Russian school, which was not bad." Then, smiling, she adds, "It was excellent education. They already went to different countries [so] they can compare; they can get whatever they would like to get in the world. It's easier because they are young, but my mother, it was impossible for her to learn."

"In Germany, my mother came to visit me and it was a big surprise." She explains that her mother had been taught that "Germans are so bad." Instead, she saw that "they have a beautiful country, they are smiling, they are not bad people. She didn't understand; how could she? She was taught during 40 years that everything overseas or in foreign countries was bad."

I ask if she is still angry about the long Soviet occupation. "Seventy years was enough to remove the memory of Uzbekistan from the people in the world and now it is just time to put our name out. I have a philosophy education and I believe in the circles of history. Otherwise, you make wrong interpretations. You have to be very sensitive and value history, value the present and value the future.

"Just today I was walking on 17th Street with my friend and we met someone she knew and introduced me. She's Uzbek and he isn't. He asked me all these questions and we talked for 15 minutes, right there on the sidewalk. He said he couldn't wait to go and look us up on a map, on the website, in the library," says this one-woman chamber of commerce who loves to make new friends for her country. "I'm satisfied because that's one more person who knows.

"I'm always introducing myself and Uzbekistan and explaining everything. I do it officially in groups like the Congressional Wives and the Muslim Women's Group and at school and in shops and stores. And even when I go with two of my friends to help with Meals on Wheels."

As much as she enjoys Washington, when this diplomatic wife goes home on vacation there are several things she finds she can't import. "The first is dancing in the streets, everywhere and all the time. We dance for birthdays, weddings, holidays—there are people dancing in the streets. We love music. And, in the airport at home they respect the diplomats very much and in Europe they respect you too. But in U.S. customs they show no respect to diplomats.

"When I miss my country, I miss the smell of the country, the smell of the food," she says, closing her eyes to better imagine the fresh bread, luscious peaches, strawberries and famous fragrant Uzbek melons. "There are all kinds of fruits and vegetables in the bazaar and they insist that you taste them to test them. They are really delicious!"

Here, she does her own grocery shopping but "can't find a good market. We eat rice once or twice a week, one rice pilaf, one rice in soup. We eat lots of vegetables and spaghetti. I make it, it's different. I never buy it in the market. We have dumplings with meat and pumpkin. Stuffed cabbage with meat and rice and kabobs with fish, ground lamb."

When I ask if her son likes American food, she says emphatically, "He makes me crazy because all the time it's, 'Mommy, can we go to McDonald's?' 'Can we go to Pizza Hut?' Pizza Hut wasn't as good in Germany but we have McDonald's, Coke, and pizza at home in Uzbekistan," says this mother who admits to taking her son to McDonald's "when I want a big favor."

All the time she's talking about her children, I'm having a hard time imagining her with grown daughters. "I have one grandson, Ibrahim," she says proudly. "But I am not a grandmother; I am the wife of a grandfather!" She wishes she were closer now. "I have no chance to take care of grandchildren; they are too far away." When the ambassador was at Harvard, she and their three children stayed home in Tashkent.

Here, they live upstairs on the third floor of the former Canadian Embassy on the most congested block of Embassy Row. The ambassador's office and the reception rooms are on the two floors below. The staff works above the residence on the fourth floor and their driver and guests stay on the fifth floor. I wonder aloud what it's like to be sandwiched in between and have so little privacy. She shrugs her shoulders and tells me it's much calmer now that she's finished redecorating the handsome old mansion.

When I ask if living so close to her husband's office means they can have lunch together, she quickly shakes her head. "He always has lunch and dinner together, one meal, when he comes up at 5 P.M. After dinner he says, 'I just need to turn off my computer,' and he is running down and we are waiting, waiting, waiting while he is working until eight or nine o'clock."

"House rules" for their 11-year-old son mean that "he's allowed downstairs only after six at night, he sometimes comes to a party or reception but he has to be dressed well, and he's only allowed one guest at a time for a sleepover." But most of the time, this diplomat's son would rather roller blade in the back of the embassy or play soccer, basketball or "American football." Even though there is a sauna and aerobic workout room in the basement, the ambassador, once a professional soccer player, mostly goes to the neighborhood "Y." His trim diplomatic wife, who bypasses the elevator to run up and down the five flights all day, says, "I don't need much other exercise."

Before we leave the Bukhara Room for a tour of the rest of the embassy, she tells how difficult it is to create ganch, this famous design work that decorated the palace of the Emir of Bukhara so many centuries ago. "This room was done in 40 days by three young men we brought from Uzbekistan. You must be very fast. It's very difficult. You have to cut the plaster [right on the mirror] before it is dry. They worked twelve to fourteen hours a day," she says, sighing.

As we walk down the wide, elaborately paneled hallway toward the first of 30 fireplaces in this mansion of marble and exquisite hand-carved designs, she tells me how the embassy stayed open while the 40 Uzbek craftsmen brought from home refurbished these five floors in "the Uzbek way." Originally, it had been the home of Clarence Moore, a wealthy Washingtonian who lost his life on the Titanic in 1912. Immediately she adds, "My son saw the movie six times. He knows everything, the story, the people on it."

As she shows me the Uzbek sculpture and paintings on the landing of the grand staircase, I notice the huge white-and-blue stained glass design stretching above us to the ceiling. It celebrates her country's most famous product, cotton. But, on the eve of the World Cup soccer finals, I admit to this soccer mom that the white design reminds me of a soccer ball.

"Oh," she says excitedly, "my son is for Germany" (one of the national teams in the semifinals). I remember they choose The German School in Potomac, Maryland, for him because, "He came from German school and his English and German are better than mine, without any accent. "My son is really a German boy," says this mother who is happy her son absorbed "everything German" while his father was ambassador there. Now he "tries to do everything from the American perspective."

Now we're on their residence floor and I finally get to meet this athletic 11-year-old named Jon. When she opens the door, he comes busting out in his Bahamas T-shirt and cut-offs, starts hopping around and showing us his latest gymnastic tricks on the handsome Uzbek carpet.

As she takes me through their living quarters, she begins to describe her Muslim prayer rituals. "I pray five times a day but I can be anywhere. God is in my heart, in the car. Only every Friday am I at the Mosque from two to two-thirty." Because her son is at school at that time, I ask whether he leaves the classroom to go with her. "No, he should grow up first and understand before he goes."

Back downstairs, we say good-bye to the ambassador in his huge office. He surprises me with a beautiful book of Uzbek architectural and art treasures, which, according to the jacket cover, have "never before been seen in the West."

Then she takes me to the entrance floor, where she's proud to show me the Samarkand Room, hung with large photos of that 2,500-year-old city and more design panels that I say remind me of the Taj Mahal.

"Yes, of course," she begins, "they are related. Shah Jahan, who built the Taj Mahal in memory of his wife, is the great-grandson of Tamerland. Shah Babur, Shah Jahan's father, was from the Uzbek dynasty and came to India from Central Asia." While I'm still taking all this in, she wants to show me something else. "Just one more picture across the hall." From the ancient city of Samarkand, we spring to outer space and an enlarged color photo of Russian astronaut Sabirgon Sharipov in a NASA space suit. "He's Uzbek," she says, beaming.

* * *

As I pull out into the rush hour traffic across from the Brookings Institution, the venerable Washington think tank, I remember the story she told me about her son: "One day our son was drawing a map of the world with his finger on my husband's back," she says, "pointing out how he wanted to go to this place and that place. I wish we could all look at the world through his eyes, the eyes of a child where everything is possible."

6

South Africa: New World Model

This is one ambassador and one interview I shall never forget.

I went in with my tough questions written down and my tape recorder running. Within his first answer, I realize that his words, his voice, his passion are extraordinary and so would be this interview. I am not the only one impressed. Ambassador Franklin Sonn of South Africa has received ten honorary degrees in less than four years in Washington and is often on speaking engagements out of Washington. A personal friend of South African President Nelson Mandela and the first nonwhite ambassador to represent his country, Ambassador Sonn has a clear mission with a major message that Americans want to hear.

"South Africa is viewed upon by the world as a model, and the extent to which South Africa succeeds other heterogeneous societies will also follow that same process. The extent to which we fail will destroy confidence," he says in a velvety tone. This man with caramel-colored skin began as a high school principal, became a college president, and went on to receive national and international recognition as president of South Africa's teachers' union. In 1992, he was former President Jimmy Carter's personal advisor in monitoring the Zambian elections.

"I got a letter from Mandela [which was] smuggled out to me from prison. It is my most proudest possession," says Ambassador Sonn, who has Mandela's letter praising Sonn's work with the teachers' union framed and hanging in the official residence. "Those are the best memories of all my life—those kinds of accolades.

"South Africa must be seen against the context of a society that has had dramatic change but is still a society in transition," says Sonn. "Often people forget that we [South Africa since Apartheid] are only five years old, the extent

South African Ambassador Franklin Sonn and Mrs. Sonn with South African President Nelson Mandela. Photo by Ken Cobb.

of the change and the challenges that are facing us. ... It is one thing to write a constitution, to change the government. But to change the behavior pattern, to marry the cultures, to affect the process of reconciliation, to build the confidences, to bring and create respect and greater acceptability within a world that often is racist is a difficult and time-consuming process.

"We have to govern effectively, deliver to the people and manage the inequities in society and reconcile our society. The most outstanding, glaring inequity is the level of development of blacks against whites. ... The essential crime of Apartheid was how it advantaged whites, and this played itself out mainly in education and training."

I ask this well-educated man, who calls himself "colored," how he was able to go to university. "My grandfather was a poor laborer," he begins. "My father and mother were teachers, so I come from a professional background. Under Apartheid, it was not unusual for families 'to eke out an existence' while saving to send a 'chosen' brother or sister to school. In white families, it was a common assumption to go automatically to university. My mother and father and girlfriend, who's now my wife, all helped me go to school."

Ambassador Sonn was 27 when he entered a university.

The more I hear, the more I wonder what he did with his anger. "I think it is impossible for anybody not to have anger if you have been systematically and deliberately disadvantaged. You live with it for the rest of your life … but you must manage your anger," he says in a beautiful voice with a charming, refined British accent.

"Mandela … selects his time to show his anger," says his disciple. "When you are angry, you are not in control. For example, when you sit in solitary confinement [like Mandela did] with a whole gambit of emotions, you start thinking that these people can only upset me if I participate. And that is the point of our struggle. It was, in fact, to get in charge of our anger and to get beyond it. That was the greatest weapon we used," he says. "People thought, 'Gee, I thought they would jump through the roof but they are so calm and calculating' … and that's disarming and that was part of our strength and our victory. In South Africa, control of anger almost became a national sport!"

My head spins with the implications of the disciple's words in the context of the United States' own racial problems. He continues, "We are aware that we have a mission in the world as black people. … Whites always feared that if they give us the rights we will do to them what they've done to us. They are so surprised if we do the opposite and it's important for us as Africans to show [that] humanness is our strength.

"Africans easily call each other brothers and sisters, because it's a world vision—as a disadvantaged brother, [you] owe it to your advantaged brother to show him the superior way. This is very much the African way, not just the South African way. That's why we were so easily colonized, because of our welcoming and open and humane attitude towards strangers."

I ask him if he has to be careful, considering what he just said, to not be too accommodating, too agreeable. "No, we just understand better," he answers. "We know where to draw the lines. We remain humane and personable, because we believe it is our greatest strength. But we realize we must modify in relation to the situation. We feel confident about ourselves; we know who we are. We have come through the crucible, the worst possible situations—we've seen human beings at their worst so we don't fear."

"My wife was always telling our children about her fears of my fearlessness," he explains. "I don't think I am driven at all by fear. You fear the unknown but when you get to the unknown it is not worse than your capacity to deal with it."

As an example, Ambassador Sonn tells me how, as union leader, he often found himself at the deathbed of a member. "I saw how fearless they were—

how peaceful. The human spirit soars beyond the worst situation if you allow it to," says this religious man who in his earlier life was active in South Africa's Christian youth movement as a member of the Dutch Reform Church.

"Whites are more surprised. They are a bit in awe that the government is doing so well, that there is so much forgiveness," he says, beating me to my next question about those on the other side of Apartheid. "If there is anything they are guilty about, it's that they had thought that we would fail—whites were totally taken by surprise."

At this embassy and at South African embassies around the world, there has been an "amalgamation of the foreign service," and as the result there are staffers and diplomats from before and after Apartheid who all work together in a new system with a new focus.

As an educator, Ambassador Sonn believes education, or as he would say, "access to education," is the key. "The extent to which South Africa will succeed and to the extent to which we will have greater self-determination for black people will be a function of education. We will [still] have racially divided schools but the mainstream will be integrated."

I ask Ambassador Sonn what it has been like for him and his family to live in a country where there is also fighting and discrimination between the races. "I feel like a fish in water. We [South Africa and the United States] have so much in common and many of the same problems. We are both heterogeneous, English-speaking democracies. And, very helpful to me particularly, it [the United States] is a country that respects free speech, where you can have your say.

"Americans are very sure of themselves. As citizens of the only superpower in a unipolar world, Americans sometimes sense that they know what's good for you. We feel it is our integrity to say, 'no.' We think the way we do it is better. We take an independent, issue-by-issue position, unlike many poor African countries who look to America for aid and say 'whatever America does is right, just help us.'"

Always the diplomat, Ambassador Sonn softens his complaint. "We want to retain our pride, sovereignty and integrity and at the same time make progress with the Americans on a day-to-day basis with trade, with business."

Now discussing economics, I ask about the rand, South Africa's currency, and his answer is honest but in no way apologetic. "Our rand was volatile, a consequence of the Asian contagion, which gave rise to investors removing some money from the Third World countries to the First World. That will reverse again. Currency in other emerging countries suffered much more than ours."

Taking the opportunity to talk business, he launches into a short list of why his country is a good trade partner for the United States. "Markets want reliability, they don't want surprises. They want stability. They want to be sure that what you say today you will say tomorrow. They want integrity. They want you to be honest and straight. They have come to understand that these features are symbolized by our president. But he's not an exception. He symbolizes in a wonderful way who and what we all are."

And while South Africa's rand has been losing some value, the country has also been losing some of its best and brightest citizens in what has been called "White Flight" or "White Exodus." Since the majority of the people educated in the past were white, most of South Africa's professionals are white. These former Afrikaners have fled due to fear of the high crime rate and the country's uncertain future. I ask the ambassador how critical the problem is.

"We don't say, 'move out.' We say, 'move over.' Our whole emphasis is not to deny people who are South African a right of access to their heritage. But some people feel threatened by black people and by change." He speaks softly but firmly. "We want to be a comfort to our previous oppressors; they are our people and I will defend them as hard as I can. Our first priority is to come to terms with them and create confidence with them and live in peace. Our second priority is to do it in an integrated community."

But due to the increase of crime in South Africa after Apartheid, I ask Ambassador Sonn if such fear isn't justified. "Crime should be seen in perspective," he answers, pointing to a parallel pattern of crime increase in the United States when "America also started loosening up, making your society more open [between the races].

"Wherever there are major changes in society, there are high levels of crime because international criminals exploit [countries with] greater freedoms, because there is bail, due process. With enough money and good lawyers they can escape. A lot of [South African] crime is blamed on transition; there are disgruntled elements in the police force, security force."

Ambassador Sonn even suggests that some of these former enforcers of the law under Apartheid have "been tempted to join the criminals."

"The point I'm trying to make is that South Africa doesn't have a crime problem because it's South Africa. There are sociological forces which … create criminality. We are dealing with it scientifically, not episodically." He cites the "forces" of poverty and low or no education that lead to crime.

"In more than 20 years in my home township—an area for blacks—where we have a big, comfortable house, there has not been one burglary. If you accumulate statistics and look at crime in Washington, D.C., we would be horrified. South Africa is a miracle," he says, suggesting that their crime rate is not bad considering the country's dramatic change in social structure.

When I ask him if events in South Africa including crime have been reported unfairly, he responds, "Yes, there is an element of journalists looking for bad stories, thinking our story is too good to be true. There has been too much journalistic concentration on crime as a downside of the South African miracle."

Surrounded by photographs of President Mandela with him and his family, Ambassador Sonn talks about his relationship with the world-famous, Nobel–prizewinning South African. "I am personally very close to Mandela. He has a way of treating me; he calls me 'my boy.' I feel personally attached to him." Although Ambassador Sonn tries not to bother Mandela with frequent calls, "his daughter tells me he misses it and that I should call him more often. I am very flattered by that but I don't [call], because I realize how precious his time is, how many people want to talk to him."

He starts describing how he felt the day Mandela finally was released after 27 years in prison. "I was there the day he was released. When he came into public view, he saw me and called out my name, and I remember the emotions I experienced." He crosses his arms as if to hug himself. "He called me himself the night he asked me to come here.

"When my mother died in Cape Town, a two-hour flight away, he came to the funeral, and he asked to speak at the funeral. When my daughter was married in Cape Town he tried but couldn't come. But he called and said they must come for breakfast the next morning. I don't think I'm an exception; he makes everybody feel personally attached."

Mandela had recently married Graca Machel and I ask Ambassador Sonn if he knew her. "Yes, I was supposed to go to their wedding but I couldn't. Their relationship is unbelievable. She is friendly, warm, loving. They are such a match … such the same people. She is a woman in her own right: eleven years minister of education in her own country, Mozambique, the widow of its president, and a candidate to be the UN's secretary-general."

Ambassador Sonn is scheduled to have another appointment and leaves to check whether they have arrived. I spend the few moments glancing around the office. Behind his desk is a big, bright crayoned "DAD" that he later tells me his grown daughter, Heather, did years ago. "It's always with me," says the proud papa. In another prominent spot, a striking picture of Nelson Mandela with Bill Cosby hangs on the wall as part of a calendar.

When I tell him how much I like the picture, he asks me if I want it and immediately turns around, takes the big calendar off the wall and hands it to me. Completely surprised by the gesture, I start flipping through the months, each one with another interesting, often historic picture of Nelson Mandela, the charismatic South African leader. When I ask him to sign the cover, he inscribes it: "To Gail Scott, My New Friend."

Throughout the interview, we have been waiting for Ambassador Sonn's wife, Joan, to join us. At one point, he calls and casually asks her to come. When his next guest is late, he shows me around the roomy office, which is actually a second-floor bridge between the chancery and the residence. Then he opens the door to his official home, where his wife is entertaining an old friend from South Africa. When I suggest that I could leave and he could join them, he says, "Oh, no, I have an appointment." After the door shuts, and we are alone, he impishly says, "You almost got me into trouble there," obviously not wanting to join the women and their tea party.

As I say good-bye, I ask him if he misses South Africa. "I can't wait to go back. I could stay here longer but I miss being part of this wonderful experience," referring to the historic metamorphosis of his homeland.

* * *

A few days later I return to the embassy to talk with Joan Sonn. I notice the dramatic difference between the indigenous African art and the more traditional European style art that is hanging on the dark, paneled walls of imported African stinkwood. Upstairs, I wait for her arrival in the double drawing room.

More than 30 minutes later, Mrs. Sonn enters through the garden in her stretch pants, T-shirt, and partial ponytail. This is a first. Throughout my research for this book, ambassadors' wives (there has only been one husband) have always arrived at our interview well dressed, carefully coifed and made-up just in case a camera was near.

"I'm so sorry to keep you waiting," she says, quickly sitting down next to me. "It's almost 5 P.M. in South Africa, and I have been working since 6:30 all morning on two responses that needed to get there before five. It's hard with the time difference. I didn't even get my run."

A lean, athletic woman, Mrs. Sonn looks down at her Nikes. When I tell her that I'm impressed she even tries to exercise with her busy schedule, she outlines her exercise routine for me, which includes shorter runs and longer walks in nearby Rock Creek Park and down to the Potomac River, several miles away. She also loves to rollerskate and wishes she could bike more. "I'd love to exercise everyday, but sometimes it's just impossible and other days I can get away for two to three hours." On weekends, her husband joins her, but "I can out-walk Franklin."

"I can't believe four years are almost over," says this former teacher and mother of two. "From the beginning, we were happy when we heard that three of the ambassadors from Cape Town were going to be here—the British, the German, and the Greek—and they made contact with us [in South Africa] even before we knew it was final that we were coming here. It was comforting and reassuring that they would be here."

"We did have some apprehension—but it made it less as they were very kind, and our tutors on Washington diplomacy in the way of telling us what to do and how to go about things, because Franklin and I are not career diplomats." In Cape Town the Sonns had a constant flow of visitors, from education or politics, because Franklin is internationally known. They wanted a "true reflection of what was happening."

In 1977–78, the Sonns came to the United States to meet with the U.S. State Department and visit his brother, Julian, who lives in Richmond, Virginia, and his sister, Marlene, who lives in Canada.

"Our nephew, Julian's son, just spent the weekend with us here," she says, gesturing around the spacious drawing room.

On that original trip, the Sonns went to New England and ended up getting snowed in. "I had never seen snow and we were snowed in for seven days! I was so excited. We were walking in a forest and I was like a child. I picked up the snow, rubbed it against my face—it was the most wonderful thing."

The Sonns have lived their entire lives in Africa, and I ask if they enjoyed the seasons here. "Yes, except Franklin doesn't like the cold, and in the winter he doesn't even go outside." Fortunately, his office is only a door away from his living quarters. In South Africa there often is no air conditioning. "We have heat but not this humidity. In fact, the hotter it is the more we are outside. From breakfast to late-night snack at 11 P.M. we are sitting out. We can't here."

When I explain that I wanted to meet and interview them for a long time but was told again and again, "The ambassador is out of town," she nods her head. "Life here has been very hectic, especially in comparison to daily life in our country. All the changes at home have put us right on the map. I don't know another ambassador who's had so many speaking engagements. In fact, I think he's booked up 'til next April, and we are supposed to leave this December! The first two years we traveled more; I think Franklin has been to all of the states, met most of the governors and mayors of your big cities and was the only ambassador invited to the Governor's Conference."

I mention to her that after interviewing him, I understand why he is a much sought-after speaker. "He's a teacher," she says, smiling, "and he loves students and all kinds of people. When people come here for receptions that are supposed to be from 6 P.M. to 8 P.M. people don't leave until 11:30," she says, squinting her eyes and feigning fatigue. "He's always telling people, 'Look, stay as long as you want to,' and they do."

"We don't take ourselves very seriously," Mrs. Sonn says, giving another reason she thinks they have been so well received here. "We know protocol, know how to do things and what's right and what's wrong, but this is our home and we are very friendly people," she says. As South Africa's first lady in Washington, she graciously encourages other diplomats in the embassy to hold their own events in this residence because, "It is the people's embassy." She tells them, "This is your home too."

Ironically, when her husband came to Washington ahead of his appointment and saw the residence, "He told me, 'We're not going to live there!' He thought it was so dark and dreary, and since we have two houses here, one for the DCM [deputy chief of mission], he thought we might live there instead. So I did nothing here at first, hoping to live elsewhere." But the paperwork and arrangements took too long, and she gave up and started to rearrange this residence. She hopes the embassy has been transformed into a much brighter, happier place. "It was so dark and sparsely decorated; only two or three pictures with all these walls, and these couches were lined up along the side of the room," she remembers. "Franklin did most of it. He's even better with interior design than I am."

Then I ask her the question she would spend the next hour answering: "How did you meet?"

She smiles and takes a deep breath. "We were both at a dance in Port Elizabeth. It was December, and I was to become engaged in March. He spotted me and watched where I went to sit and realized I was with a woman he knew, my cousin's wife, Shirley. While I was dancing he went over to her and asked who I was, declaring, 'I'm going to get married to her!' Shirley said, 'You're crazy, you're mad. She has a steady boyfriend and she's getting married in March.' When I came back to the table Shirley told me. The next dance he came over and he started talking, asking me who it was in Cape Town that I was going to marry and he said he knew him. He told me, 'Look, I have just met you and I have told Shirley that I am going to marry you.' I thought he was arrogant, I hated him! He went back to Shirley and reported, 'I've spoken to her, and she's hating me. But he's not the man for her. I really can't let this happen.'"

"But that's Franklin—he takes charge," Mrs. Sonn vows, explaining that her husband even tells their friends how to redo their homes. "My sister says, 'You married the worst man. Unfortunately, he's always right.' Then she adds, laughing. 'And if you don't listen to him, you'll be sorry.' Everyone knows it. Somehow, he's right. It's as if he has a genie. People respect and resent him for it," she says. "Not that he wants to take over. He's just so powerful, not dominant. He doesn't want to be that way. He gets beautiful letters all the time saying, 'Only in the last few years with you … I've realized my potential.' He changes peoples' lives."

She tells me of a secret meeting in 1971 when South African blacks and whites, academics and businesspeople gathered to "talk about what are we going to do to make miracles happen." One well-known white intellectual, Willy Esterhuyse, was there as well as her husband. Esterhuyse is an author and a professor at Stellenbosch University, where only whites were allowed. "Franklin walked and talked with him through the night and changed his mind."

She returns to her story of courtship. "Shirley came to tell my mother and then Mother told me, 'He's a good Christian youth.' At the time we were both in the Christian Youth Union and he thought he was going to become a minister of religion. During holiday we would all get together and go and have services on the beach.

"Unfortunately, Arthur [her fiancé] had olive skin, green eyes, and black hair and looked like a Greek god," she says, lifting her shoulders. But Franklin, who knew him from their sports club in Cape Town, insisted both to her and to Shirley that Arthur drank and wasn't good enough for the girl Franklin wanted to marry. "I was a girl from the country, Arthur and his family came from Cape Town," she adds, defending her naivete.

Then Arthur's family gave a dinner dance for the young Joan in Cape Town, and she saw for herself what Franklin Sonn had warned her about. "All his friends were women and he was drinking too much," she says. "I found him in the dancing room dancing 'the blues' with a girl. You don't do the blues with someone else," she says, explaining that when the lights are low and usually blue, and the music is slow and romantic, that's "the blues."

She immediately left the dance, returned to pack, "wrote a note and left in the night." After being "very sad" for more than a year, this young teacher from the countryside returned to Cape Town when city cousins invited her again. "As I walked in, they said, 'Aunty Violet just sold her house around the corner to the Sonns.' But Franklin was away on a Christian Youth Trip."

Ironically, during the future Mrs. Sonn's visit to Cape Town, Franklin Sonn was at her home in George, in the Cape, having dinner with her family! "My father met him and several other students when he went out to buy vegetables. He heard these students saying that they had nowhere to stay that night. So he invited them home for dinner." During a wonderful chat over dinner, Joan's mother realized that this Franklin Sonn was the same young man who had vowed to marry her daughter.

Finally, years after they first met, the two found themselves at the same dance where Joan's escort that night turned out to be Franklin's brother, Julian.

"Franklin and I ended up dancing the whole night together." Once again, Franklin Sonn was right after all.

They married, helped each other go back to school, and had two children. She's eager to show me their pictures. When I see her daughter Heather's college graduation picture, I recognize "the Quad" at Smith where my daughter Indrani graduated the year before. We talk about our daughters' college days.

"I remember her crying on the phone, calling us in South Africa from college," she says. But when Mrs. Sonn first arrived on the Smith campus in Northampton, Massachusetts, for Heather's graduation, "I wanted to cry. It was so lovely," she says, wishing she had been able to visit her daughter during the four years she was there. Heather's vice principal [in South Africa] had gone to Harvard and encouraged her to apply when she asked him about a Smith notice on the school bulletin board. "She won a scholarship," says her proud mom, who herself had to settle for a "commercial degree in accounting," because in her generation, "only sons got the education."

Their son, Crispin, has a telecommunications business in South Africa, and Heather is married and works for Merrill Lynch in New York. Her mother adds hopefully, "Merrill Lynch is about to open an office in Johannesburg, and Heather may come!" Interestingly, today Mrs. Sonn uses what she learned in business school "checking with our broker in South Africa on a daily basis."

All the talk about our children and their colleges sadly reminds me of Amy Biehl, the young American Fulbright scholar who was killed in South Africa when she drove some black friends home. I had just seen her parents on *Good Morning, America* and was so taken with their grace in forgiving her killers in the spirit of the Truth and Reconciliation Commission. I tell Mrs. Sonn what is going through my mind. "You just want to cry if you put yourself in their shoes," she says. "They are wonderful people; I have met them. The Biehls say they have forgiven, but they can't forget."

Then she stops and looks straight at me. "It all could have turned out differently; it could have been such a bloody revolution. Mandela has such striking qualities. I'll never forget the first picture I saw of him when he came out of jail. He was shaking the hand of the person who had locked him up for 27 years—the expression on his face. I just broke down. The spirit of forgiveness. It can only come from people who have suffered so much. I'd love to say, 'I can do that,' but I'm not sure I can."

We continue looking at pictures of the Sonns with famous Americans like Sidney Poitier and Harry Belafonte. Then she tells me about the origins of the dark, heavy Cape Dutch style hutches, bureaus and tables that came all the way from South Africa to this embassy. I have already heard that the magnificent oriental rug was a "hand-me-down" from their former neighbor, the Iranian Embassy. As Mrs. Sonn tells it, "With the fall of the Shah of Iran, they didn't know what to do with this huge rug so they approached our ambassador and asked him if he wanted to buy it since it couldn't be sent back."

When I ask about the red dots on the picture frames, she answers, "We're about to pack." As she prepares to reenter South Africa's new society, I ask how she feels about all the changes she has witnessed in her homeland. She closes her eyes and begins, "I never knew it would happen in our lifetime. I still remember, as a newly married person, when they refused to do my hair in a beauty salon.

"And, worst of all," she continues, "I remember when our daughter was just six weeks old and she was crying so hard because it was so hot. We stopped at a petrol station to get a little cool water to put her in. The toilets were locked and only opened for white people but nobody was around. Franklin went around the back where he saw a young mechanic. He said, 'Excuse me, sir, but I need some cool water for my baby.' And this young, uneducated mechanic said, 'I'm boss. Who do you think you're talking to?' Franklin came back with tears running down his face. It was so degrading, so humiliating.

"Franklin said, 'An animal in the woods can provide better for his offspring. Here I am educated, a principal of a high school, president of a 22,000-member teachers' union, people come to me from all over the world to get the true perspective on change in my country. I'm this guy and I can't provide for my child.' He felt so hopeless and helpless."

But, typical of Franklin Sonn, as Mrs. Sonn goes on, "He wrote to the company, Caltex, and demanded to see the CEO, who invited him to come see him. And they created the idea for a symbol, a white rabbit, that would go on the bathroom door to signal that both whites and blacks could use it."

Once again, Franklin Sonn made a difference. "I think and I hope that I have made a difference," Mrs. Sonn says. "I wanted this residence to be open. When people come here they often tell me they have been here before—but this is the first time they have ever been invited inside. They tell me, 'The last time I was here I was picketing outside and I got put in jail for it.'"

* * *

Ambassador and Mrs. Sonn have returned to South Africa where he and his son Crispin have an international consulting business together.

7

The Baltics— Estonia, Latvia, Lithuania: A Three for All

The Baltic states—Estonia, Latvia and Lithuania—are like three brothers, distinctively different in personality but still obviously from the same Northern European family. Bordering the Baltic Sea across from Sweden and south of Finland, these three countries and their ambassadors are tied together by their precious independence regained from the disintegrating Soviet Union in the fall of 1991. Their continuing concern about keeping the Russians out of their backyards makes full membership in the North Atlantic Treaty Organization (NATO) the number-one issue for all three.

It was easy enough to reestablish diplomatic ties with the United States, because America never recognized the Soviet occupation of Estonia, Latvia and Lithuania when the Soviets forcefully took over with Hitler's complicity in 1940 and stayed more than 50 years. "The Balts," as they call themselves, woke up in a bit of a time warp in the early 1990s and today they hurry to pick up their national lives, which were squelched for more than half a century by Soviet troops, dogma and intimidation.

All three were independent nations before the Soviets marched in and began to mysteriously "relocate" hundreds of thousands of Baltic citizens to Siberia and other infamous gulags. Soviet rule decimated more than one-third of the Estonian population. Other Baltic citizens escaped by emigrating to the West. In fact, over one million Lithuanians now call America home.

Today, as they cherish and openly celebrate their pre-Soviet heritage, Estonia, Latvia and Lithuania each rush to recover economically as they create market economies, compete against one another and hope to enter the millennium with pride and solvency. The metamorphoses of these three countries are somewhat alike but as interestingly different as are the three distinct personalities of their ambassadors.

Ambassadors Ilves, Liljegren, Kalnins and Eidintas with the author at Ambassador Ilves's farewell party. Photo courtesy of Diplomatic Photography by Albert.

Since I first interviewed with them, only one, Latvian Ambassador Ojars Kalnins, remains in Washington. He is now dean of the European Diplomatic Corps, a helpful position for a country that is still trying to convince itself and many others that it is an integral part of the European community.

Toomas Ilves, the Estonian, left Washington in late 1996 to become Estonia's foreign minister until the government changed. Both his colleagues and Baltic experts say they would not be surprised to see this former Washington ambassador run for high office in Estonia. Alfonsas Eidintas, the Lithuanian, is now ambassador to Canada.

Two of the three original ambassadors had to give up their American citizenship to represent their newly independent countries. All three are well-educated, middle-aged men who brought their families to Washington. One used to be a Chicago advertising executive who became a well-known activist, another was a Radio Free Europe broadcaster based in Germany and the third was a leading historian and author battling Soviet rewrite artists daily to tell his students what really happened.

For more than five years, when the U.S. State Department did something these three men disliked, they would march in together and complain in chorus: the cool but blunt Estonian with his freshly starched white shirt, prim bow tie, wire spectacles, straight back and fancy vocabulary to match; the newly wed Latvian with the beard he grew as a protester plus his easy manner in negotiating "win-win" solutions he learned in advertising; and the

Exterior of the Embassy of Estonia on Washington's Embassy Row. Photo courtesy of the Estonian Embassy.

jolly, less-polished Lithuanian, who is not as sure of his English but is sure of the pain he witnessed in his homeland and knows Baltic history firsthand.

Of course, what they have in common is their passion for freedom, their gratitude to the United States for never recognizing the Soviet domination and their determination to help their countries be proud and popular nations while still answering the needs of Americans of Baltic heritage.

* * *

Besides the friendly hand extended by the United States, they happily substituted for their former Soviet "Big Brother" a kinder and wise neighbor, former Ambassador Henrik Liljegren of Sweden, to guide them.

Toomas Hendrik Ilves, the former Estonian ambassador, had an extra reason to feel a kinship with this Swedish ambassador. "He is half Estonian and I was born in Sweden," explains Ilves, who came to the United States when he was only three, grew up in New Jersey, graduated from Columbia

University and received his masters degree in psychology from the University of Pennsylvania, but had never lived in Estonia prior to becoming ambassador.

When I first meet him, I ask what it was like for him to give up his American citizenship at age 40. "I think the U.S. officials around me were more upset. For me, it was a test to one's commitment to Estonia's independence."

We are sitting one floor directly below his circular office in the embassy's new Kalorama chancery, a handsome Washington landmark that once was the Landon School for Boys. "Eleven or twelve countries tried to buy it before us," he proudly explains, "but we worked with the neighborhood association, invited our immediate neighbors in, and from the beginning, offered to rent garage space." That did it! District residents are understandably disgruntled when embassies move next door and all nearby parking spaces are declared diplomatic property.

"This building is one of the few buildings here that reminds us of Tallinn, the largest medieval town in Europe with 46 towers. The Saudis have their minarets. For us, it is a medieval old town for which this part of northern Europe is known." The academic ambassador drives home his point, "I wanted the impression of an old country, not newly independent country. ... I wanted the ethno-psychological effect that would evoke old Europe." This young ambassador pulls from his years of translating "the psycho-pathological" themes in Estonian literature, which even he admits to being depressing, especially during the years when the Soviet-suppressed country was losing so much of its identity, including its own language.

But now, here in Washington, Estonia is not only surviving but thriving. On a small but "important" point of land jutting out to Massachusetts Avenue, this formal ambassador may have a new embassy, but the look is of established diplomatic dignity. And, inside, he has achieved an impressive interior. Whether it's clever diplomacy or just the "Yankee ingenuity" of this former American, Ilves admits to regular weekend forays into suburbia's yard sales and closeouts to find the fancy furnishings within budget. His goal was to conjure up the memory of the main hall in Estonia's beloved national university built in 1632, and many Estonians vow he did just that.

We walk around the curved wall and read an old letter from Calvin Coolidge, another framed document from the Consul of Estonia dated June 1926 in San Francisco and another from the Consul of Estonia in New York, 1918.

In contrast, up the rebuilt spiral staircase, four diplomats run as modern and computerized an embassy as possible. "In a sense, I'm 'in' all day. My e-mail is always open; the link with Estonia is never closed. We are far more computerized than any other embassy," says the former professor. "With our webpages we functionally increased our size." All over Washington this new technology is leveling the diplomatic playing field and making smaller embassies especially effective.

"I log on at home, check out *The [Washington] Post's* website, our own news agencies and read the next day's three main Estonian newspapers on the web by seven or eight at night," says the ambassador, who does his own analysis. "I am much closer to being a journalist or a minister-counselor for political affairs," says this forty-something intellectual who did on-air political play-by-play for Radio Free Europe. "I do the same thing here; I process a hell of a lot of news and write reports."

Unlike professional diplomats of bigger countries who come up through the ranks and reach Washington as a career coup, these brand-new diplomats of smaller nations don't have any time to party. "My big treat is to sleep in on Sunday morning until nine!" He almost smiles. "I work long hours, twelve to fourteen a day, nights and weekends," says the father of a pre-schooler and a nine-year-old, who already speaks three languages, wears a bow tie at embassy functions and looks just like his dad. Similar to a lot of American dual-career couples, Ilves met his wife, Dr. Merry Bullock, in graduate school. While in Washington, she is a prominent senior scientist at the American Psychological Association and, according to the ambassador, "DAR material." In addition to mirroring many dual-career Americans they also have a nanny.

Back to business. "We are the future Singapore," he claims, sounding now more like a salesman than a statesman as he lights another cigarette. "We have no tariffs, no import duties, foreigners can buy land, own currency, which is 100 percent convertible, and we just dropped the need for a visa." He continues to praise his country's 100 percent repatriation and strategic location. "We have three times the investment rate of Poland."

I can tell it's time for me to go. He answers five questions in a row with "Yep." He's proud that "Littany," an Estonian group, has the number-one CD on the classical charts and is a previous Grammy nominee. And his favorite vacation is anywhere that mobile phones don't work. He admits he is more stern, stoic and dry-humored than his Baltic brothers. "Like Lutherans," he says. I close my notebook.

I leave this little bit of Estonia through the heavy iron and glass door and walk away into the sunshine.

* * *

In comparison to my visit with the cool, distant Estonian, those with the Latvian and the Lithuanian ambassadors touched my very soul. I cried twice

The author with Latvian Ambassador Ojars Kalnins and Mrs. Kalnins. Photo by Gail Scott.

while listening to the Latvian's stories, something I haven't done in more than 30 years of interviewing. The Lithuanian ambassador kept my attention for more than three hours. At the end, I felt emotionally drained.

"I'm a born-again Latvian," says Ojars Kalnins, the 46-year-old former American advertising executive whose high school buddies back in Chicago call him "O.J." He was born in Munich, Germany, in a U.S.-controlled refugee camp and emigrated to America with his parents when he was only two years old.

The first time he ever stepped on Latvian soil, he had already graduated from an American college and was working in a Chicago advertising firm. He had come back to Latvia with his young wife to meet his new in-laws. He had no family left in Latvia.

"It was 1978. I didn't speak Latvian very well … but, I remember the exact moment I realized that this was my country. We were riding in on a bus from the airport to the hotel. I saw a huge neon sign that said 'milk' in Latvian. That was the first time I ever saw anything in Latvian like that. I thought, this is a legitimate, real country," he says softly. "Then, I saw the Soviet troops, and the anger came."

Growing up as an only child in one of Chicago's poor, ethnic neighborhoods, this young immigrant lived in two separate worlds. "In the daytime, I went to school and spoke English but in the evenings and on weekends, I lived in the Latvian community." His father was a construction worker by day, but "at night, he put on his tuxedo and was a musician in a dance band. At all the Polish and Lithuanian weddings, my mother and I sat at the back table with all the other families and got a free meal.

"My father wanted me to play the piano; I wanted to play baseball." Kalnins was the only Latvian among his daytime friends. "There were Poles, Ukrainians, Greeks, Czechs, Germans. But when my friends asked me about my name and I said it was Latvian, they figured it was Lapland or something. No one knew who we were. In history class, they didn't talk about us and we didn't appear on the evening news. The whole idea of Latvia seemed remote, like a mythical country to me."

What an incredible, touching story, I thought—to go, in one's lifetime, from feeling you were from a pretend, invisible country that no one knew, to becoming that country's ambassador with the official mission to make everyone in America and its capital know and appreciate Latvia and its capital, Riga, a cosmopolitan port city with a thirteenth-century pedigree. And how to do this on a meager budget, with a tiny staff, from an ordinary-looking brick house hidden back in a forgotten neighborhood off upper 16th Street? Once again, the story unfolds and this house takes on historic proportions.

Kalnins's predecessor, Anatols Dinbergs, who for more than 50 years kept Latvian hopes for independence alive, bought this modest home for $28,000 in 1953 from the original cache of 50,000 ounces of gold that Riga moved to the West before Stalin's crackdown.

Through wise investments, Dr. Dinbergs, a lawyer by education, was able to buy the current embassy and then entirely finance the legation's complete activities for all those years from the interest earned on Latvian assets. According to *The Wall Street Journal,* when Latvian independence was restored in 1991 and the new government was able to reclaim those original 40-pound gold blocks, they were worth $18 million.

But for five long decades, exiled diplomat Dinbergs became white-haired waiting for attention while the White House and U.S. State Department entertained Moscow's envoys. Dinbergs watched American presidents come and go, from the ailing Franklin Roosevelt to feisty Harry Truman through West Pointer Dwight Eisenhower to Hollywood's Ronald Reagan.

On November 18, 1991, Latvia's Independence Day, Ambassador Anatols Dinbergs returned to his homeland for the first time since 1937 to be honored for his 50-plus years of service in exile. Already in his eighties, Dinbergs remained ambassador of his newly recognized country for only one year before retiring.

In the meantime, Kalnins had already renounced U.S. citizenship to become Dinbergs' minister counselor and deputy chief of mission (DCM). Before that, he served as his press spokesman and public affairs liaison.

In 1978, after seeing the Soviet repression firsthand, young Kalnins returned to Chicago ready to fight for Latvia's freedom. "I asked myself, 'Why was I so lucky? They suffered all their lives. I visited for two weeks but they had to stay.' I decided, 'I've got to use my opportunities in the West, my writing and my advertising to help.'"

Ambassador Kalnins's parents had died but this newly inspired patriot started telling anyone who would listen about Latvia. He wrote letters to the editors, got on talk shows, marched in demonstrations. He wrote feverishly for the *Chicago Latvian Newsletter* and became its editor. He started to look like the pro-independence quarterback for Latvians in the United States.

So when the American Latvian Association, the largest Latvian organization outside Latvia, decided the time had come for a full-time director of public relations, Kalnins was it. He followed his heart and moved his wife and young daughter to Washington for half his annual advertising executive's salary—$15,000 and a storage-room "office" in the basement of a suburban Maryland church. Appropriately, it was nicknamed "the Bunker."

"I thought I'd do this for a few years and then get a real job. But I became a fanatic. I was totally taken. I started going to Latvia. I went dozens of times," he remembers defiantly. And, always, with the KGB watching every move this passionate American made.

He vividly and proudly remembers "the spark that got things moving." Mikhail Gorbachev was at the helm and glasnost was in fashion. It was September 1986, and he was one of seven Latvian Americans to attend Chautauqua '86, a U.S.-Soviet sponsored event in Riga. "The Soviets threatened us and that's when it became a story. We starting passing out American-Latvian pins and that made the KGB livid."

Philip Taubman of *The New York Times* did a story and "when we came back, we were treated like conquering heroes. That led to the first demonstration [in Latvia] one year later."

Flipping through Ambassador Kalnins's family photo albums, I see the dance band and the little boy in an American cowboy suit on a fake pony; the bearded, long-haired student demonstrator on TV protesting Soviet occupation; the Latvian-American lobbyist driving activists up to Congress in his beat-up Honda; and finally, the new Latvian ambassador presenting his credentials to the president of the United States.

But something is wrong with the picture; he is alone. Usually ambassadors presenting their credentials at the White House make it a family celebration with their parents or spouse and children and everyone is smiling. Not here. His parents had died and his first wife and young daughter had left him

Latvian Embassy Team, Race for the Cure: Ambassador Kalnins; Mrs. Kalnins and her daughter, Ingrida; Latvian Prime Minister and his foreign affairs advisors; embassy staffers on the roof of the Canadian Embassy overlooking the U.S. Capitol. Photo courtesy of the Latvian Embassy.

somewhere along the way when politics took over. He celebrated one of the biggest moments of his life by himself.

Today, he is happily remarried to Irma, a Latvian born in America whom he met while she was organizing healthcare for Latvia. They make their home with her three children. He plays volleyball once a week with his old Latvian buddies and he no longer has to tell Latvia's story alone. She is as passionate as he about Latvia finding its new identity in today's world.

During my three years of research, I had the privilege to know them both and watch them both grow in their jobs.

"As the wife of the ambassador of a formerly occupied country, I have seen firsthand the need to empower women," says Irma Kalnins, the international director of The Race for the Cure. "Women's issues, especially as they pertain to women's health, are not really addressed in the public forum, only in the clinical forum in these countries." This new diplomatic wife embraces the challenge of "educating, teaching about early detection and the need for research."

She adds, "Just being in Washington and being an American citizen is a unique opportunity and I intend to use it to the max to help Latvia!" In 1988, she joined Latvian Renaissance, a humanitarian effort that with Project Hope and Americares has sent "more than four million dollars [in] medicine, medical supplies, clothes and books to Latvia. We helped organize prenatal care and started a Lamaze program. We want to bring dignity back into these peoples' lives.

"I look at this as a duty," this ambassador's wife explains, "not a time for me just to sit back and enjoy life. The main thing is that I am doing it for love—for my husband and all the Latvians who didn't get the chances abroad that I did."

"It is hard work for wives of diplomats from smaller, lesser-known countries whose governments don't have the money to buy their way into Washington society. Unless you have friends in high places, you have to work very hard to get exposure here," she reasons, mentioning that richer, bigger countries are already known and "everyone comes to them to host charity balls."

In addition, when she married Ojars Kalnins and moved with her three children to Washington, "I had no guidance, nothing was written down at the embassy. There were no guidelines on how to do a reception, what to do for the 18th of November [Latvia's day of independence].

"My father was a friend of Ambassador Dinbergs," she explains. "They were part of the same social circle, and, in fact, Ambassador Dinbergs was very happy that Ojars and I were together.

"But otherwise, it was much harder than I thought it would be to be a diplomatic wife," she confesses. "You always have to be on your toes; this is not just social chitchat." To prove her point she adds, "I never want to miss an opportunity. My number-one question when I meet an ambassador is always, 'What is your number-one health issue?' Some are not prepared for such a question but at least it gets them thinking about it."

Ambassador Kalnins's past is still close to the surface. So is the sadness. "I grew up very quickly," he says. "I remember getting out of grade school to go to the unemployment office with my mother who didn't speak English. I was my parents' teacher about America. After my father died, I worked construction, got scholarships, and supported my mother. She didn't want me to get into any controversy. ... She was afraid the KGB would come and take you away," says the former dissident. "But I kept telling her this is America. She'd even go in the closet and hide when there was a big storm. She died scared."

That first time Kalnins went to Latvia he saw a woman who knew his mother. "They grew up in Majori, the same resort town. But when my mother got on the train to escape to the West, her friend got off and went back because her mother was sick. Forty years later, I met that woman's daughter. It turns out that my mother's friend had been raped by a Russian soldier and this young woman I met was the result of that. That's when I decided that these were my people, my family."

For this ambassador, telling Latvia's story is his life's work. Latvia is his one client, and he uses every public relations and marketing trick he knows. "You have to be a PR man and get Congress on your side, the American people on your side," says the ambassador, who, while lobbying for NATO membership, trades quips with President Clinton about Hillary's and the ambassador's favorite Chicago baseball teams.

As far as Latvia's old oppressor, the fear is not so far away. "Russia always scares us," he admits. "It's like sleeping with an elephant who could roll over you."

* * *

"I am not a politician, I am a historian," says Lithuanian Ambassador Alfonsas Eidintas, who has published more than forty academic articles on Lithuanian emigration, Lithuania's national revival and "the inaccuracies of Lithuanian history as propagandized through Soviet stereotypes and myths," as his official embassy curriculum vitae boldly states. He is the author of eight books, mostly published in the West, and has lectured at important conferences and universities in Finland, Sweden, France, Germany and the United States.

We sit in his third-floor office overlooking noisy 16th Street in this old, ornate, Italian-style mansion that has housed Lithuanian diplomats, without interruption, since 1924, despite Russian occupation at home. The consulate-*cum*-residence has been through two modest renovations with the help of American-Lithuanian artisans and generous donations from large, loyal Lithuanian groups throughout the United States. But the neighborhood isn't grand anymore, and not too safe either. Across the street is a decaying mansion, and recently, when the Italians decided they needed more room, they abandoned their embassy here to build their contemporary palazzio off of safer Massachusetts Avenue.

In November 1993, when Ambassador Eidintas first arrived, he saw "wild trees" taking over the garden, and one cold month later the pipes burst in the old five-floor walk-up. "I *defected* from the building with my family to a hotel" to keep warm. The cold wasn't all bad, he admits. "Maybe the comfort of the hotel inspired the birth of our third child, Monica!"

He considered selling the old mansion. But first he wisely asked the American-Lithuanian community whether to attempt expensive renovations or give up, sell and escape the "bad neighborhood." "No, no!" they responded passionately.

"'All these years,' they said, 'as long as we had a legation in Washington, we knew there was hope for independence. We had this building and we would take the kids every year to National Day.'" To them, this building was "part of real Lithuania" for almost 60 years and now for four generations.

So, they got saws, and the ambassador and several "amateurs" from the community tamed the garden. Three American-Lithuanian architects took over to "keep the integrity" of the 31-room building, while installing new heating and, for the first time, air conditioning, as well as a cherished basketball backboard in the new parking lot. Lithuanians are passionate basketball players, and Eidintas and his teenage son, Donatas, often shoot baskets but forget the exercise equipment in the basement. There was no money for an elevator. The ambassador pats his belly and admits, "We live upstairs and it is five flights down and there are so many beers and sausages at all these parties." He laughs, takes another puff on his Marlboro and loosens his tie.

This famous historian finished his Ph.D. at the University of Wisconsin in Madison eight days after Lithuania's declaration of independence in 1991. But he was surprised when he was asked to become Lithuania's ambassador in Washington. "Teaching history is very different from being a diplomat, but history is very connected with diplomacy," says the man who tried to keep his country's diaries honest during those long, hard years of Soviet control.

"History was falsified. There was no 'socialist revolution.' Smetona was put out by an ultimatum and Soviet troops entered. At that time, history was part of politics and every article I wrote was important. Everybody was buying [my] books. ... I had the time, the chance to write, and we became the most important enemies of the Soviet ideology in the Academy of Sciences. Our Lithuanian books were printed in the West and KGB men kept coming to take my tapes. ... I was limited in lectures. They made rules. They said you can't say that. ... Our history was being written in Moscow."

"I would go to the archives and this lady with an iron face would give me only one book at a time," says this history professor. "I had to take notes by hand and then, they would take my notes and check them and say something to my university. There was always 'the official version,' bourgeoisie history. We were working between the lines."

When the phone rings, the ambassador gets up, stands over his desk piled high with papers and yells into the speakerphone. It's late and the small staff has gone. He lights another cigarette, shaking his head. "The paperwork kills. So many overviews and analyses."

I ask him, as a historian, if he knew when freedom was coming. "We spoke openly between our friends. It was finally clear, the empire was dying. The bad quality of life: lines in shops, pipes bursting." He smiles for a quick moment and we relish together the irony of his pipes bursting here. "The state system didn't work and will crash one day—maybe in 10, 20, 30 years, our hope. The military and the politicians looked very strong, but with information, more and more of us started to think how to quit this limited life."

I ask him why he didn't just leave. After all, he was often abroad lecturing. "How to leave," he laughs, shrugging his shoulders. "I always have two children at home, my wife, and very, very old parents."

Now that he and his family are here and free and he is in a powerful, prestigious position, I ask him how it feels. I get a surprising albeit honest answer. "It is a burden to have so much freedom. You have so much more responsibility for your life," says the intellectual who fought so long with words to free his country.

Now he sees his role as continuing to fight for NATO membership and national security with his Baltic colleagues. "It sounds different when you say, 'Three ambassadors are coming,'" he says, referring to the ad hoc Baltic lobby. Months after this interview, I saw Ambassador Eidintas with his arm in a sling. When I asked him what happened, he charmingly answered, "Oh, it's nothing. I guess I was just knocking too hard on NATO's door!"

This ambassador feels strongly that it is his embassy's job, however time-consuming and tedious, to help the one million Lithuanian Americans find their roots and locate their lost family members. After his diplomatic experience in Washington, he hopes one day to return home and create a professional diplomatic corps for Lithuania.

"I would like to teach very practical classes on how to run an embassy. That way, they would be ready to go and we could change ambassadors faster." He already has his class syllabus in mind: job descriptions, teamwork, financial planning, creative—not competitive—production, basic public relations and the primary American free enterprise principle—the customer is always right.

Calls and letters constantly come in, demanding the whereabouts of lost relatives and asking questions regarding the restitution of lost lands. "We are not a genealogical society but we must help these people whether their question is crazy or not. They are the customers and we have to answer to them. The staff must understand even when a caller says, 'I'm expecting your response 26 November, because I go to Lithuania 27 November.' She is not guilty of eating our time. These are nice people seeking their roots and we must help.

"Every [Lithuanian] family has bad emotions that time will help heal. My father's brother was killed in 1947, my father and many cousins lost their health serving in the Red Army. The Soviet regime used the Russian-speaking people … but our Baltics are ours again."

I ask about his family here and how they relax, living above the consulate. "An evening off, just being home together with the children," he vows, "or a good nap" after the nonstop days. "On weekends, we visit a dairy farm of an American Lithuanian near Culpeper, Virginia. We love the silence there," says this country boy, who grew up with lots of cows, green grass, dogs and cats in a small town in western Lithuania. "My wife is from a seaport but had grandparents in the countryside. The first week here we had a terrible time sleeping—our bedroom is right on the street."

And what does this father think about bringing up two teenagers in America? "In six years, how many changes in this one Lithuanian family. Our children teach us American slang. My son doesn't even speak Russian. I think he even dreams in English and is better writing in English. When we play basketball in our lot, I give orders to pass the ball in Lithuanian but he answers in English." He smiles. "He swears in English but I swear in Lithuanian!"

But the hardest thing about being Lithuania's ambassador in Washington "is that I have to behave. And some moments that kills you." I ask him how he feels when he has to attend an event at the Russian Embassy. "They are too familiar. They smile and finally they come over and say 'How nice it will be when we are all one family again.' This is not funny. Yes, we are neighbors, but we are also two *very* different countries now and Lithuania is *finally* independent again."

8

Sweden: Negotiating for Others

Over the past two decades, three Swedish ambassadors have made a difference in Washington's diplomatic dance, both on the dance floor and behind the scenes. You might say they each danced very different dance steps to very different tunes, but they each ended up with the White House as a partner. Each ambassador, in his own style, knew how to get things done in Washington for Sweden and often did much more than that.

Count Wilheim Wachtmeister, a favorite tennis partner of President George Bush, served Sweden for 15 years in Washington and was dean of the Washington diplomatic corps from 1986 to 1989. He and his wife, Countess Ulla Wachtmeister, chose to stay here after his retirement and are still revered by Washington's old guard as the ultimate diplomatic couple.

In 1993 a more unusual couple became Sweden's diplomatic "Dream Team": Henrik and Nil Liljegren. He was the seasoned senior diplomat who didn't look very Swedish and she was the blonde granddaughter, daughter and widow of Turkish diplomats who looked more Swedish than Turkish. Together, the Liljegrens charmed their way to the top, and once again, one of Washington's most popular diplomatic couples was Swedish. In this new age of diplomacy after the breakup of the Soviet Union, he helped the Baltics negotiate the departure of the Soviet troops and, together, the popular Liljegrens proved that good parties still make good diplomacy.

Then in September 1997, Ambassador Rolf Ekeus, immediate past executive chairman of UNSCOM, the United Nation's Special Commission for Iraq since 1991, moved with his wife, Christina Oldfelt-Ekeus, into the big white Swedish residence. He arrived just in time to help the Clinton administration successfully handle Saddam Hussein in his latest threat of biological weaponry.

According to Staffan Heimerson, Swedish Broadcasting's former Washington correspondent and well-known Swedish author, "There is a long tradition and history of Swedish diplomats and negotiators acting on the international arena." Heimerson, who is both a respected war correspondent and a great storyteller, says that as far back as 1791 during the French Revolution, Sweden's ambassador to Paris, "Axel van Fersen, who by the way was Marie Antoinette's lover, smuggled ... the French king and queen out of the Paris turmoil."

During World War II in Budapest, Raoul Wallenberg had only a junior diplomatic status when he "saved a hundred thousand Jewish lives—and he himself was caught by the Russians in 1944 and disappeared into the gulags." Out of the Swedish royal family, Folke Bernadotte saved more Jews by organizing rescue operations for Nazi death-camp prisoners in the months just before the end of World War II. In the 1950s, Dag Hammarskjöld was UN secretary-general, and Prime Minister Olof Palme "flamboyantly tried" to negotiate peace between Iran and Iraq in the 1980s. There are many more.

* * *

The Liljegrens are one of my first interviews for this book. We meet around Easter in 1996 when, as a member of the American News Women's Club, I am invited to tea and a press briefing by the ambassador himself.

The black iron gates are already open as my car enters the circular drive. At first, I think I have the wrong place—the orange roof tiles make the long, two-story, white stucco residence look more like a Spanish hacienda than the home of the Swedish ambassador. Built in 1923 for David Lawrence, then editor of *U.S. News & World Report,* this house and the impressive grounds were acquired by the Swedish government in 1950 and renovated in 1989.

I am met at the front door by their charming butler, Alipio Paras, who will welcome me many times over the next two years. In the dining room, which opens out onto their gracious terrace and long expanse of lawn, Nil Liljegren greets each club member warmly and encourages us to sample delicious little Turkish meat pastries and scrumptious Swedish sweets. But there is no Ambassador Liljegren.

While we wait for his arrival, she invites us to wander around the spangling residence. We inspect huge antique wall hangings, the Swedish art on loan from Stockholm's National Museums and charming vistas from under the festive yellow-and-white-striped awning that stretches the length of the long terrace.

In the ambassador's study, I notice the personal photographs. There is the formal picture of Sweden's Queen Silvia, intimate family pictures of this glamorous diplomatic wife and her handsome husband, and some of their college-age daughter, Nilden.

What surprises me most are the bunnies. All over the embassy, stuffed animals snuggle up against huge, elegant, fresh spring bouquets. You see, the ambassador's wife collects stuffed animals. For me, this is the first sign that "real life" can exist in an official residence.

At five o'clock, we start to leave. Just then, the ambassador sweeps in the front door and we were all shepherded down the elegant front hall, past his antique hobbyhorse (it goes to every post with him) and into the blue-and-gold ballroom. He and his wife hurry across to the prized Malmejo grand piano, turn around and begin an impromptu news conference.

I am sure he is breathless and she is relieved, but they are pure diplomacy—grace under pressure. I notice then, with a room full of reporters, how forthright he is about the Swedish economy and how symbiotic the relationship is between this ambassador and his diplomatic wife. She stands at his side; they finish each other's paragraphs and sometimes, even each other's sentences.

* * *

Soon after that, they invite me back for tea and our interview. As we sit in the study one Friday afternoon, Nil Liljegren keeps offering me champagne to "start the weekend." They are candid and charming.

Immediately, the ambassador puts his post in perspective. "Washington is totally different from the other capitals. You can't just call up and say, 'My PM would like to see your president.' Here, you have to work with so many institutions."

The mustachioed Liljegren describes how it took him three months to get a response from the White House about his prime minister's upcoming visit. His right eyebrow arches up as if to give facial punctuation to the problem. "You send a fax and they 'never receive it,'" Mrs. Liljegren jumps in.

"It goes on and on, but we don't give up," he says with a charming lilt and finally a smile, "You can choose to be upset or ignore them, and this town is full of resentful, frustrated diplomats. Or, you can adjust to the environment, forget about protocol, adopt a hands-on approach and do all the necessary phone calls yourself. A personal call from an ambassador … stands a better chance of receiving results."

Just then, Al appears with tea and homemade Swedish jam cookies warm from the oven. Nil (as she asks me to call her) smiles when I succumb to the luscious calories, and she sends the rest home with me. With a nod of approval, the ambassador continues to explain and I'm impressed how these three entertain in concert: no one skipping a beat.

Ambassador Liljegren continues, "It's like a big board game." With so many embassies in such an important post, "in order to be relevant, you have to pose a problem to the international community, be a strategic outpost, or have influence, clout through ethnic presence. Or, have a gimmick. In my case, I have a secret weapon: my wife, Nil."

* * *

At first glance, Nil Liljegren seems to be just a social butterfly whose beverage of choice is champagne. Wispy blond hair, good legs and couture in between. You think, not a working wife. Well, forget it. She definitely "works the party" and is not afraid to venture into unknown territory, even alone.

Shortly after they arrived in 1993, she contacted Tipper Gore's office for an appointment. After all, the vice president's wife is a Swedish American and this savvy diplomatic wife didn't want the connection to be missed. "Everyone said I shouldn't do that, that I should wait for her to call me or for Henrik's credentials to be presented to the president first.

"But, she saw me and has been friendly ever since," says Nil, who wore a blue jean dress and gold boots to the vice president's casual diplomatic do—a 7 P.M. barbecue. "My dear, no one knew what to wear. The diplomats showed up all dressed up. I mean it is seven o'clock and it is the vice president of the United States!"

Her adoring husband admits, only half-jokingly, that maybe she is "sometimes a little proud and aggressive," but he also appreciates her Circassian heritage from the former Turkish area north of the Black Sea, where tall, blond, blue-eyed Vikings ventured 1,000 years ago on their way to Constantinople.

As Americans might say, she hasn't grown up in a family of diplomats for nothing. She is named after the great Nile River and expects to play an important part in diplomacy.

When Sweden's dashing ambassador to Turkey married Nil Kirectepes 17 years ago, she was a young widow with a young daughter. All of Sweden watched her every move. But she soon proved herself and won Swedish respect even though she has never lived in Sweden, except for summer visits. She speaks four or five other languages better than Swedish. Interestingly enough, she says her Turkish is also not perfect. She left Turkey when she was only six and has spent most of her life outside her homeland.

"Because German was my first language, I speak Swedish with a slight German accent," she admits. She realized it was a surprising advantage when

Swedish Ambassador Henrik Liljegren and Mrs. Liljegren. Photo courtesy of Diplomatic Photography by Albert.

she first met the Swedish royal family. "The Swedish queen, who is half German and half Brazilian, also talks Swedish with a German accent!" When the royal couple does come to Washington, there is a royal suite in the residence awaiting them. (The ambassador vows that "it is really quite plain.") Not surprisingly, their chef and upstairs maid are Turkish.

To add to this international intrigue, the ambassador himself was born in Estonia, not Sweden. His Estonian father was a decorated war hero in the war for Estonia's independence. Coincidentally, Estonia's Ambassador Toomas Hendrik Ilves was born in Sweden. He calls Liljegren his mentor, "a big brother" to the Baltics and says, "It's almost as if Estonia has a second ambassadorial presence here."

When Ambassador Liljegren's Swedish mother remarried a Swedish diplomat who became cultural counselor here, teenager Henrik Liljegren got his first taste of embassy life in Washington, often visiting the residence as a young student at St. Albans.

More than 40 years later, Henrik Liljegren returned as ambassador and, with his wife, quickly became well-known for their parties in this same residence. *Washington Post* diplomatic reporter Nora Boustany declared them "the hottest embassy couple in Washington." Word spread and they became natural targets for local socialites who needed an embassy to host their charity events. But after having 15 large, separate functions in just four months, the ambassador proclaims, "We plan to not do as much … the exposure creates a background music, it adds exposure for Sweden. But, now we'll do smaller dinner parties with people who can really help Sweden." Bad news for this town's society mavens.

The Liljegren's delicious buffets were always full of Swedish salmon and meatballs with a touch of small Turkish meat or spinach pastries. "Darling," she explains to me, "we are on such a tight budget, my chef is a genius." Later, when I'm invited, party after party, I notice she often fills in the menu with a delicious albeit less expensive pasta and tossed salads and has taught her staff to create clever, unusual floral arrangements with her garden flowers.

Together, they continue to charm Washington, all the while making major inroads for Sweden. King Carl XVI Gustaf, a noted environmentalist who had read Vice President Al Gore's book, was coming to visit the United States. After days and days of phone calls by the ambassador, a luncheon was set up in Philadelphia, where they both would be. The eyebrow goes up and you know a story is about to unfold. "But, early that morning, I got a phone call that the king's plane was stuck in Iceland." So, after all that arranging, "they ended up meeting for five minutes at Andrews Air Force Base instead. They shook hands, that's all! But they met in full view of the press and that is all that's important.

"It's marketing, making your country seem relevant. It doesn't help to distribute leaflets; you have to come up with a clever solution." For instance, it took eight months to set up the first time, but Henrik and Nil Liljegren are proud that each fall when Sweden's famous Nobel Prizes are awarded, the American winners are flown in from around the country, feted with a ceremonial tea at the White House and a black-tie dinner at the Swedish residence.

"When the ambassador asked the state department to arrange a meeting between Prime Minister Bildt and President Clinton in 1993, the answer was a polite 'No,'" the ambassador reports. "The president would first have to meet several prime ministers from NATO countries."

"However, Nil and I found a way out. We invited all the American Nobel Prize winners that year to a black-tie dinner at the residence. When they had all finally accepted, I asked the White House whether President and Mrs. Clinton would be interested in meeting the Nobel laureates. It turned out that the president and his wife were delighted with this idea. They immediately invited the laureates, my wife and myself to a reception at the White House and added: 'By the way, if you have an important visitor from Sweden, why don't you bring him along?' I asked 'How about my prime minister?' and that is how a meeting between the president and Prime Minister Bildt combined with a tea party hosted by Mrs. Clinton for Nobel Prize winners was arranged."

Probably the most important legacy of this Swedish ambassador was his discreet negotiatory role involving the White House in efforts to get Russian troops out of the three newly independent Baltic countries. "The withdrawal of these troops was considered one of President Clinton's first major foreign policy successes," he says. "This makes us more relevant. It was only courtesy visits before for our prime ministers at the White House. Now we have very close cooperation on a major issue [Baltic independence]. The relationship between the United States and Sweden has never been as close."

Quite a feat for this Swedish ambassador, considering Washington still hasn't forgotten Count Wachtmeister, who has a European title and was dean of the diplomatic corps. Plus, he had the ear of President Bush each time they played tennis together.

Ambassador Liljegren doesn't even play tennis but he too charmed Washington and created his own way to the White House. To his knowledge and experience, this modern ambassador added creativity and nerve. "I've learned the last 20 years that if you avoid a fight or risk, you'll always live to regret it. If there's a major cause and it involves a risk, take the risk and deal with the consequences," advises the wise 61-year-old, who obviously still loves a challenge. "This is why I—in spite of some application at home—accepted [the invitation] to appear before Senator [Alfonse] D'Amato's committee to defend my country's record during the Second World War.

"One learns by not winning, but you have to be philosophical about it. Pick long-term goals, two or three objectives and at least you'll win one of them," he adds with a sparkle in his eyes.

Not surprisingly, Liljegren is popular with the press, at home and here in Washington. *Daqen Industri,* a leading Swedish publication, hailed Liljegren as "a heavyweight" who always seems to have everything under control." Reporter Hans-Inge Olsson called him "a great diplomat [who] works intensively, and discreetly, in quiet." Olsson's story, "The Spider in the West," suggested that this clever ambassador weaves his web of diplomacy watching every detail, staying focused on the final pattern.

Staffan Heimerson, who has followed Liljegren's career for more than 20 years, calls him a "diplomatic lion." They first met "in the middle of the night" during the 48-hour siege of the luxurious Ledra Palace hotel in Cyprus, where more than 300 reporters were trying to cover the 1974 coup. "Greeks were attacking from the front [of the hotel] and Turks were attacking from the gardenside. It was an unbelievable movie scene."

"At the time I was a young, eager, brave war reporter in the midst of a bunch of bad-behaving journalists," remembers Heimerson, "and here comes this tremendously polite, properly dressed young man from the foreign office with such a cool attitude. I was impressed." As it turned out, Liljegren was equally impressed. "Henrik mentioned me in his official report, he was so amazed that the first thing I did was fill my bathtub with water … elementary when you're under siege."

Years later in a divided Berlin, they met again. Liljegren was already ambassador there when Heimerson arrived at his new journalistic post, knowing no one. "We had lunch and talked about East German politics," says Heimerson. "Henrik told me who to talk to. He's a shrewd security expert and a social genius" with "a political brilliance to cleverly find a way … to introduce people for their mutual benefit and for Sweden's, too. This is all good public relations but it also happens to be a good political course and makes Sweden a little more important."

Almost indefatigable and undefeatable, this couple hoped to convince Stockholm to finally build a permanent chancery here. After all, the Swedes are second only to France in having the oldest diplomatic ties with this upstart, the United States.

For 20 years, the Swedes rented space at the infamous Watergate complex. In 1993, after trying to build on Massachusetts Avenue for many years, the Swedes lost a lengthy zoning battle and couldn't find other suitable land. So they asked their Swedish-American design team to take two floors of a new office building and make them look and feel like Sweden. Inside, the look is Swedish but outside, there is nothing visible—not even Sweden's handsome blue-and-yellow flag to denote what's inside. So much for the public diplomacy in which their Scandinavian neighbor Finland excels with their showcase on Embassy Row.

The Liljegrens had dreamed of a dramatic spot overlooking the Potomac River between the Kennedy Center and Watergate to the south and Washington Harbour and Key Bridge upriver. This could have been a wonderful chance to show off Swedish engineering and design while being the first embassy to be built directly on the riverfront. But, the expensive project died abruptly when Ambassador Liljegren was posted to Turkey in August 1997, after five highly successful years in Washington. Liljegren was disappointed and still holds out hope for Sweden's riverside chancery. "In every country," he explains, "you have a bureaucrat or two in key positions, who act like Sir Humphrey in the British TV series 'Yes, Mr. Prime Minister.' They prefer to pursue a policy of passivity rather than what is good for the country."

Henrik and Nil Liljegren left many Washington friends behind, but it is difficult to imagine a major capital other than Ankara where Turkish-born Nil would be a greater asset. It is a romantic ending.

* * *

Even before Rolf Ekeus came to town as Sweden's new ambassador, I heard why: his life had been threatened and Sweden wanted to move him to keep him safe.

Hearing that, I had to meet him. But to my surprise, his staff kept telling me he was "shy" and that his wife "doesn't ever do interviews." Finally, they both agreed to talk with me after we all met one hot and humid Washington night at Staffan Heimerson's farewell party in Georgetown.

* * *

For me, it is odd to return to the Swedish residence and not have Nil and Henrik Liljegren there. But Al, as always, opens the big wooden front door just as I arrive, wondering if this time I'd have to ring the doorbell.

Ambassador Ekeus, a spry, white-haired gentleman, was comes down the stairs from their private quarters and ushers me into the study. "I'm sorry, my wife couldn't join us after all because she is at the doctor's. Her appointment was changed." I say I am disappointed not to talk with her and that I had heard she was recovering from an illness.

I am surprised how different the room looks and find myself cataloging what is new in this charming study overlooking the long expanse of green.

I begin by asking the ambassador if he was really on 24-hour call by the White House, the State Department and the Pentagon when he first arrived and Saddam Hussein was threatening to use biological warfare. "I came directly from the battlefield," says the diplomat who had just left UNSCOM. "It is obvious that we keep in close [contact] with the Administration. It's very difficult to say where the curiosity about my knowledge starts and [where] the political reality [begins] that Sweden temporarily is an important country." He reminds me that, until the end of 1998, Sweden was still a nonpermanent member of the UN's Security Council and that, "there is always a play with majorities and minorities."

"But obviously, ... as ex-chairman of my old job, I was a natural contact for the U.S. government. We depended upon the U.S. for support; we had to finance everything ourselves. We didn't get one single cent from the UN budget," he says. "It was a very expensive operation," he adds. The United States didn't give money but supplied equipment like high-altitude, U2 aircraft and pilots, support teams and technical advisors, while Germany and Chile gave heavy helicopters so necessary for success.

"Our yearly budget was 30 to 40 million in cash. The U2 operation was run by the U.S. from Saudi soil with about 100 people as support team. We had to build monitoring networks from scratch," says the Swede who raised

Swedish Ambassador Ekeus presenting his credentials to President Clinton. Official White House Photograph.

the money from several Arab nations, Japan and Germany while constantly commuting from his offices in Vienna to the UN offices in New York and to the field headquarters in Baghdad.

When I asked about the reported assassination plans against his life, he calmly says, "They treated you like an enemy, it was dangerous but I don't know if that's true. The press reported plans for [my] assassination."

He is not surprised that once again Sweden and its diplomats are playing the role of negotiator. "First of all, Sweden has the priviledge of not being dragged into the wars. During the Cold War, we were not part of NATO. … It became natural to turn to the citizens of Sweden" because "Sweden seemed neutral."

"You see, the country that is not part of an alliance … has to work out its own understanding of international conflicts and international marriages. So, of course, our diplomats have been trained to have an independent judgment. In an alliance, you form a coherent philosophy, a coherent policy.

"We have a tradition of diplomacy," he says, summing up Sweden's long history of being "a unit, a solid state" since the mid-1500s. "As a semi-great power we were heavily involved at this time in throwing our weight around." He mentions that, except for France, many other European states like Belgium, Holland, Switzerland and Italy are "relatively new."

I wonder aloud how independent Sweden will survive in the European Union. "It is really a difficult thing for us to adjust. Sweden has an extremely strong democratic tradition. In 1435, the Swedish parliament was created and has been unbroken since then," he explains, adding that "not just the aristocracy but small business owners and farmers were always members."

"Now suddenly, the decision of various significant trade policies, the age-old tradition to tax themselves and run their own business is tied to and is to be decided in context. It is heart-burning to have to adjust with the flow of history. The French could say the same thing."

But when it comes to trade, Ambassador Ekeus says, "It is in our broader interests to support globalization ... for our own self-interest. Sweden has always been known for its large industries"—like Ericsson, Stora, Electrolux, Volvo [recently bought by America's Ford Motor Company] and Saab, even IKEA. "That means they are depending on the foreign market and so by necessity. Sweden is in the forefront of liberalizing trade."

Now we are into commercial diplomacy and this ambassador doesn't miss this opportunity. "We are an ideal country for investors. As far as company taxes, we are one of the lowest—lower than America," he says, emphasizing Sweden's "high quality, well-trained, noncorrupt workers." And, "We also have the legal system, the needed infrastructure, and cheap electricity." But he concedes, "What is expensive is the individual tax," which makes many Swedes "tend to move abroad."

When I ask about Sweden's socialized lifestyle and if the country will continue to take such a big bite out of everyone's paychecks, he justifies the Swedish system. "Swedes see the link between taxes and what they get. They are socially educated. They know a tax cut is painful," he argues. "Swedes know that if you take from the schools, the hospitals, the good police force, they get lower quality." Then he adds with pride, "Sweden has high defense spending in its class." Swedes ask themselves, "How do I want my country to look like to the rest of the world?"

He chooses daycare as a good example. In Sweden, "every working mother has access to childcare. That's an enormously powerful incentive. If she doesn't have a job, she loses her place in the daycare center. Working mothers get help; we treat them much better than your country."

Now I really wish Mrs. Ekeus were with us to answer my questions, because she has had not *one* but *three* impressive careers while rearing their four children and his two from a previous marriage. But I am delighted to learn how open he is to discussing their personal life with me.

Al has just served us each a luscious piece of apple creme tart and I begin again to feel comfortable in this residence. This career diplomat speaks about his family with the same ease and energy that he speaks about Sweden. "We are always together for the holidays," says this grandfather as he samples the tart.

"When we had three little ones in The Hague—eight, six and two—I looked after them and their mother came from Brussels on weekends." At the time, she was a senior diplomat in Sweden's foreign service, her first career. "But then when we had another baby, they all moved to Brussels and *I* commuted for five years."

Later, "they had a great time in Geneva when she was director of the UN's environment program and even spent lots of time in New York." That's when he was ambassador and head of the Swedish delegation to the Conference on Disarmament in Geneva. "But that's before she jumped ship and became an analyst," he says, lightly referring to the seven years his wife trained at the Jung Institute in Zurich, Switzerland, before opening her private practice in Vienna.

I can't resist asking him if she helps him "diagnose" other diplomats and if they discuss everyone's "real" agenda on the way home from the endless list of diplomatic events they must attend. "She never talks about her patients but it is quite funny to talk about other people … their patterns, types. We enjoy it," he admits, with a little laugh.

And, what about rearing the children? Does having an analyst in the family help? "Well, hopefully, we did it through example but there were moments in their teens when you look at them with fresh eyes. We love them just the same." He smiles warmly.

I ask if any of his six children, aged 18 to 34, are tempted to become diplomats after all this living abroad. "No, they know the drawbacks; they are the victims. All six suffered in various forms. … They know how it is to get friends and then lose them. But," he says smiling, "they also gained so much, friends all over the world, language skills, and we lived in lovely places so we don't complain." His children, several of whom live in New York City, "love to come here for the weekend, they treat it as a spa."As for sports, this lean ambassador loves to play tennis with his new Argentine son-in-law who's married to his daughter Helena. "I belong to the hard-hitting school [for tennis]—less consistent, but I love singles."

When I ask him if his wife plays, he makes a face. "She's bored with it. In Holland, one time when we were playing on the queen's tennis court, I served and she yawned! I said, 'If you yawn when I serve, I'm not playing with you anymore!'"

Because I know the Japanese ambassador loves a competitive game, I ask Ambassador Ekeus if he has played tennis yet with his next-door neighbor. "No, I hear them play but I can't see them. You know, when we built the fence between our properties we had a door put in … but they made a key for themselves. We don't have one." He raises his eyebrows on that note of international one-upmanship and finishes off his apple tart.

As for his personal goals, "It's important to deepen our relations with the U.S. because we were not allies during the Cold War. We want a cordial and warm relationship with the new generation. … We are deeply democratic, active on human rights, the United Nations and for free trade." To emphasize Sweden's attractiveness as a dance partner for America he adds, "Our history as a democracy is second to none." Ekeus underlines additional similarities between the two countries: advanced technology, defense and nonproliferation interests. Not a surprise since he has spent much of his diplomatic career improving Europe's defense security and working toward global nonproliferation of nuclear weapons.

About first arriving in Washington, "I couldn't believe how much I had to read—foreign affairs briefings, cable traffic," says this lawyer who has published numerous articles and received various awards, including the Wateler Peace Prize from the Carnegie Foundation in 1997. "The pleasant part [of being an ambassador here] is the quality of the people one meets in the think tanks, state department and in the press corps." Ambassador Ekeus says he especially enjoys participating in seminars and giving lectures in Washington.

As far as his hopes for a new Swedish Embassy, on the river or anywhere else, he is refreshingly frank. "It is slightly embarrassing. We have one of the oldest diplomatic relationships with America, dating back to Ben Franklin"—and yet, never a permanent embassy chancery. Although the riverfront idea is alluring, he votes for Sweden to choose a site less confining when it tries again to build an embassy in Washington.

We've had a good time talking, but I make sure not to overstay. Outside, the ambassador's handsome limousine, a navy blue Volvo, is running and his driver is waiting to take Sweden's ambassador back to his "invisible" embassy.

As I drive away, I remember Staffan's words: "Rolf Ekeus is one in a long row—and probably the most important of them all. Ekeus put up UNSCOM … and his knowledge of Iraq and Saddam Hussein's thinking is outstanding. When crises in Baghdad are flaring up, Ekeus is on a daily basis consulted by the UN's Kofi Annan, the State Department, and often by Madeleine Albright personally and the White House."

Maybe he isn't going back to his office after all. Maybe the long dark-blue Volvo is on its way to the White House.

9

Finland: Sauna Diplomacy

There is one embassy you must not miss: the green glasshouse of the Finns. On Massachusetts Avenue, across from the vice president's official home and next door to the very traditional Nunciature of the Holy See (Vatican Embassy), Finnish architects Mikko Heikkinen and Markku Komonen have taken this funny little triangle of land that disappears down into Normanstone Park and created a Scandinavian showcase of engineering ingenuity and artistic nerve.

Washington Post architecture critic Benjamin Forgey called it "a breath of fresh architecture in Washington," while William Morgan in *Architectural Review* declared it "the U.S. political capital's best building in 50 years." Herbert Muschamp of *The New York Times* concluded that Finland had constructed a building that has the nerve to be a work of architecture, unusual for an embassy.

Internationally acclaimed architect I. M. Pei came to see it and ended up staying and studying the building for two straight days. Not only is this building a great architectural addition to Embassy Row, it has become a symbol of the new "public diplomacy" and the Finns love working here.

"Absolutely," agrees Ambassador Jaakko Laajava. "They are very motivated … and the physical surroundings are part of it. The building has changed their horizons," says the man who served as deputy chief of mission (DCM) from 1986 to 1990 when the Finnish Embassy was a nice but nondescript building in a residential area near American University. Former press counselor Yrjö Länsipuro recalls endlessly giving odd directions because, "It was the only embassy in Washington best described by saying it was across the street from a favorite Washington deli." Obviously, that's not a problem anymore.

"Our embassy is part of the 'public diplomacy' concept where awareness, perceptions do matter," says Laajava of his embassy, which is often open to the public. With today's "foreign policy decisions being announced through the media for public scrutiny and to be reviewed and assessed" by other countries, public diplomacy is the stuff of CNN and the Internet. In addition, this veteran career diplomat thinks that "Madeleine Albright is the prime example" of how today's top diplomats operate in front of cameras as much as behind closed doors.

"Without public diplomacy you cannot entertain hopes to be effective," says this career diplomat who served most recently as director-general for political affairs in the Helsinki Ministry of Foreign Affairs. "It will never replace regular diplomacy but it is immensely important."

With handsome banners touting their latest art or consumer exhibit, the Finns regularly invite visitors in to see their latest show, be it a celebration of saunas or ageless Finnish design. It's a "polite billboard" for everything Finnish, great PR and a fantastic venue for charity events. In addition, with the best technical sound stage and video equipment available, many performances have been recorded live for an embassy CD series, and even other ambassadors ask Finland to host video conferences.

When embassy websites were becoming all the rage, Finland hosted the Scandinavian countries for an interactive briefing and press conference promoting these countries' online capabilities. (Iceland was one of the first to have an embassy website, followed quickly by the six other Scandinavian countries. Today, there are more than 40 Washington embassies on the World Wide Web.) Just a note of caution for visitors. As welcome as you are to come inside, you are not welcome to park in front. A hard lesson to learn considering the spacious green ramp beckoning you. But the architects insist it is part of the overall design and not to be stained by car oil leaks.

Since opening in May 1994, the most talked-about part of this new embassy has been its facade—a copper trellis that was supposed to become covered by climbing vines of blue and white flowers, the national colors of Finland. But with Washington's relentless summer sun, the embassy's southern exposure does not help create what was to have been a natural green filter from the heat. "When I took this job in Washington," says former journalist Länsipuro, "never did I expect fifty percent of my job to be answering questions about this new building and ninety percent of those queries to be about those vines!"

One of the embassy's architects, Mikko Heikkinen, proudly gives me a tour, emphasizing that "this building, like the people it represents, does not reveal all its charm at first. We wanted it to be a 'window into our country' and a cultural center, not just an embassy," says Heikkinen. Neither he nor his partner had ever designed an embassy before. "We like to always do something

Exterior (top) and interior (bottom) of the Finnish Embassy. Photos courtesy of the Embassy of Finland.

different, one of its kind," he explains with a thick Finnish accent. "We had done an airport, a fire brigade training facility and a film school."

As we descend the dramatic hanging staircase, I understand what he means about the embassy's "hidden charm." With each step down I get a larger look into what he calls the "Grand Canyon," the reception hall below with its tall walls of glass opening onto the woods. At night, outdoor lights atop sleek pylons of varying heights visually bring the outside in and further create an illusion that the floor continues beyond the building into the night. A brilliant touch that makes the room always sparkle.

But the real secret of this building is the diplomatic sauna on the ground floor where staffers and visiting dignitaries retreat and sometimes find answers to the most difficult problems. In "sauna diplomacy," according to architect Heikkinen, you can't stay more than 15 minutes because it's too hot, so you come to conclusions quickly! Traditionally, only Finnish families sauna together naked; otherwise, Finns always take a sauna separately by sex, "unlike the Germans," says Laajava firmly. So how does a country that prides itself on sexual equality use a workplace sauna effectively?

"You must organize two sessions," says this top diplomat, undaunted. "Sauna diplomacy" is maybe a little bit exaggerated but remains a proven way to "smooth the atmosphere." With seven top-ranking women out of 22 diplomats in this embassy, female colleagues must sweat separately from their male counterparts. So strict is the Finnish sauna code that if Secretary Albright joined in she would have to be with the women, not the ambassador.

This sauna, which can comfortably accommodate 10, is an actual log cabin built by a Finnish American from Maine with Virginia pine. "So, it is a building within a building," explains Heikkinen.

* * *

Former Ambassador Jukka Valtasaari, the "father" of this unusual embassy, was responsible for successfully shepherding this project from the start. First, he had to find an available lot on crowded Massachusetts Avenue. As Valtasaari, now Finland's secretary of state, tells it, "Late one night driving home, one of my senior diplomats saw the new 'For Sale' sign in front of what locals nicknamed 'The Texan Embassy.' It was a big brick home built in the 1950s by then-Congressman Clark Tomson of Galveston." Valtasaari made sure Finland snatched it up.

But purchasing the property was just the beginning. Zoning and neighborhood approval would not be an easy feat in Washington, where embassies are notorious for being bad neighbors. "Embassies mean traffic, foreigners," Valtasaari admits, and lots of parties and parking problems. "The Japanese

The back terrace of the Finnish Embassy.

were the last to get an embassy built on Massachusetts Avenue," says Valtasaari. "The Swedes failed, two blocks up, after eight embarrassing years of trying and major expenditures." Neighbors said, 'No' because "it would have an adverse effect" on the busy residential neighborhood already burdened with embassies. Plus, "Washington hates glass boxes."

So how did he do it? "Old-fashioned charm," he says, smiling. "I joined the neighborhood association and invited the neighbors over," says this shrewd diplomat whose residence is within walking distance. He learned from the Swedish ambassador "what went wrong and what he would do if he had to do it all over again." From the beginning, the neighbors were included in each step with plans, drawings, tours and even a model that had little smiling people, miniature lights and real twigs. "I used real ones from my yard."

"We started with a concept, not a building," Valtasaari says. "We wanted an intimate interplay with nature, a Finnish tradition." He gestures widely to the dramatic staircase, "I wanted everyone to feel like they were making a grand entrance," a very diplomatic idea. He also appreciates all "the humor" these architects tucked into this efficient building. Little windows in individual office doors frame charming vistas for officemates outside. Under Finnish regulations, as in most Nordic countries and Germany, all offices must have natural light and private workstations. The ambassador's office is modest, only slightly bigger than everyone else's, with a thin balcony where "I walk because my brain works faster when I walk."

Finnish seafaring and shipbuilding details throughout the embassy include a sail-like canopy shading a balcony that extends into the trees like a pier on a green sea. The main hall's clever dividers turn into tables and are the architects' answer to "every ambassador's nightmare": too many no-shows making your event look like a failure. Here, the room size can be almost anything you want it to be, even as guests arrive.

To Valtasaari, gracefully mixing daily embassy work with unlimited cultural activities and events is the modern-day recipe to the pressures of public diplomacy. "You need something going on, you need the tools and the stage to produce something which takes you to the headlines," he says.

* * *

Ambassador Laajava agrees and adds that Finns are well known for successfully mixing work and pleasure. "We just dance and sauna, sauna and dance," he says, joking with me and his wife, Pirjoriitta. After teasing me for the past year and a half every time we met at various embassy parties about whether we're ever going to talk, Pirjoriitta and Jaakko Laajava and I are finally sitting in their contemporary living room for "the official interview." He and I had talked when he first arrived, while Ambassador Valtasaari was still here, and we have already danced together at "Swing Night," when I learned how passionate Finns are about ballroom dancing. Not only had I danced with her husband, but Mrs. Laajava never lets me forget the night we first met. "You tried to poison me," she always jokes, referring to the time I poured her a wine glass brimming with aquavit, the powerful Scandinavian drink, thinking it was only innocent white wine.

As I arrive at the yellow brick Cleveland Park residence, their little jump-up-in-your-arms Cavalier King Charles Spaniel named Sandy enthusiastically greets me and proceeds to jump up on her favorite white couch, inviting me to sit next to her. I begin by asking the ambassador to compare the current U.S.-Finnish relationship to what it was in the late 1980s when he was here before.

"The U.S. was very friendly with the Finns. … We always have excellent access, mutual understanding," he says. "It works to our advantage being Russia's border country." During Reagan's reign, things were "quite tight with strict export controls" because the United States worried about the Soviet Union's capability to export military weapons to rogue states. "We cooperated with the U.S.," he says, only obliquely referring to the tight rope Finland walked for almost three-quarters of a century between the West and Finland's immediate neighbor, the former Soviet Union.

Pirjoriitta Laajava remembers how her husband returned to Finland in September 1990 just in time to finalize arrangements for the Bush-Gorbachev Helsinki Summit. "We in Finland have the knack of handling smaller, practical things; we know what works and what doesn't. ... As far as foreign policy, the traditional American way is to talk strict, to raise your voice, which you do from time to time. The Finns have softer methodology."

I ask him to further compare his country's foreign policy style to that of his Swedish neighbor. "The Swedes react very vocally; the Finns develop relationships. The relationship between the Baltics and Russia is a two-way street. In spite of so much suffering, somehow we must do a better job than just incriminate former imperial hosts. The Swedes have a different mentality. You know from 1600 to 1700 they were the great power of the North."

After discussing the role America played in the late 1960s and 1970s he concludes, "The United States is responsible for our European security. In many instances, we helped the Western agenda," he says, counting the ways. "On the borders, being the informant, and the humanitarian, helping with the reunification of families."

Finland, still haunted by all the years it kept its hard-won independence after World War II by separating itself from the rest of Europe to appease its big Soviet brother, is not sure it still wants the reputation of what *The New York Times* called "East-West Headwaiters."

"We don't need these summits," says the ambassador, "but we do give 'good parties,' and the party given doesn't have our own agenda, we place no demands. When you think about any other European country, if you met there you'd have to meet the leaders and have hour-long discussions."

"Finns are very good at organizing things," Mrs. Laajava adds. "We are very efficient. Nothing goes wrong in Helsinki. People are trusted. If the plane is supposed to leave at 4:15, the plane will leave at 4:15." Finns do things, "in a quiet way, we don't want to brag about it." The ambassador remembers in the late 1980s when Secretary of State George Schultz stopped over in Helsinki on his way to talks with Soviet Foreign Minister Andrei Gromyko. But there was a bad snowstorm in Moscow, and his plane couldn't fly. "In less than two hours we arranged a special train with a special presidential car. Then next morning, Schultz arrived refreshed having enjoyed a nice dinner on the train."

"But, at times," he says, "we are too direct." He recalls how in 1995 at the European Union's General Affairs Council meeting the long agenda prompted the foreign ministers to take off their headphones while others talked, concentrating instead on the pile of papers before them. "It was a terrible waste of time," he says, waving his hands about. "Blah, blah. But when the Finnish minister took the floor he said what's happened the last two to three months in just 45 seconds. They quickly learned. Whenever he started to speak, they grabbed their earphones and listened intensely. He captured the essence."

The Finns, according to Mrs. Laajava, "Do everything in a Protestant way. We obey. We are disciplined. If we are told we have three minutes, we take three minutes, not 13 or 30."

"But," jumps in the ambassador, "the Americans want to 'over-organize' ... like a teacher." He uses a joint session of Congress as his example. "We like to show respect, so when there is a joint session and foreign dignitaries are invited we go, but we waste more than five hours, our calendar is ruined and I have to go to sauna after it to recover," he says shaking his head.

"They ask us to be at the State Department by eight for drinks and coffee, then we all go to the Hill together, two hundred of us and it takes two and one-half hours to get organized. You get to know which guys are before you and who's after and then we get on buses," reports Ambassador Laajava, who especially dislikes being herded back on the buses to come back to the State Department, where it all began. "We all have our own car and driver and could find our own way to the Hill."

However, when an ambassador wants to meet with a U.S. senator or member of Congress, the courtesy is often not returned. "In most other countries you would not say 'No' to an ambassador; it is considered an honor to meet with them," he says. "But somehow we are not considered very useful here. They think we ask for favors or are there to somehow mislead them."

His wife adds, "One time the British defense secretary came to the Hill and the only person who met him was one staffer, and he was only 22 years old!" The ambassador continues, "During the Bush administration, the cooperation with foreign countries was closer. Bush had a strong background, he had been one of us and was very, very talented in foreign policy."

* * *

The eldest of their three children, 24-year-old Minna, recently received her masters degree in political science, which this diplomatic father says "translates into diplomatic relations." But Minna's mother adds, "She doesn't know yet what she will be doing." Son Mikko, 21, is a graduate student at London School of Economics, and 20-year-old Milla is studying medicine at the University of Tampere.

"We sound like the 3M Company," says the ambassador, laughing. With an empty nest this time in Washington they look forward to family reunions during the Christmas holidays just like other families. When I ask this Finnish mother what they do together when the children are home, she answers, "Shop! They want to go to The Gap, Banana Republic and see all their old friends here."

During warmer vacations or back home in Finland, Dad and Mikko love to play golf. "We go to the course and pick up a game, not telling them who we are. My son just says, 'I'm Mike, this is Jake.'" Finally, I have the nerve to tell them how difficult it is for me to correctly pronounce their names. Pirjoriitta Laajava gracefully answers, "Then you'll just have to call us Jake and Rita, like all our American friends do."

"In the last ten years, golf has become very popular in Finland," the ambassador says, perhaps trying to legitimize his intense interest in the game. "In Finland, you can get in nine holes before work or after," he adds, explaining life in "The Land of the Midnight Sun." "We can play late, until midnight, or start at four or five in the morning. It's not expensive. Sixty dollars would be the most expensive."

But back in Washington, "I play at the Army-Navy Club less than once a week." We discuss a possible foursome with the German and Japanese ambassadors, who are also passionate about the game, but he says, "We talk about it all the time but that's *all* we do! Ambassadors in Washington very seldom have time just for themselves."

"Washington is different from anywhere else. In other countries, we compare notes all the time. We very seldom do that here," he explains. "In small European capitals we're almost in constant contact with other diplomats." In Washington, "The delegations are coming and going all the time," Rita adds. "We are always busy entertaining people."

"Plus," the ambassador says, raising an eyebrow, "in this regulatory environment we have a big increase in 'commercial diplomacy.' … In Finland we concentrated early on with research and development and tried to do the microeconomic thing, deregulating things like telecommunication where we were among the first. It gave us the edge in competition and that partially explains why Nokia is a world leader."

Later he tells me, "Everywhere I go in Europe, from Helsinki to Portugal, I use my cell phone. In information technology, Finland's Nokia is number one worldwide in cellular phone production. Per capita, we have the highest number of users of the Internet and are number one, again, in owners of cellular phones."

"Everyone just thinks of us as a few years ago having 'Winter War' with Russia," he says of Finland, the world's most northern country, with one-quarter of its land above the Arctic Circle. "But we have 100 percent literacy, the highest in the world, and we are very well organized. We are very homogeneous and have developed a high level of education," he adds proudly, noting that all education from kindergarten through graduate school is either free or highly subsidized.

"Of course," he begins, "we often have been accused of overdoing welfare. ... Now, we have to cut, reduce the role of government, relying more on individual responsibility without losing healthy fundamentals," putting a positive spin on Finland's economic slowdown.

"In Scandinavia, it's hard to find household help—babysitters, nannies, nurses, maids, waitresses," Rita explains. "No one wants to work in other people's homes and be a 'servant.' And everyone in Scandinavia is on a first-name basis, a reflection of our democratic society. In schools, you always call your teachers by their first name," adds this mother who has worked with hundreds of exchange students. "For our foreign exchange students studying here it is very hard for them to start calling their American teachers by their last names."

I ask what else they want Americans to know about their country, given that a 1990 Gallup Poll reported that Americans are extremely positive about Finns but know very little about them and Finland. The ambassador begins. "We have a hundred thousand lakes. Every twelve hours you can take a cruise line, like the 'Love Boat,' to take you to Stockholm overnight. We have the Savonlinna Opera Festival in July and Kuhmo, the Mecca for musicians, where hundreds of musicians play way out in the countryside, twenty-four hours a day they play, officially and unofficially. Musicians love to go there."

"And," Rita adds, "we have fur and great design, like Marimekko."

"And," the ambassador counters, "Porsche's Boxter is made in Finland and our Saab convertibles, so popular with Americans, and Nokia, the biggest maker of cell phones in the world, are all Finnish."

Then, he looks at his watch, and he's off for an important meeting. Only his Finnish punctuality protects me from a never-ending list.

Rita offers me a tour, another opportunity to show off Finnish design like the coveted chairs by famous architect Alvar Aalto. Sandy wants outside and so do I. The sauna, a rugged-looking "playhouse" in the back corner of the garden, beckons us. A delicious place to escape the pressures of Washington, especially on winter days.

It seems Sandy is a sauna devotee too. "I take her collar off," says Rita, "and she goes to the sauna. When we're at our summer cottage on the lake at home, you see four or five kids and three dogs running back and forth! Of course, in summer here, Washington *is* a sauna," she says, laughing.

With a masters degree in education, Rita has specialized in teaching textiles and has translated 20 books and many articles in the field of fashion and textile education. She is passionate about quilting and doesn't hesitate to run upstairs to fetch her favorites.

"All our beds are covered with my quilts, here and in Finland," says this artistic mother who began quilting with the Beauvoir Quilters, a group of moms from the private elementary school at nearby National Cathedral, where her children were once enrolled. "I dive in and love to work twelve hours in a row," she admits, showing me several of her favorites.

"When my husband said that he might come back to D.C., I told him he could start quilting; I've had a male student for seven years," she says. The ambassador's response? "I'll start quilting when you start playing golf." At last report, she's "trying" golf, but he hasn't started quilting.

* * *

It's almost dark now and Rita and Sandy walk me to my car. Then, they're off for a spin around the neighborhood. Next time, she wants me to bring my beagle, Bagel. As I drive away, in my rearview mirror I can see them walking past their old house next door where they used to live before, when the ambassador was DCM and the children were young. But, tonight, with no parties to give or attend, the ambassador working late and their grown children an ocean away, diplomacy seems like a very lonely business.

* * *

Ambassador Valtasaari is currently Finland's secretary of state, serving as his country's highest-ranking civil servant in the ministry of foreign affairs.

10

Israel: One-Item Agenda

According to protocol, each ambassador must "present credentials" to the president in a White House ceremony before doing anything "official" in the United States on behalf of their country. Today's diplomats often complain about how they have to wait, sometimes weeks but more often months, cooling their heels. And even when their time comes, they may be herded together with other ambassadors only to have little more than a "photo opportunity" with the president of the United States. Few countries can "skip the line."

Israel can. "I had already met President Clinton twice before I presented my credentials," says Ambassador Eliahu Ben-Elissar, barely unpacked before Israel's then brand-new Prime Minister Benjamin Netanyahu arrived to meet with President Clinton. Many countries, fighting for attention, are envious of Israel's legendary access to power in Washington.

When I ask this proud grandfather how he celebrated the occasion, Leora, his secretary, suddenly interrupts us. "I'm sorry, it's the prime minister on the phone for the ambassador." Immediately, this gracious ambassador grabs his notebook, excuses himself and asks Leora to kindly stay behind and entertain me.

While he is discussing the latest peace possibilities in the adjoining office, Leora, a pretty mother of three, and I are discussing how she manages to work full-time at such an intense job and still get her nine-year-old daughter to the ice rink four times a week for practice and expensive private lessons. "I knew I would pay a price," says Leora, who at home in Israel is a pediatric speech and hearing specialist but must settle for office work here while her husband works with an American defense contractor.

More than any other embassy I have visited, the staff here somehow seems more focused and cohesive, believing their daily work is of utmost importance.

Especially the young, handsome guards on the sidewalk and those downstairs in security act as if each of their jobs really matters, that they are on a mission, together. One purpose, one team, serious business. Not like some embassies, where bureaucracy reigns and turf battles are commonplace without any regard for the bigger picture. And not like some other embassies, where, regularly, phones go unanswered and faxes go unread.

Soon the ambassador is back and eager to answer my question. But first I ask about his call with Prime Minister Netanyahu. Sidestepping the content, he says he usually talks with the Israeli leader once a day and that they are on an "excellent, first-name basis." I am struck by how quickly he switches channels and is already back in interview mode with me, remembering my last question and anxious to talk about his official Washington welcome.

"While I was still in Israel. I called up … the State Department protocol office to see if I could go immediately afterwards [from presenting his credentials] to lay a wreath at the Tomb of the Unknown Soldier and at the Holocaust Museum," says this child of the Holocaust. "I had to pay homage to those Americans who gave their lives for their country and for saving the world from two evil empires. And I had the obligation to remember all the Jews who perished in World War II."

When I ask him to tell me his story of survival, his voice gets softer; his eyes, bigger. "I was saved by being taken to Palestine, as it was called then by the British, in place of a boy who was not anymore alive," he begins. "It was 1942 and I was ten years old. I had to call a woman who I hardly knew, Mother. I didn't ever see my parents again and my grandparents were killed; but this is Jewish destiny."

He still carries with him the picture of Nathan, Golda Graucher's young son whose untimely death gave Eliahu Ben-Elissar the chance to live. He translates the Yiddish inscription on Nathan's picture for me: "Mommy, they are taking us away, Good-bye."

Together, we observe a moment of silence. Then, he begins to tie those indelible personal experiences to his political being. "I can link it with Desert Storm in 1991. As a member of the Knesset [Israel's parliament], from the rostrum I said, 'I will never forgive Saddam Hussein for having compelled one million Israeli children to use gas masks,' and everyone got the point," the ambassador reports.

I see a visceral reaction when he says, "Every Jew, every Israeli is inspired by the thought that Jews ought not to be weak again." Otherwise, he vows, "Jews are not enamored in power, in force."

"Our system, in spite of the wars, is basically a democratic nation and free. A military coup in Israel is impossible to think about. Everybody will start laughing. Why, why is it that military and force is necessary? For life, [not] extinction," he declares.

With a Ph.D. in history and political science, this ambassador is the author of several books, including his most recent work, *No More War*. It is his personal account of the Israeli-Egyptian peace treaty and his experience as the very first Israeli ambassador to Egypt. Interestingly, he often writes his books in French and they are translated into Hebrew.

I ask him if he honestly expects to see peace with the Palestinians in his lifetime. "I remember times when I thought peace with Israel and Egypt was impossible and it took place. It took place when Egypt realized it cannot undo the state of Israel," explains this five-term Knesset veteran who "feels at home" in the U.S. Congress. "This is where I come from; I love to go up there and see the commotion.

"With the Palestinians, they have to realize the same thing and they have to realize much, much more. It is totally different. With them, we have actually a very bitter conflict, an acrimonious conflict, not a conventional conflict. It is not on territory or raw materials, not boundaries or space or oil. Basically, these are two groups of people who are absolutely certain that this land belongs to them.

"Peace won't come without the presence of the United States," he predicts. "Experience shows we can't consummate peace without the Americans. We can start the process. We started alone with Jordan and Egypt and the Palestinians, but we need the Americans for the final touch."

Then I ask, "Was it Jimmy Carter or Anwar Sadat who made the difference?"

"Sadat was a man of vision and a lot of courage much ahead of his generation," he begins. "We had a very, very special relationship: very, very close; very friendly, very open, very candid. He knew he could raise everything he wanted with me and I knew the same.

"Our talks were always one-on-one. Nobody took notes, no assistants, nobody. We were all alone. I was always rushing immediately afterwards to write down everything; I used to spend the rest of the day in reconstruction of our conversation.

"He was a realist. He understood before other Egyptians that he could not have both; going to war with Israel and [Egypt] building itself, it was either/or. Egypt was actually on the verge of ruin: very high fertility and birthrate and economic and social pressures because of the state of war. No investments, no tourism. The Suez was closed."

Since Sadat's widow, Jihan, lives nearby in Virginia, I ask if they are in touch. "Yes, we have a close relationship. Jihan told us that the morning her husband was assassinated he was not only not worried, he was absolutely relaxed. She had asked him to put on his bulletproof vest and he refused, saying, 'Everything is in the hands of God, Allah.' And he didn't put on the bulletproof vest."

"I understand this kind of attitude: It's in the hands of God." I ask Ben-Ellisar if he wears a vest now or has a bodyguard. "I have a bodyguard, no vest."

* * *

The day before, Nitza Ben-Elissar and I had tea together at their residence. I remembered her volunteering how "insulted" she was not to not have any Israeli security in Egypt when her husband had as many as eight body guards and always traveled in an entourage with two cars in front and one behind. "That being a woman [a wife] is not important enough." She continued, "I was part of the show and I kept wondering how come nobody pays attention to me. When we went out to charity functions they would grab him and take him away but nobody gave a damn that I was there. So I would go in a corner and sit and smoke and look at that carnival going on," said this independent Israeli woman who founded an Israeli school in Monrovia, Liberia, and organized Zionist chapters all over Europe for the World Zionist Organization.

"Finally after we were there three months the Egyptians gave me a bodyguard," she said, obviously still feeling slighted by the Israeli government and "furious with my husband." That's why she decided to write her book, *The Parting of the Red Sea.*

"When he read my book he had tears in his eyes," she told me. "He didn't realize that while we were there he didn't have any time for me."

* * *

Back in his office, I wonder about the next generation of Jews and Arabs, both those growing up in their own country and those living outside their symbolic homeland. I ask Ben-Elissar if these younger Jews are brought up being taught hatred or distrust of their neighbors and historic enemies. My research assistant Peter McMahon was a counselor at "Seeds of Peace," a camp in Maine where the ambassador had spoken the previous summer to the young Jewish and Palestinian children who are flown here to learn about each other.

"Jews are never brought up on hatred to Arabs," he vows, quickly adding, "Of course, terrorists are different. Terrorists should be expelled from human society." He remembers that while he was at "Seeds of Peace," there was a terrorist attack [in Israel] and the Arab campers sent condolences to the Israeli campers.

Israeli Ambassador Eliahu Ben-Elissar. Photo courtesy of the Israeli Embassy.

I ask him if he could imagine being a Palestinian. He throws his hands up in front of his face and turns his head to the side, as if he is literally ducking my very words. "I am not ready to play this role," he says, dead serious. "I have a one-track mind, I am an Israeli Jew ambassador."

But, "Realizing basically that attitudes will not change, we are doomed, Palestinians and Israelis, to live together. Refusal is mainly coming from the Arab side," he says, making a preemptive strike. "We must imagine new formulas and create something new, something different. We will be able to live separately but nevertheless together."

"Maybe the best formula was Moshe Dayan's: The Arabs have to realize that they will not be able to throw us into the sea and the Jews have to realize that they will not be able to throw the Arabs into the desert."

He speaks passionately, firmly. Because most of this interview has been very serious, I mention that when I first called to inquire about interviewing him and his wife, everyone told me how strikingly different they were. And talking with his wife just the day before, I understand what they meant. Now, I get a big smile.

"Yes, yes, we don't always agree," he says, laughing, and looking like he feels a bit ambushed. "At home, my wife is the ambassador!"

I see this very serious man can be jovial. And I learn again what a great advantage it is to chat with an ambassador's spouse first, even though some may consider it a protocol misstep.

When he finds out she already told me that they met in a supermarket, he decides to tell the rest.

"Yes, she saw me signing my book but I didn't see her. We really met at an Independence Day celebration in Geneva at a friend's home."

I ask him if I understood correctly that at the time they met they were both still married. He shuts his eyes and holds his finger up to his mouth, making an almost inaudible, "Shhhhh," but surprisingly he does admit, "It was immediate electricity, high tension."

Nitza Ben-Elissar is a woman with dramatic, big, black eyes and a thick mane to match. She is an enchanting storyteller who specializes in candor and intimacy. "It's important that I like people and people know that I like them. I look straight into their eyes," she says leaning close, "and don't look behind to see if there is someone more interesting to talk to."

He, on the other hand, shrewdly weighs every word and doesn't choose such public exposure to his private thoughts. I ask him to explain why his wife told me the day before, "My husband is relaxed only once a year when he is like me, and he dresses in costume for the annual Israeli Carnival." (He wore her sister's red jogging suit, pretending he was Lenin.)

"From my studies of history, I am not ready to assume uncalculated risks," he says, melding his personal demeanor with his political persona. "Consider the margin of maneuvering that I possess is much narrower than other nations. I don't consider myself more hawkish than necessary or more [hawkish] than Madeleine Albright. Americans make concessions where security is involved."

He admires Albright for "her determination, she knows what she wants. She's an intellectual with a past. Perhaps I feel close to her because she was born in Czechoslovakia and I was born in Poland and she's first-generation American."

But when I ask if she has ever talked with him about her newly discovered Jewish heritage, he answers, "Never." He describes coming close to the issue, though. "I mentioned to her that we have something in common … that we are both children … products of the Munich Era; the Munich Accords, 1938, that sold out Czechoslovakia."

We start to talk about his daily schedule and he dramatically rolls his eyes and takes a deep breath. "I get up at six and read Israeli press releases because they are seven and a half hours ahead of us. Then breakfast and *The Washington Post* and *The New York Times.*" He regularly eats lunch in his office, "a sandwich brought from home," and has an exercise bike at home but doesn't use it. When urgent phone calls often awake him during the night, he falls back to sleep, "like a soldier."

"You ask me how I relax, I take cat naps," he says pointing to the couch where I'm sitting. He explains that with Knesset late nights and nonstop book writing, he survived with "siestas." "My method for writing a book is that I don't care about the hours. I write day and night and then I make a pause" for a refreshing nap.

His comment that he sleeps "like a soldier" brings him to another conclusion. "I have devoted half my life to fighting the Arabs. It's only the other half that I'm trying to make peace with them."

The phone rings again and he moves to his desk immediately, leaving me sitting on the black leather couch while he doesn't hesitate to answer, in Hebrew, even though my tape recorder is still running. Either it's Leora again with a polite way to say my time's up, or maybe it's some part of the peace process that can't wait.

While he's on the phone he sees me looking at the three-panel black-and-white photo of Jerusalem that is overhead. It has traveled with him to Cairo, then back to Israel and on to this post. "You can tell it is at least twenty years old," he explains, "because there are still no TV antennas." Around his office, I see other reminders of his country's history and serious goals. On his desk, there's a silver letter opener from Sadat that needs polishing. A picture of Auschwitz is inscribed, "Fifty years too late" and "This will never happen again." An antimissile missile from the chairman of the Foreign Affairs Committee and an Israeli F-15 model are prominent among the many defense mementos. A Jewish mezuza and an open Bible, with Hebrew on the right side and English on the left, also help set the stage.

But it is the haunting sketch by French political cartoonist TIM that I shall never forget: a man in his black and white concentration camp stripes with the blood-red word *RACISTE* emblazoned across his chest. "It is the artist's copy and signed, 'Cordially,'" says Ambassador Ben-Elissar. He reminds me that then, in 1975, the UN General Assembly adopted a resolution "equating Zionism to racism."

And still he smiles when we say good-bye. Ironically, as I leave, Leora has a call for me from the Egyptian ambassador, who needs to reschedule our interview. (Coincidentally, I was to have visited him next, only a short walk away on International Drive.)

As I cross the atrium to pick up my credentials and go outside through the courtyard to the outer security booth, Nitza's stories from yesterday are swirling around in my head. I find myself transported to their living room, replaying her vivid accounts.

How they couldn't find a house in Cairo because "Egyptians were afraid to sign a contract with us. Peace was only a few months old and they didn't expect it to last. They didn't want to be put on a black list in case it [peace] didn't last. Egypt had a black list," she said. "It was easier to sign a peace contract between two heads of state than sign a house contract."

"We lived in a hotel, a bit isolated outside the center of Cairo, away from the action," she said, remembering her long days alone when her husband was so busy and so well guarded. "My cigarette was my best friend."

"One day I decided, 'This is enough,'" and she left their hotel suite and went down to the lobby in search of a cab. The hotel security man asked incredulously, "Are you alone?" And only after the doormen consulted the chief hotel security officer did they allow her to leave in a taxi. "I saw them write down the number in case they have to have the body traced!

"I had no papers, no passport, only a bag with about 20 Egyptian pounds. I didn't speak Arabic and I had no map. About 5 P.M. it started getting dark and I decided to look for a cab. It's Cairo with 11 million people, no taxi and I don't even know where my hotel is. If I say, 'I'm the wife of the Israeli ambassador to Egypt,' the traffic policeman will immediately put me in an insane asylum!

"Finally this old Peugeot station wagon stopped with six or seven people in it. I pushed my head in and said I needed to get back to the Sheraton. My God, in Israel, I would never go in a car in the evening with strangers, but they were very nice. When they started to talk to me in Arabic," she says, "I let them continue to think that I was Mexican."

Then there was the time "the wife of the L.A. bureau chief and her husband invited eight couples and us to dinner … and none of them came." Members of Egyptian society didn't want to take the chance. "I didn't take any friendly gestures for granted," Nitza recalls. "The U.S. ambassador's wife, Betty Atherton, was like my mother. She knew we were in this business together, that Americans were our partners."

"Nineteen seventy-three was our worst war, the Yom Kippur War, and seven years later we're representing Israel in an Arab country. It was short notice: We had only a few weeks to pack, little time to learn about Egypt," she remembers. When she went out to shop for leather handbags and five-dollar shoes, carved silver and copper pots she discovered a bustling Cairo that was totally foreign to her. "Every day was a lifetime, no Israeli, nobody had ever experienced what I experienced before.

"On Friday the whole of Cairo became a mosque. The first Friday I went to the street of all the shoe shops, I was pushed by angry people because I was stepping on a [prayer] mat."

But her story has a softer ending than her husband's. "I learned the enemy is a human being and the enemy has a father and a mother. When the Egyptian chief of staff, who was head of the army, was killed in a helicopter accident on the Libyan border, I went to pay my condolences to his wife. Two years before, the same event would have been a happy event for me. But now I sat and cried with her.

"My Egyptian experience made me more open," says the former Zionist organizer who adds, "Mrs. Sadat and I cry together."

While Nitza Ben-Elissar and I are having tea together in this Upper Northwest Washington contemporary residence, these vivid stories keep taking me to the crowded, diagonal streets of Cairo.

"The peace process is limping now. I call it a 'Cold Peace.' I hope the ice will dissolve. It is a peace without relationship but still it is a peace," she says. "It was such a historical time," she continues. "But here, people ask, 'How was Egypt?' and you say one sentence and they immediately start to exchange recipes. Nobody's very interested.

"I'm a 'glorified caterer.' I open my house and my heart to as many people as possible so more people know that Israelis are not so bad," she says. "It is hard work but it is fun. It's constant work twenty-four hours a day. What I'm in charge of, it can't be put in office hours."

"We get a lot of state visitors. Our first year here most of them showed up because there was a new government," she explains referring to when Netanyahu became Israel's new prime minister almost overnight. "The prime minister was here six times in one year and the president once."

Her guest list for receptions at the residence looks like a "Who's Who in Washington": Katherine Graham, Senator Ted Kennedy, Justice Ruth Bader Ginsburg, National Security Advisor Sandy Berger, CNN's Wolf Blitzer, former UN Ambassador Jeane Kirkpatrick, Alan Greenspan and NBC's Andrea Mitchell, and, of course, the secretary of defense, the chairman of the joint chiefs of staff and the White House chief of staff. Not a list many embassies can boast.

In addition, she has organized a "Bible group" of about 70 women who meet monthly at the residence. "After all, this is [Israel] where the Bible was written ... we start at twelve and they leave at two. We serve lunch but my cook calls them 'bird ladies' because they eat so little."

Unlike some other ambassadors' wives in Washington, "There's a big difference for me because there are five million Jews in this country and a big demanding Jewish community and I am theirs." She and her husband have endless invitations from Jewish charities and other Jewish organizations all over the country.

But when the Ben-Elissars get a night off, "He goes to sleep and I take a friend and go to the movies," said this energetic wife. "I call it 'my little bonus.' I drag him too sometimes to concerts, opera. You know Placido [Domingo] is ours; he started his career in Israel." During the rare days when she isn't committed to going to some luncheon or fancy tea, she loves to "sneak out" and take herself on walking tours of Washington's museums and famous monuments or simply nose around Dupont Circle or Foggy Bottom. "The Library of Congress and the National Cathedral have lovely concerts," she said, showing her knack for tracking down a city's lesser-known but charming events.

For Egypt, they both decided to learn Arabic. "He said that first he wanted to learn the alphabet and read. I wanted to know how to talk with the cook, the maid, leave messages, chat with the shopkeeper and the man at the shoe store. I made lots of mistakes, grammatical errors, but I can carry on a conversation. He is still learning the alphabet!"

But, she doesn't tease him. "As a Holocaust survivor, he is very tough but he doesn't like teasing, what would be commonplace in a normal family, in a normal childhood.

"We have no children together, but we tell everyone, 'We have three grandchildren together.'" The two grandsons and one granddaughter, children of the ambassador's daughter Hem, who lives in Connecticut, especially liked going to the White House ceremony when their grandfather presented his credentials and then driving around Washington in the limousine afterward.

"My husband is totally a different person with children. It's as if he broadcasts that love, those rays. We sit at the airport waiting for a flight and he can just look at a child and the child will come over and talk to him and maybe crawl up on his lap."

At the residence, there are lots of pictures with all three grandchildren and their proud grandparents, including some with President Clinton. There's also the one of the ambassador dressed up as Lenin. But one 20-year-old picture alone symbolizes peace: the one with Anwar Sadat and a much younger-looking ambassador. About this photo, Ben-Elissar's fashionable wife said, "That's before my husband had white hair."

* * *

The Ben-Ellisars are enjoying their new post in Paris, where he fondly remembers his student days, and together they can stroll to the romatic city's sights and famous museums and galleries.

11

Egypt: First-Rate Hospitality

Anyone who thinks that ambassadors don't work hard should visit Egyptian Ambassador Ahmed Maher El Sayed. When Patty, his American secretary, first shows me into his office, I can barely see him behind the pyramid of papers on his desk. In fact, as he pushes his reading glasses on top of his bald head, he playfully reaches up with his elbows and puts his chin on the stack to make his point more dramatically. "See how much work I have do today!"

Then, without moving, he asks me to sit down right in front of his desk. Throughout our interview, he stays seated behind his desk, with his glasses on his head and with that paper pile between us.

I thought, at first, that this was going to be a short interview. But Ambassador El Sayed not only gave me his full attention and lots of his time, he gave me some of the best quotes and insights of any of the ambassadors.

"The ambassador's worst enemy is CNN," he tersely begins when I ask this veteran diplomat how instant, 24-hour global communications has changed diplomacy. In fact, "CNN is really the competitor of the ambassadors," he says, half laughing at his comment. "They get the news and you're asleep and you get, from Cairo, a call saying, 'What is this or that?'—and you don't know. They have watched CNN!"

When I ask him how he protects himself from such wake-up calls, he shakes his head. Today, "An ambassador doesn't really [ever] leave his job for many reasons—when events happen there, [it] is a difference of seven hours between here and Cairo. When they want something it is eight or nine o'clock in the morning in Cairo and it's two o'clock in the morning here!"

This ambassador, who has served in the Egyptian Ministry of Foreign Affairs for more than 40 years, says the biggest change in diplomacy is how heads of state "telephone each other, fax things and have direct contact," bypassing their ambassadors. "We are left trying to keep up, learning things after the fact."

Besides playing catch-up by watching CNN, I ask this veteran diplomat how he manages. He points to the pile of papers between us and shrugs, "This is the part of the job I don't like."

Does he get up early? "Yes, but it is not very early by American standards. I have not yet gotten accustomed to this 'barbaric custom' of having working breakfasts; I am not able to conduct intelligent conversations with anybody that early. But I do wake up early. I listen to the radio, I watch the news on television, I read the papers and I usually come here at about 9:30 for a staff briefing, including lead dispatches. A seven-hour difference leads to a lot of mail in the morning."

When I ask if his staff compiles a condensed version of the morning news for him, he answers, "Yes, but I like the *feel* of newspapers, the *feel* of books. You get articles and things from the Internet, but it is very different."

Then he looks at his calendar and gives me a briefing of the rest of his schedule. "Today for instance, I have an appointment with representatives from the Jewish community and after you leave, the new ambassador from Tunisia is coming here for a courtesy visit. But fortunately, tonight I have nothing; last night I had three receptions!"

Looking forward to a night off, I ask how he relaxes. "I love movies! I am a movie fan but I don't go as often as I like," says the man who liked *LA Confidential, Mad City* and *The Rainmaker.* "I like to read but unfortunately this pile of working papers makes reading [to relax] a difficult exercise."

When I mention how Sir John Kerr, the British ambassador, and his wife, Lady Kerr, also love to drive themselves to the movies he interrupts me. "I don't drive because of parking problems; we take the Metro. Your Metro is one of the nicest metros I have ever been in," says this low-key ambassador who loves to take the underground for a quiet night out with his wife, wherever they are posted—Paris, London, Cairo—but Cairo's underground "is only an infant, but it is a very good system."

"I like to walk too, although I have a problem with Washington," he begins. "Downtown Washington after-hours is empty. You can walk in any other city," says this top Egyptian diplomat who has lived in Zurich, Kinshasa, Paris, Lisbon, Brussels and Moscow.

Another difference for foreign diplomats in Washington: "It is not a question of mingling with other diplomats. Every country here has its own obligations, commitments and their own problems that are the gist of everyone's efforts to deal with the American side."

In other capital cities, "Members of the diplomatic corps need each other for information, for tips on how to make life easier," says the ambassador, who served in Moscow before coming to the United States. "In Moscow, we gang together to import meat from Argentina, tell each other to look in this shop or that shop, the tips on how to make life easier. So you make friends," he says, adding that when they came to Washington, "We already had good friends here: the Italian and the new ambassador from the Netherlands—we were in Moscow together."

Because of the growing size of the Washington diplomatic corps, "You acquire friends from the smaller groups. The Arab ambassadors have a formal meeting every month and also I have to attend the formal meetings of the African ambassadors."

Ambassador El Sayed thinks Washington is very different because ambassadors here need to keep in touch with all the branches of government, in addition to their constituents. "In Europe, you don't have much contact with the legislature, the parliaments. Here, you have to be in constant touch with members of Congress ... each member."

Elsewhere, according to the ambassador, "There is a rational system because there is discipline: One votes according to their party's beliefs, unlike here where each congressman has his own agenda. It is very time consuming but it is very important."

In addition, "The press plays an important role—and you have to establish some sort of relationship with them. Some become friends, some are just contacts." Again, "It is very, very time consuming, all these contacts, but very important."

Still, "This is one of few cities where the ambassador is considered important. You are solicited by charities. The first year, I couldn't refuse anything. Now I have become more choosy. But, charities are a good thing," says this man whose sister died of cancer at the age of 32 and who himself has undergone two major heart surgeries in the United States. "You meet new people, you become part of a community, and you help a cause." The ambassador and his wife were particularly active with cancer charities and those involving children, "since we unfortunately have no children ourselves."

When I ask about his health, he leans back in his chair and puts his hands in his pants' pockets. "My first heart trouble was in 1982. Dr. Cooley in Houston was my surgeon; his assistant was an Egyptian." As I begin to ask about his daily exercise routine, he puts his hand up to stop me. "I'm supposed to exercise. I have a treadmill and I like to stroll. I have to stick to a regime." But then, he tells me he doesn't really like to exercise.

Egyptian Ambassador Ahmed Maher El Sayed and Mrs. El Sayed. Photo courtesy of Mrs. El Sayed.

As a young boy, "My family tried in each and every sport and hobby to interest me. It was difficult to make me a sportsman. I was hopeless on the violin and so they tried gymnastics, then football [soccer], then riding. I had asthma and was overweight." I am charmed by his candor.

Although he is naturally on the healthy "Mediterranean diet," much touted in America, he finds it hard to control his weight. "We have an Egyptian cook at home who makes lots of stuffed things with squash, tomatoes and we eat lots of rice and beans and, of course, pita with hummus." But when he sneaks away to the movies, he loves to have "a small bag of popcorn."

He reminds me that he hasn't given up yet on exercise, at least when it comes to golf. "I played golf in Portugal but that was ages ago. In Belgium, the weather was not very helpful for golf and Moscow was hopeless. Since I came to Washington carrying my clubs and everything, I promised myself that next month I'll start again. I still dream. I like biking but I never do that too."

Back to business, this seasoned diplomat wants to make sure I understand that all ambassadors have two important roles. "First, he is the ambassador to the authorities and a relationship must be established from which the ambassador has to explain why upon certain circumstances, his country takes positions that may not coincide with those of the host country or please that host country.

"Second, he is ambassador to the people. He has to go to the grassroots, talk to the people and try to explain positions across the country. He must submit to their questions and illuminate the issues for the next generation by meeting young people, students and most of the people who come to the embassy." He pauses for a moment. "This is perhaps the most gratifying role."

Even though the Washington Arab community is reached and can keep in touch through five Arabic TV stations, this ambassador's schedule is full of community events. "They like personal contact also, so they want you to go to them."

For successful commercial diplomacy, it is also important "to cultivate the business community—all ambassadors today do that because of the commercial and economic side of diplomacy. Diplomats used to look down on businesspeople. Money was something you didn't talk about. But now, trade plays an important role in any relationship, so an ambassador has to have contacts with business people and you discover businessmen can help with the politics."

Due to the distance of his ancient country from the United States, "What we do not do here, unfortunately, is the cultural. Europe was easier to bring dance troops and orchestras and things like that. Here it is too expensive." But the ambassadors' wives organize a crafts bazaar that gives them the opportunity to speak about their country, get exposure and sell some products and handicrafts for charities at home.

I had heard that Ambassador El Sayed participated in the famous Camp David Peace Accord negotiated between Egypt and Israel during the Carter administration. At that time, he was chief of cabinet for the minister of foreign affairs. I was especially interested in his recollection of those days, because I had already discussed the same Mideastern summit with Israeli Ambassador Ben-Elissar, who was also present at this history-making event.

"I'll tell you what it felt like—a prison. We were really confined to this camp for 13 days, meeting, eating and going to the movies. It was very oppressive when the relationship is as tense and tight [as that was] and when you are discussing very serious matters," he reports. "In the end, there was some fraternization and there was the agreement but we all had to go through this.

"The first day in the common dining room we had an Egyptian, an American, and an Israeli table. We rarely moved," he remembers, "at least, not between the Israeli and the Egyptian table.

"But since we were living together, we had to talk together and then you discover in front of you is another human being who can share feelings. Then people showed pictures of their children, talked about their families. Because, independent of the political atmosphere, you sort of create a human bond that I think is extremely important."

"Was Sadat the crucial ingredient?" I ask.

"He was a man of vision. It was the conjunction of Sadat's person and vision and Begin's sense of history and courage and Carter's messianic tendency to do good and his determination to do good."

Again putting his thumbs in his pants' pockets and leaning back in his chair, the ambassador seems to be stepping out of the pressures of this day to properly remember this man he admired. "Sadat was a unique personality. He had an amazing degree of calm and self-confidence and you didn't feel him tense. He liked theatrics and enjoyed the grand gestures. He loved the media; he was the center of attention and they [the media] loved him as they sensed his love." In comparison, he thinks Egypt's current president, Hosni Mubarak, is "even more approachable, more relaxed and listens a lot."

After so many posts and so many years serving Egypt abroad and at home, this ambassador is thinking about writing a book himself about diplomacy. "When I was young I wanted to be a journalist but my problem is that I wanted to start at the top." His book might be about his experiences in Moscow and Washington, maybe a sort of "Tale of Two Cities." "My only problem is that I don't keep a diary," he says, so maybe "I will write a novel."

Before I leave, I ask this hardworking diplomat what it was like for him when he heard about the terrorism at home in Luxor involving a busload of tourists. "It was 2 A.M. Washington time," says the ambassador, who then immediately flipped on CNN. "I was on the phone with Cairo and with the State Department. It was a terrible shock as details came out and my first worry was, 'Were there any Americans [killed or hurt]?' The human side is that you regret anyone dying but I did have a sigh of relief [when hearing no Americans were involved].

"Terrorism is so un-Egyptian," he says emphatically, "and this kind is even more un-Egyptian. Usually with terrorists, people are killed and the terrorists then try to escape. These [people] were deliberately killed and these terrorists were in no hurry—they took their time, they mutilated the bodies, they shot [their victims] in the face," he says in disgust. "This is very, very un-Egyptian and makes me wonder where this comes from—who these people are, and where did they learn this horrible way [of killing].

"This is not terrorism, but savagery. All terrorism is savagery but there are degrees and I sometimes wonder if this is a new trend. Is it something imported?"

The ambassador then suggests that a new breed of "international terrorists" were created and encouraged by the war in Afghanistan. "Afghanistan, the CIA and the Arab countries found it expedient and useful to encourage people to fight against Russian occupation in the name of religion [as well as] to finance them. So it gave them courage—and when the war ended, it was very difficult [since] this genie had been let out of the bottle to get her back in again," he says of the Arabs and Muslims who fought in Afganistan. When these terrorists, the so-called mujahideen, returned to their countries, they decided their countries were "nonbelievers." So among themselves "they exchange experiences, they exchange money, they exchange weapons and maybe now, they are exchanging persons—some of them are brainwashed.

"It's very, very sad. Egyptian people are hospitable; they like foreigners and have no place for xenophobia," he says firmly. "We resent violence and especially the barbarous manner in which these people were killed."

He agrees that the well-publicized incident was terrible for Egypt's tourism and bad for the economy, but most of all he wants to emphasize how "un-Egyptian" it was. He shakes his head and is quiet. He says, "Terrorists will not prevail; they will be defeated by the people themselves."

It is time for the new Tunisian ambassador to arrive and for me to leave Ambassador El Sayed with his next visitor and his never-ending pile of papers. As I slip into the elevator, the ambassador's guest steps out.

I leave marveling over how modern ambassadors work around the clock, day after day, fighting information-overload, the endless paper pile and their 24-hour opponent, CNN.

* * *

She has a beautiful face and gorgeous skin. But best of all, she has a wonderful sense of humor. Mrs. El Sayed looks even younger than the 11-year difference between this diplomatic couple.

She is already worrying about "the nightmare when we move." It seems that the pile of papers I saw on the ambassador's desk comes home every week and his home office is a final resting place for all this reading, along with all his books and newspapers.

"I've gotten used to sleeping with earplugs and a mask," she says when we begin to talk about the late-night calls from Cairo. "Sometimes we leave the TV on all night and the fax machine is in the bedroom," she says good-naturedly, laughing about her unusual home life in America.

"When [President] Bush collapsed in Japan, it was two or three in the morning here. They called from Cairo and asked the former ambassador what's wrong! He said, 'Bush is fine and he's in Japan.' They responded, 'He's collapsed.' It was late morning in Japan, late afternoon in Egypt, and midnight here. But they called Washington to find out about Bush in Japan!"

She remembers "the tension, the excitement" she heard in her husband's voice each time they talked during the Camp David Accords. She was back home and he was at the Presidential retreat in nearby Maryland. Even though he couldn't discuss any details he was able to keep in touch with her. "I'd read about it in the newspapers and then when he called he couldn't say anything about the progress except, 'I think we're coming back in one or two days.'

"It was a very complicated situation," she continues. "The two leaders didn't want to see each other. President Carter wanted them to meet," and she says, laughing, that they even contrived a plan to send the famous leaders out on bicycles to meet on the wooded paths somewhere.

By now three plates of Egyptian pastries, piled high in delicate pyramids, are in front of me. Enough for two dozen guests. She laughs and reminds me how hospitable Egyptian people are.

"I am proud to be Egyptian," she says sincerely. Then without sounding at all like a commercial, she explains what it means to be from this modern republic, once the fertile center of an ancient civilization. "We are a peaceful people. We love laughing. You can see what you think is a miserable little boy with no shoes but he is happy, laughing.

"We have old roots. You feel the age. Cairo is dusty, is dirty but you know the city is eighteen hundred years old. Egypt and Cairo have been there since the creation of civilization.

"Unfortunately, we have a big gap between the very rich and the very poor but we had a 'civilized revolution'—opposite the French Revolution. There was no blood, no death. The resistance surrounded the king and told him, 'You can't remain like this.' The negotiations took two to three weeks and then he was escorted, as king, to Alexandria. With their money and their jewelry, they went by boat to Italy. He was saluted as king when he left and Egypt was a republic."

She says that years later when members of the royal family wanted to return to have their baby born on Egyptian soil, "They were very welcome. There was no fear. He's an Egyptian."

Remembering Nitza Ben-Elissar's account of her experiences in Cairo, I ask this diplomatic wife if she and the Israeli wife are friends here. For the only time in the interview, Mrs. El Sayed turns cool. "No," she says, explaining that she had heard how much the wife of the Israeli ambassador "complained about her time in Egypt" and she didn't want to make her "more miserable."

All of a sudden, we are talking about anti-Semitism. "I can't be an anti-Semite because I am Semitic. I don't feel any difference. My aunt, Aunt Marcel, who is Jewish, lived with us," she says, referring to her childhood.

I had already heard from the ambassador a short version of how they first met. When I tell her his version, she starts to laugh. "Our families were neighbors; I knew him all my life," says the handsome woman who is 11 years younger than her husband. "His father was a gynecologist and brought me into this world. When we were married he said, 'I can't believe I'm marrying my son to the baby I brought into this world!'"

Back to the beginning. It seems he asked his mother-in-law to ask her daughter if she minded him coming to call on her. But when her mother broached the subject she said, "Mother, don't make any problems for me," thinking her old family friend was "too old."

And "when he came to the house it was a little embarrassing. I loved and respected him so much," she says that it was hard to think of him romantically. Plus, she had many friends, many of them young men, and she didn't want to lose her friends by marrying an older man.

"I said I want to keep my friends, *my friends,"* and he agreed. When I tell her how many times I tried to set up an appointment with her and was told, "She has a friend visiting from Egypt," we laugh. "It was true," she says, dramatically opening her arms up wide.

When I ask her about her childhood, I see a whole new part of this 50-year-old woman. "In my generation, we were never forbidden to do anything. I grew up like a boy," says this sole sister of three brothers. "I was always swimming, riding horses." She tells me a story about a jumping accident when she demanded a horse that was much too strong for her because, "I thought I could do anything." But here, with all her official duties and busy charity schedule, this former athlete has little time for sports.

"In Moscow, where there was less to do, I took up painting, piano. There, an ambassador is so well treated that they gave me the highest music professor. I really got the best." And although she brought her paints with her to Washington, she has not had time to open her paint box.

By now I have had two glasses of a tasty limeade. "We have it all the time at home," she says when she sees how much I like it. "I'll give you the recipe: fresh lime juice, sugar, water and a few drops of mint extract." This hostess anticipates well what her American guests might like on a hot summer day. I take time to taste the mishaltit and gorayeba and baklava, all homemade sweets. She laughs when I tell her that it's not fair that she puts all of this between us on the coffee table but doesn't take a bite herself.

She's proud to tell me, "Puff pastry is Egyptian. Napolean's cooks saw this type of bread and the soldiers loved it," so the French learned to make it. "Their recipe is lighter than what we have."

When I ask about her specific charities and other interests she tells me about her indoctrination into Washington's social circles. "When we first arrived, expecting to only stay a year, all sorts of groups asked me to have them for tea. My house was like a catering facility with herds of people coming and going."

Then they were asked to stay longer and she started accepting only certain charities such as the Race for the Cure, Very Special Arts and several local hospitals. I ask if she ran in the Race for the Cure. "I tried to run but I couldn't. When I started to run, people behind me ran over me like buffaloes," she says, laughing.

She loves to garden but thinks it "looks too silly" to wear her gardening clothes and be out in front of the embassy on Massachusetts Avenue. She did love her "beautiful garden in Moscow where our home was bigger, really a palace. And in Portugal, where we had an enormous garden with fruit trees and a cook's garden."

Now, she hopes her next garden will be home in Egypt when her workaholic husband finally decides to escape from his pyramid of papers and retire.

12

Japan: Economic Jitterbug

Early in my research, June 1996, I interviewed the ambassador of Japan. I recently had had knee surgery and that Friday, the day of our interview, my doctor decided he had to remove my stitches that same morning. While my research assistant Nicole Giugno tried to change my appointment with the ambassador, I tried to change my appointment with the doctor. But neither could reschedule. So I explained to Mr. Tsukasa Uemura, the ambassador's press and information officer, why I might be "a few minutes" late for our noon interview.

* * *

A full waiting room at the doctor's office and bridge construction on Massachusetts Avenue makes me much later than expected. While I sit standstill in traffic two blocks away from Ambassador Saito's office, I review my notes, streamlining questions and wishing I were going instead to an embassy where punctuality is not such a national obsession.

It is already 12:15 P.M. when I pull into the circular drive at the embassy. I limp up to the glass-enclosed security checkpoint only to be greeted sternly by a small Japanese receptionist, dressed from head to toe in lavender. After several phone calls and negative glances toward me (I am sure everyone there knows I was late), she hands me a parking pass with my exact parking space number and printed directions for their underground garage. It is now that I realize how ridiculous my cross-town dash has been and how this is one embassy where I should have arrived a half an hour early just to get through security.

Down, down I go deeper into the parking garage, past the men chatting while they shine the ambassador's black Lincoln limo and finally to my parking spot, number 56, far away from the ambassador's office.

When the elevator doors open upstairs, the woman from security is there waiting for me. Now I am in an inner sanctum, next to an atrium courtyard with daylight streaming through the big skylight. She asks me to wait. After a few more minutes, my contact, Mr. Uemura, appears but begins by admonishing me, "You know you are very late and the ambassador does have another appointment at one. The ambassador has been waiting for you." I try to explain as we quickly weave our way through the office maze, past another Japanese garden, through the messy press office filled with lots of young Japanese faces, until we finally arrive at the ambassador's door. After all this rushing around, my knee throbs in terrible pain, while my ice packs melt in the car five floors below.

Once inside his huge office, Ambassador Kunihiko Saito is polite but businesslike when I apologize. He points to his watch and we began our no-nonsense interview immediately. We sit down, facing each other in the far corner of a huge beige horseshoe sectional sofa. Mr. Uemura joins me on my right side.

"My job," says Ambassador Saito, "is to make Americans understand Japan better ... particularly the Japanese market. Our market," he continues, "is not closed to foreign products. That is an old notion. But it is not easy to penetrate unless you understand. There are a lot of opportunities if they try hard."

No matter what question I ask, Ambassador Saito will give me an answer with an economic twist. It is June 1996, before the Asian financial crisis has hit his country, and he wants to talk trade.

He tells me that the bilateral relationship between the United States and Japan is so important and so intertwined, "politically, economically and on security and other global issues [that] they are bound to have problems between governments from time to time and I try to solve problems as soon as possible."

He speaks in a calm, contained way. When I ask him if he ever gets mad he looks at me incredulously. "I try to remain calm," he vows, adding, "I seldom get angry even with my wife. I have a personal conviction that I am a bureaucrat and I am more than happy if I can play a part. I have no personal ambition and should not try to get personal achievement with this or that. I see this as a continuous process for our foreign ministry."

Ambassador Saito is much different from the "showboat" ambassadors I have met, who use the Washington spotlight for their own political or professional gain.

There are no flowers, silk or fresh, and no bonsai plants grace his oversized office. A young woman brings in tea and kneels as she places it on the low coffee table in front of us. In a far corner, there is a naked VCR but no fancy Japanese big screen or entertainment center near the table for twelve. Over the ambassador's shoulder in the opposite corner of the room, I see his spotless desk with three newspapers perfectly laid out as if they belonged in a fancy hotel lobby: *The Wall Street Journal* is, not surprisingly, on the top with *The Washington Post* and *The New York Times* underneath. But, oddly, next to the papers is a stuffed animal—a tall, spotted giraffe.

I have been sneaking peeks at my watch and am determined to end the trade talk and discover what makes this ambassador tick. Now, we have only six minutes left.

"Do you collect anything, Mr. Ambassador?" He looks around me to Mr. Uemura and repeats my question, asking his aide for clarification. I explain "collectibles" as being things such as stamps, rare books, old guns, stuffed animals.

"Mr. Ambassador," I persist, "do you collect stuffed animals?"

"Stuffed animals?" he echoes, again looking at his aide for some feasible explanation.

"Yes, like that giraffe on your desk," I explain.

"Oh," he says, beaming and nodding his head. "Toys 'R' Us! Chief executive officer came to see me. In 1991, Toys 'R' Us opened their first stores in Japan. Now they have 37 and plan another 13 by the end of the year. That's 50!"

So, we're still on the economy. But, with only four minutes left, he is warming up and starts to talk about his personal interests. "I love to read detective stories," he says. "I have read all of Agatha Christy's; I was very sad when she died. I also play golf but only about once a month, and tennis doubles on our courts at the residence and bridge. My wife is much better and often beats me, but I beat her at golf," he says, proudly. He loves golf, and he loves to win.

Our time is up, and as I stand and say good-bye, I ask him about his unusual tie. Again, he beams and pulls it up to his face so he can see it too. "It's wheat and chickens," he says, delighted that it is he who is puzzling me now. "It's an American tie from your agriculture department. I had my choice: this one or one with cherries and pigs."

We laugh. And, I thought I could get him off trade!

As I walk near his desk, I see his slippers hiding under his desk. Later, I find out from his wife that he hates to dress and works at home in his pajamas and bare feet.

Just outside the ambassador's door, Mr. Uemura seems relieved the interview is over. I kid him about the "I Love Virginia" sticker on his file cabinet, and he asks me about good weekend side-trips around Washington.

* * *

It is almost two years later, June 1998, when I call on Ambassador Saito again. Japan is suffering from the Asian financial crisis and its economic picture is no longer quite so rosy. We've all learned that the global economy is much more interdependent than we thought. This time, I expect the ambassador will want to talk to me about anything but trade.

I plan to arrive early. But an accident, more construction and the embassy's own remodeling torpedo my good intentions. In addition, the embassy is in the process of adding yet another layer of security, a direct result of the hostile takeover of the Japanese Embassy in Peru. It takes even more time to check in.

The same Japanese lady greets me at reception and seems to remember me, smiling this time as she hands me the parking pass. Aya Nakamura, a recent Amherst College graduate on the job as a press officer for only two weeks, leads me back to the ambassador's office. As we wait for the ambassador's door to open, we trade secrets about our favorite restaurants and shops in Amherst and Northampton, Massachusetts, and she tells me why she likes working for this particular ambassador.

"When I first arrived, he invited me and a new protocol officer to lunch," she says. "I was so impressed with his attitude to work and his staff. He told us how he is always reminding Tokyo [on the phone] to not work so hard. Whenever I see him, he always takes time to ask me how I am."

I am glad I have a second chance to talk with this ambassador, who seemed all business before. Perhaps I was wrong in thinking he only cared about trade. Maybe I had read too many *Wall Street Journal* stories about workaholic Japanese businesspeople.

The door opens, and the ambassador greets me enthusiastically. When he notices me looking to see if his giraffe is still there, he laughs and says, "Yes, I remember you!"

Ambassador Saito and I take the exact same seats, and, again, just over his shoulder and across the room, the giraffe guards his desk. As I explain that I have returned to get an update on the Asian crisis and Japan's recovery, I am surprised how congenial the ambassador is in light of the sober subject.

But first, I ask him, as a citizen from the country that endured Hiroshima, how he feels about the nuclear testing in India and Pakistan, the story of the day in Washington.

"I was horrified, because to me it seemed to be such a stupid action out of India," he says, speaking more forcefully than I remember him. "I wish all these people, everybody in the world for that matter, knew more about the extent of damage caused by nuclear bombs. I am sure if they had known they wouldn't have done such a thing.

"They thought by carrying out nuclear tests, they would be able to raise their status in international society, but they were completely wrong," he says. "With the Japanese media there was disbelief, anger and there were many demonstrations in Hiroshima, in Nagasaki and in Tokyo in front of the Indian and Pakistani Embassies." After the explosions, Japan quickly moved to suspend ODA (Official Development Assistance) to both countries.

I ask Ambassador Saito how he will feel the next time he sees the Indian and Pakistani ambassadors. "We have been trained not to reveal our feelings, so I don't think I'll have any difficulty doing that. They are my good personal friends. Every time we meet, I mean the Pakistani ambassador, we talk about playing golf."

I apologize for bringing up two sad subjects in a row but must ask the obvious question about the economy. "It is depressing," he begins. "Our economy has been in recession for more than seven years. … We thought that finally our economy was picking up and then we went deeper into recession. … I was disappointed and that has made my work more difficult." Then he admits, "It might even get worse before it gets better."

We both take a sip of tea and he adds, "Sometimes we do not agree on the specific measures proposed by our American critics. The U.S. government … tries to avoid telling us specifically what we should do. Critics, scientists, economists sometimes give us specific prescriptions and … we do not necessarily agree."

Since much of the media talk has been about how to get the "thrifty" Japanese to start spending their money and stop saving so much, I ask for his opinion on tax cuts in Japan. "Unlike in the U.S., tax cuts do not necessarily lead to increased public spending. … It works here, but not necessarily in Japan." And as for Japanese thriftiness, "I don't agree that by nature that we are 'thrifty.' Since our economy is so bad and our society is aging rapidly, we cannot but have concern and anxiety." Citing lack of public confidence in the yen, he continues, "They feel they have to be prepared for the twenty-first century when fewer people will have to support more aged people."

But, this major Japanese negotiator is happy about the progress he has seen between the two countries. "We always had economic issues—automobiles, semiconductors. It is natural for us to have economic disputes from time to time. But now we don't have any major bilateral disputes. … The U.S.

is justifiably worried and giving advice, because our economy will affect Asian economy and, eventually, the U.S. economy. Our relationship is very close, even closer now. Not because we are in trouble. Our interests are identical. We share the same ideas, therefore we are concerned about each other."

Aya nervously points to her watch and tells me, "You have only two more minutes," but this time the ambassador dismisses the time limit with a small wave and continues on, leaning closer to me. "Our policies towards China, towards Korea, and recently about Indonesia, and more recently about India and Pakistan, are very close. We have a cooperative relationship and we ought to keep that."

Unlike our first interview, Ambassador Saito seems to be enjoying himself and asks for my next question, despite the time constraint. I ask aloud if he is disappointed President Clinton didn't include a visit to Japan on his China trip. "Oh, no," he says, but "some people in Japan" may feel that way because "these people fear China would take the place of Japan as the U.S.'s ally and partner. I think they are wrong. … Japan and the United States have much more in common than China and your country."

Now he agrees he must move on to his next appointment, but he has one more thing to tell me. "The Japanese will be stronger" when they come out of this financial crisis. "We have a high level of educated and well-trained work force." And, unlike some Washington embassies representing Asian countries, he hasn't had to downsize.

Only after we say good-bye and I turn and hurry out do I remember that I should have bowed and backed out of the room, per Japanese custom. That's what Aya does.

* * *

Since 1977, the Japanese residence has been on Nebraska Avenue across from the NBC studios and the National Presbyterian Church and next door to the Swedish Embassy. Covering nearly eight acres, the grounds include the 70,130-square-foot residence with its authentic tea house, both European and Japanese gardens, a pool and cabana and a tennis court where the ambassador and his wife still play doubles with guests. The late Japanese architect Isoya Yoshida designed the building to emphasize the elegant simplicity Americans expect from the Japanese. Inside, the high ceilings and huge public rooms make you feel more like you're in the Kennedy Center or a four-star hotel than a residence. The interior is striking. All Japanese designs, the imaginative chandeliers, specially designed rugs and furniture and artwork by the country's most famous artists create a fabulous showcase that enables the guest list to number in the thousands.

When my research assistant, Shawn Rabin, and I attended the Japanese National Day reception here, the crowd was large but you never felt crowded. The food was fabulous but hard to manage for Westerners using chopsticks—huge trays of delicate, fresh sushi and sashimi and lots of shrimp.

The most special part of the evening was participating in an authentic tea ceremony in the picturesque teahouse visible from the main hall but divided from it by a serene Japanese garden with a peaceful pond. Embassy wives wore traditional kimonos and performed the elaborate, delicate ceremony, explaining each step. Every move was studied and well rehearsed like a slow-motion ballet.

* * *

When I return to the residence for my interview with Mrs. Saito, I have the entire front parking plaza to myself. The butler is already holding the door, welcoming me with a big smile. The residence, built down a slope from busy Nebraska Avenue, is almost impossible to see as you drive or walk by the handsome fence, which is softened by the familiar Japanese cherry trees.

Akiko Saito meets me just inside the front door of this enormous residence and is especially curious about our interview since she is a journalist too. When I see the teahouse again from the main hall, I tell her how I still cherish that evening ceremony. She nods, and says, "I would like to do it more often, but I hate to ask embassy wives because it is so much work for them."

As we settle in the small salon, I am surprised when she asks to answer my questions in Japanese with Press Officer Kaori Inui translating. I know this will take twice as long as well as distance us.

In more than two years of research, this is the very first time in dozens of interviews with ambassadors and their families and staffs that I have had to use a translator. However, as Mrs. Saito finds it cumbersome and intrusive in our conversation, she interrupts her translator or try English, asking Kaori to help here and there to find the "perfect" word. By the time she shows me their ten official guest suites and private quarters, everything is in English and we are having a good time talking about our children and writing. I decide that she, as the former chief editor of Japan Women's University Newspaper, just wanted to be careful.

In the "small salon" (which isn't small at all), we sit under an inspired contemporary chandelier by Minami Tada that looks more like a ceiling sculpture than a simple glass fixture. From my vantage point, I look directly out into the trees through a curved wall of floor-to-ceiling glass that gives the

To celebrate the Birthday of
His Majesty the Emperor of Japan
The Ambassador of Japan and Mrs. Saito
request the pleasure of your company
at a reception
on Tuesday, the third of December
from five-thirty to seven-thirty o'clock
4000 Nebraska Avenue, N.W.

R.S.V.P.
By enclosed card

Business attire
Please present this card

An engraved invitation to the official birthday celebration of His Majesty the Emperor of Japan. Courtesy of the Japanese Embassy.

room a rounded character. Matching cloud-patterned curtains, carpet, and wallpaper in cool blue contrast with the gold lounge chairs in which we sit.

Tea is served with miniature pastries. I find it impossible to resist sampling them, but she never touches the sweets. Mrs. Saito looks fit and is smartly dressed in a short skirt, black turtleneck and beige chenille jacket with a handsome gold leaf pin. She laughs when I ask about her exercise routine. "I don't do things which are not fun like exercises to build your muscle. I like sports in general, especially tennis and skiing," she admits that most of her days in Washington are long and without time for exercise. Their two sons, Hiroshi and Jun, sometimes ski with them on holiday in Switzerland or France.

Thirty-one-year-old Hiroshi is married and works for the Bank of Japan, keeping typical, banker's hours so she finds it easy to stay in touch. Twenty-six-year-old Jun, a television director with NHK Broadcasting in Tokyo, is difficult to catch at home because he isn't married and "doesn't have a 'regular' life," as she puts it. She also admits that her husband is "not too interested" in Jun's creative profession and much more understanding of the older son's more traditional professional and private life.

I ask her if her older son had an arranged marriage. "No, he met his wife in the bank," she says, adding that her second son is not interested in having help with his social life.

She laughs when I wonder how she and the ambassador met.

"We had an arranged marriage, but it's not so different because after you meet, you date. It's just the beginning." She laughs again and admits, "He told me, 'It would be more interesting to be my wife than an ordinary wife,' and I was intrigued with living overseas."

Looking back on her life she says, "There are more pluses than minuses. The good aspect of diplomatic life is meeting various kinds of people that otherwise you would not see. On the other hand, the bad aspect is that you don't have much private life or privacy.

"In Washington, it is even harder," she continues. "Diplomatic life here is so demanding, you have less time for yourself. The United States is the most important country to Japan. Everyone is looking, they are watching back in Japan. It's worthwhile, and you're lucky to be assigned here. You could be stationed in a tiny country somewhere, write a report, and maybe nobody would care."

She admits that she and her husband prefer quiet evenings and weekends at home reading, playing piano duets, or watching videos from *A Passage to India* and *Casablanca* to *Forrest Gump* and *Toy Story.* And even though the Saitos have two cooks—one who creates Japanese delicacies and one with classical French training—the Saitos sneak out for their beloved sushi to a neighborhood Japanese hangout.

I suggest that their schedules must be extra hectic during the Cherry Blossom Festival, when dignitaries and visitors from all over the country descend upon Washington, busload by busload. U.S. high-school seniors join this annual spring rite, which revolves around the Tidal Basin's romantic pink blossoms from the famous Japanese trees. In 1912, three thousand trees were presented to First Lady Helen Taft by Tokyo Mayor Yukio Ozaki, but most of the original trees died and a new shipment was underwritten by a wealthy Japanese businessman.

"I remember my husband's first speech during Cherry Blossom Week when he said, 'Imagine if not cherry blossoms from Japan, imagine bamboo from the Chinese or cactus from Mexico. Then, Washington would be a very different city.'"

When Mrs. Saito does get a chance to shop, she picks up what her sons request from The Gap or Banana Republic, because they are much cheaper than in Japan, and always tennis balls, which are three times more expensive back home. Surprisingly, American bed linens with the wide variety available are wonderful to take back East. Coming back, her suitcases are full of food: favorite Japanese cookies, vacuum-packed eel and "special vegetables, Japanese horseradish, and other ingredients the chef wants."

She graciously takes me on a tour of the guest wing with its ten numbered guest suites and private lounge. The most elaborate suite is "Number 1," which was redecorated in 1994 when Emperor Akihito and Empress Michiko visited.

We discuss what it's like to have dignitaries staying upstairs who are coming and going all the time. I mention how Lady Kerr, the former British Ambassador's wife explained that, "First of all, you have to realize that this is a hotel, not a home." She nods in agreement.

"When I come out [from the private quarters], I come out to work. I dress differently. I am satisfied with this way of living," she says, diplomatically. "After I wake up, I have to make up my face everyday. In Paris, I didn't have this number of guests, and," she says, smiling, "I was young and didn't need the makeup. Now, I never meet other people without makeup."

I think how awful it must be to always be dressed up in your own home. I suppose hiding behind big sunglasses à la Hollywood to avoid eye makeup would be too weird but perhaps tempting in this proper profession.

As we peek into their private living area, I notice how simple their apartment is. The best thing about it is the continued expanse of glass overlooking the spacious terrace and endless garden. I see not one but three sets of the Ambassador's golf clubs, a plethora of video movies and books in the library. When I spot an oversized, stuffed cherry-red lady bug, I explain how the ambassador and I first met talking about his pet giraffe at the office.

Speaking of pets, I can't find any. "We can't have any pets here officially," she says, "When the ambassador went to Iran we had a watch dog, a big dog named Niki. He was a German shepherd we had for protection."

She tells me that Japanese homes in general have more dogs as pets than cats. I remember how it's just the opposite in Russia where cats are welcome inside but dogs are not. Mikhail told me that because he was enjoying having a dog while he was here in America.

As the butler gets my coat, I ask Mrs. Saito if she misses not having a career in journalism; her interest has been so keen in how I am going about writing this book.

"I am still interested in journalism, only freelance," she answers, adding, "because I don't want to work under anyone. I like to be in charge, like I'm in charge here of the residence."

"Today, many Japanese women are independent. My husband is very understanding of my independence, but I don't consider myself as independent as long as I am his spouse," says this petite woman, who claims she was "a very independent child, a pure spirit."

"There is not such a difference between being a journalist and an ambassador," she explains. "Journalists who are women are also well-trained to suppress, hide how they feel," and the women who are diplomats, "have to adjust to the system."

She and Kaori walk me to the door, and I suggest that she start thinking about a book full of her diplomatic secrets. I have the feeling she would like to continue the discussion without witnesses. I say good-bye, and she says she hopes to see me again soon. As the butler holds the heavy glass door open, she calls out to me, “I love your car, I have always wanted a Jaguar.”

I offer her a ride sometime, embarrassed that my dusty old friend is on display with no place to hide in this huge parking lot. I honk and wave as I depart this symbolic part of Japan and head out into the evening traffic at Ward Circle, wishing I had told her that my other car was a Honda.

13

Singapore: Lion City

I first met the Singaporean ambassador in *The New York Times.* There, in the "Letters to the Editor," and in other important newspapers, she regularly speaks out for Singapore, often about issues of the media and libel and Singapore's style of democracy.

* * *

Ambassador Chan Heng Chee is not afraid to speak up. "If the newspaper is unfair, we have the right to say, 'Hey, you are wrong.' Our libel laws are based on British libel laws, where there is greater protection to the privacy and reputation of the individual. In the United States, it is very difficult to prove libel. I understand it is virtually impossible to win a libel case in America," she says.

I ask about the much publicized and discussed 1994 caning case when an American teenager was punished, by caning, for vandalism—defacing pricey automobiles. "Most Americans had positive comments," she says, adding that discussing this case became "one of my jobs" as Singapore's chief spokesperson in Washington. For Americans, "The question was not whether to punish him or not, only how … the type of punishment. This is the law in Singapore for a Singaporean or an American or any foreigner. Should the law be differently applied for an American in Singapore? Are you asking us to change the law because he's an American?"

First Secretary Jean Tan, my contact with the embassy, later explains to me, "In Singapore, a car like those vandalized is a precious, prized treasure, an investment, an important commodity. A Mercedes like those would cost a half million dollars or more. And if a family had a car, they would only have one. Many people use only public transportation."

But Leon Hardar, Washington correspondent for *Business Times,* Singapore's only daily business newspaper, thinks that whether you are speaking of the much publicized caning case of an American student or something else, Singaporeans want control over their news stories. "This notion of sending letters to the editor seems to be the modus operandi of the Singaporeans, somehow getting the last word. I'm not sure to what extent it has any effect," says the Israeli-born journalist. "There isn't a large Singaporean community in the United States so the ambassador is the main voice."

This former UN bureau chief for the *Jerusalem Post* adds, "The American press is pissed off with Singapore because they are tired of being sued. That's why there aren't many news bureaus in Singapore and things are rarely covered there." Hadar travels to Singapore only "occasionally, because it takes two days to get there." According to the ambassador, "There were suits brought against *The Wall Street Journal* and *The Economist,* but the problem never reached the court. However, *The Herald Tribune* did lose a suit to the Singapore government."

Hadar did his Columbia University doctoral thesis on "Television Diplomacy" and has taught this subject here at The American University. According to him, Asian countries more often send good negotiators who work well behind the scenes, while Western countries tend to focus more on "public diplomacy" and choose diplomats who perform well on TV.

"Many Asian countries, not just Singapore, are still not very familiar with the way the media diplomacy game is played," says Hadar. "It goes against their grain, culturally, they have a quiet way. So, they shy away from the media and don't usually do very well. They think they don't know enough, so they hire PR firms.

"The new generation will do better with the media, the young kids who study in the U.S." I remember that Jean Tan got her masters degree in science and communications from the well-respected Newhouse School of Communications at Syracuse University.

Hadar concludes, "She [Chan] is more conscious of the media than the elder statesman before her. I have a feeling she is putting a growing emphasis on public diplomacy to get her message across."

Ambassador Chan is certainly interested in talking to me. She is obviously proud of her city-state, often called the "Garden City of the East," and is happy to talk about Singapore's reputation as a safe and clean place to live.

"Singapore is tough on law and order. It's the price you pay for living in a safe society that keeps crime down. You have a better-behaved society," says

The Singaporean national symbol.

the single woman who travels alone, carrying her own bags, often forgoing her chauffeur-driven limousine to drive herself around Washington.

She has already experienced New York City, first as a Cornell graduate student venturing into the city on weekends to go to the theater and later as Singapore's permanent representative to the United Nations—the first female UN ambassador from any Asian Pacific country.

Surprisingly, except for crime and cleanliness, modern Singapore and New York City have a lot in common. They are both important international centers, and both are densely populated. Singapore also is an island (but with 50 islets), rivaling Manhattan's skyline with its own modern skyscrapers from its financial district. It is home to the world's tallest hotel and is Southeast Asia's largest port.

While living in American cities, Ambassador Chan says she is careful but far from afraid. "I am not reckless," says this slight woman who looks fashionably thin in her long, silk, native Chinese dresses. "I am an optimist, avoiding trouble areas but nothing more."

This high-profile academic agreed to become Singapore's first woman ambassador out of "a deep sense of purpose from seeing Singapore being built from scratch. People of my generation grew up when Singapore became independent. In '65, I was in university."

This trading post established in 1819 by Sir Thomas Stanford Raffles first became a British-crown colony, then was occupied by the Japanese during World War II and ended up as part of Malaysia before becoming a sovereign nation on August 9, 1965.

"Singapore is more successful economically, financially" than she expected but "is still very new. I wish it had more manners, more grace. There is a lot to be done and there aren't enough people to do it. We are only three million people," she says of this modern city-state. "We need depth. That is what a small country does not have. We are very aware of that. Singapore needs all the talent that it can have."

As she is speaking, sitting neatly, away from her desk in her pristine, contemporary office on the top floor of Singapore's new embassy, I feel she is speaking about a living, breathing thing; there seems to be a direct, symbiotic connection between this woman and her country.

I ask her what she loves the most about Singapore. "I like the 'can do' attitude." She's proud of Singapore's ethnic diversity, its efficiency and especially its competitiveness. According to the Swiss-based "Global Competitiveness Report" by the World Economic Forum, Singapore ranked as the most competitive society in the world in 1997 and 1998. The report listed Hong Kong as second and the United States as third.

But, she adds, "It is very hard to be graceful when you are poor." She notes that Singapore's wealthy are one generation away from poverty. "When free gifts are offered, everyone rushes. This shop will then have a big crowd. We are a new country with nouveau riche." She hopes the consumerism will be "toned down" with time. According to this ambassador from this young democracy, "court cultures" like England, France and Thailand can thank "a royal presence, aristocracy" for naturally leading the way to a more gracious society.

But Singapore is understandably proud of how well it has weathered the current financial storm. "In spite of the regional economic crisis, Asia is still a good investment," says Ambassador Chan. "Singapore has fared better than most of the countries in the region because of our sound economic management. Singapore is a good brand name," she says and smiles, sounding like an American PR executive planting a plug in the *Asian Wall Street Journal.*

She mentions that much of her country's economic investment development is shepherded by Singapore's Economic Development Board with offices in Washington, New York and California. To emphasize Singapore's strong economic global position she says, "We are the eighth largest export market of the U.S. and a participant in the G6 with the United States, Australia, Japan, China, and Hong Kong."

A perfect time to ask about Hong Kong, also a former British colony. "It will remain a thriving city, a place of business," she predicts. "Hong Kong is dynamic and driven and will serve the hinterland of China." But she does forecast some room for international companies, especially high-tech industries, to be lured away from Hong Kong by Singapore and other countries in the region who "are all in the same game."

As far as the Chinese mainland, "Because of China's size, they will be a colossal economic power in the twenty-first century. It depends a lot on what the U.S. does. The U.S.-China relationship will be the key determinant of peace and security in the Asia-Pacific and will have a major impact for the rest of the world," says this political scientist who has Chinese ancestors.

But, she adds, "If you're looking for the New York City fast pace, Singapore is not New York City. We have three cultures—Malay, Chinese, Indian—and we are English educated. We are a multiethnic, multiracial society ... with meritocracy. We have adopted a policy of accommodation. Every group has its equality but there is a larger, general assimilation into a Singaporean identity. There are Singaporean values the way Americans assimilate to American values.

"For diplomacy abroad, anyone can be elected to be ambassador but clearly language skills do matter. I am Chinese and my DCM [deputy chief of mission] is Indian. At the Singapore Embassy in China, the ambassador must be able to speak Mandarin and read Chinese.

"I like to think that I have a sensitivity in dealing with multiethnic staff ... where the Malays are Muslim; the Indians, Hindu." (The Chinese are usually Buddhist or Christian.)

"In a small embassy we must work sharper, be more focused, and can't sit around," says Chan, who has 38 staffers including "some in defense, and my driver. We each do things your secretary would do." From the outside, I tell the ambassador, this doesn't look like a "small embassy." Opened in September 1993 in Washington's new 38-acre International Center, the 55,000-square-foot Singapore Embassy answers the State Department's basic request that new embassies built here should architecturally evoke their particular countries' cultural heritage.

According to Benjamin Forgey, *The Washington Post*'s architecture critic, this modernist embassy of light beige brick and black granite is "a wonderful example" of how that can be done and still fit into Washington's landscape. Enthusiastically, he proclaims it "a winner in Washington, an unusual combination of boldness and a certain delicacy ... a treat for years to come," even for passersby who never get inside.

The embassy's American architect, D. Rodman Henderer, the principal designer from RTKL Associates, adds, "We were told that anything we build should reflect Singapore as a gardenlike country and as a progressive country." And designing an embassy to be a "machine in a garden" is not an easy task.

Built backward on a corner site, the large curved walled garden, sitting in the corner of the embassy's two wings, serves as a gateway to Washington's

Exterior of the Singapore Embassy. Photo by Scott McDonald, RTKL Associates, Inc.

new embassy district. Teak-louvered, recessed windows and the deep overhanging roofs on this four-floor office building are reminiscent of Singapore's two-story bungalows built by the British colonists and lovingly referred to as "black-and-whites." (This original turn-of-the-century design in Singapore kept out the rain while allowing open windows to help cool homes from the intense tropical heat.)

You enter this spacious embassy through a courtyard and walk into a marble-floored, wood-paneled reception atrium overlooking the dramatic open staircase that descends down into the high-ceilinged Raffles Hall and the two garden terraces beyond. Throughout the embassy, commissioned artwork by Singaporeans, dramatic lighting, specially designed rugs and furniture accented with fresh, oriental floral designs welcome you to appreciate Singapore's unique blend of nineteenth-century British colonialism, tropical lushness and the efficiency of a modern city with a soaring skyline.

The ambassador does entertain at home but uses this chancery to showcase Singapore for bigger receptions and charity events. Her long work days include keeping her eye on Congress and the White House while monitoring the media and think-tank publications and still attending nightly social functions or "flying the flag" around the United States for good public relations. "Washington is a town where people put in 12 to 13 hour days," but "you can't stay only in Washington and think you know the U.S."

Chan believes her academic experience of teaching and mentoring young scholars helps her run a more democratic, open embassy where each staffer regardless of their position or age is expected to speak up. "I expect brilliance to come from even the youngest person. Brilliance and age are not necessarily correlated.

"This is not easy in an embassy," she says, because "embassies are much more bureaucratic. I always welcome good suggestions, good ideas and encourage discussion at meetings." However, with think-tank peers, "I have no qualms telling my colleagues what I think because I am an academic." Being an ambassador and an academic, she is often asked to speak on American college campuses and has lectured at Harvard University.

* * *

When we meet again, this time in her residence over coffee and mint-green "Pandan" cake, she reminds me, "I am not a career ambassador. I remind myself to keep my feet on the ground, wear the title lightly, because many ambassadors take themselves too seriously, believe the pomp. With the think tanks I say, 'Please, don't call me Ambassador.'"

I wonder aloud how this accomplished academic, who comes from such an efficient and competitive society, relaxes, or even if she does. "I love to dance, but being single it is difficult to go to balls. I am not a woman ambassador who has a spouse, that's much easier because I don't have to worry about family," says this aunt who tries to at least remember her nieces' and nephews' birthdays but doesn't shower them with gifts from America because "too many material things spoil the kids."

"I don't think I'm being antifeminist by saying that I think it is the nature of women to worry about their families more than men. It diffuses your attention to have a family."

However, being an ambassador, she must still be a good hostess and entertain. Giving a dinner party at least once a week, she doesn't worry if she has an equal number of males and females. "I think it is more important to have an interesting mix of people." In her formal dining room, her table seats "only" 18, for which she hand picks her guests from the administration, the media, Congress, business and Washington think tanks.

"I am very hands-on, doing both roles," she says of being the ambassador and the party planner. "I have to keep an eye on all the everyday details of living in the residence and make the decisions." I ask her if she would label herself a good cook. "I 'cook' a lot in theory," she answers. "I let my wonderful cook 'practice' on me with the recipes." I can just see her standing by in the kitchen, tasting, and substituting spices to make it taste more like home.

But when the entertaining is over, what does she do for herself in this newly built red brick Georgian home bordering Rock Creek Park? "I have to listen to music every day," she says walking into her study, where her handsome desk is totally covered with CDs and her sound system is center stage. "And when I listen to music I don't read or do anything else. It is not background music. It is my way to decompress." I ask this granddaughter of a Cantonese opera singer her favorites out of all the 1,000 long-playing records in her collection. "I have very catholic tastes," she explains. Wynton Marsalis, Enya, folk, jazz and even rock mixed with her collection of arias, Baroque classics, Gregorian chants and her native Chinese folk songs to help end her day. "On weekends, I go to movies, concerts, plays, operas."

Describing herself as an "insomniac," she uses those late, quiet hours alone to read (*The English Patient, Remains of the Day, Cairo Trilogy*) and call her family and friends in various time zones around the world. "My friends say I'm very intellectual … but I come from a different generation. I am not the e-mail generation. I like to hear someone's voice, their tone."

Although she "hates shopping" and doesn't do mail-order either, she picks things up for herself, her nephew and three nieces in "sure shops" like The Gap. Otherwise, her cheongsam, the handsome silk Chinese national dresses, are all sewn for her when she returns to Singapore.

For less cerebral activity, "I feed the fish in my lily pond and water my own plants." She takes her cook shopping for specialty items like fresh coconut but still can't find the right soy sauce here.

She is so lean and trim, I ask about her daily exercise routine. "I do no exercise," she admits, rolling her eyes, "I have high metabolism. I have a step machine I brought from Singapore but don't use it. I do go for walks. I worry that I am not an exercise person."

This midlife divorcee lives here alone, keeping herself amused much as she did growing up. "As a child, I was left alone to play by myself, watching the world go by. I did a lot of things solo. I grew up with my grandmother in the house. I was her favorite and we shared the same bed. Until my brother came along, she would take me everywhere. We played mah jong together. She had a passion for mah jong."

"She had great authority without saying very much," the ambassador continues about her grandmother. "It was the way she carried herself. No one disrupted her. Everyone was dead scared of her. Growing up I wished to have her dignity."

According to Jean Tan, "The ambassador once remarked in jest to an outsider about her staff, 'I don't think they listen to me; they're not afraid of me.'" Says Jean of her mentor, "She really pushes us." But, "I don't think we work hard here out of fear but from a deep respect for the ambassador, her experience, her drive, her vision, her effectiveness—and our own sense of mission."

14

Sri Lanka: Resplendent Land

In the early 1970s, I used to come to this brick residence bordering Rock Creek Park when bachelor Ambassador Neville Kanakaratne asked me to help him host parties. Jayantha Dhanapala was the embassy's hard-working First Secretary with a young family then, and I was a Washington TV anchorwoman. One particular evening, I came to meet Mrs. Sirimavo Bandaranaike, not only Sri Lanka's prime minister but the first woman prime minister in the world. I was to interview her on my show the next day. But that night of dark tea and "short eats" (Sri Lankan hors d'oeuvres), I also met a young, talented Reuters' reporter. We were introduced on the entry staircase. That brief encounter turned into marriage and a wonderful daughter named Indrani. Ranjit de Silva and I have gone our separate ways now but this cup of Ceylon tea instantly takes me back to this "Resplendent Land"* in the Indian Ocean, halfway around the earth, and twenty-five years ago in my life.

Our tea arrives, as dark as coffee. I dilute it politely with lots of milk, an old trick I learned twenty-five years ago. Now, it is thick and silky and a warm welcome to the cold, wet April day outside.

Today our children are grown. The Dhanapalas' daughter, Kiran, is now married and has spent several years in Sri Lanka's capital, Colombo, working as a development economist. She hopes to study for her Ph.D. abroad. Their son, Sivanka, is a lawyer working for the UN High Commission for Refugees in Geneva. My daughter, Indrani, worked in India and Nepal as a budding cultural anthropologist and has returned for graduate school.

**Translation of "Sri Lanka" from Sinhala, a language derived from Sanskrit.*

Now, Jayantha is the ambassador and Maureen, his wife, is upstairs packing for the last time to leave a diplomatic post. He has just announced his retirement. And I am the reporter again. In a wild array of thoughts and feelings, my personal and professional lives converge over a cup of Ceylon tea with an old friend about to leave my half of the world again.

To this career diplomat who has distinguished himself on the international conference stage, the role of today's ambassador has changed dramatically over these 25 years from being the human information channel to the on-site evaluator. But, according to this ambassador, the need for ambassadors and senior diplomats in foreign posts is still critical.

"This aspect of diplomacy will never be supplanted by the revolution in computer technology and instantaneous communications," reasons Dhanapala. "The need for reliable analysis and evaluation of that information is made even greater, [making] the human element … as vital as ever. Personal chemistry is never on e-mail."

We discuss "the old days": fewer countries, fewer embassies, easier for ambassadors to make their mark in Washington. Ambassador Dhanapala tightens his lips and talks about what it takes to get the White House or the U.S. State Department to listen. "With over 180 countries and the U.S. as sole superpower … access is extremely difficult. The combination of the two breeds a certain amount of complacency.

"In the Clinton administration," he continues, "Latin America is hardly mentioned and they're your immediate neighbor. Today, with the Cold War over … there is a lack of need to be engaged in smaller countries. Unfortunately, the U.S. is not being the leader it needs to be: responsible, setting good examples. The UN is hobbled by the delay in the U.S. paying its dues. There is a general malaise after the Cold War. The U.S. needs to be like a good team captain: respecting all the players, knowing them by name and what's important to each."

Ambassador Dhanapala is particularly upset by the tendency of the United States and the western media to write off certain countries by labeling them "rogue states." In his mind, "that's just an excuse" not to deal with them. "Maybe they are undemocratic regimes but the people of that country should not be stigmatized. It is temporary. Washington is the center stage of the world, the vortex of international affairs so there is [for any ambassador] an intensive demand of your professional capabilities to figure out how to put your country on the radar screen."

With the Dhanapala era came a completely computerized embassy and helpful direct voice mail. But always there was still a receptionist to help the uninitiated. For general visability, the embassy has a monthly newsletter, a telephone news report of Sri Lankan current events, and a daily updated website. Many larger embassies and richer countries do not offer these new services.

Even a week-long food festival with imported cooks, indigenous cookware and ingredients, and native classical dancers made the long trip to Washington to add visibility for Sri Lanka. This festival coincided with the finance minister's official Washington visit. The embassy's commercial secretary, Asoka Dharmawardhane, is creative and determined that trade with the United States, Sri Lanka's number one export partner, continues to be healthy. Forty percent of this Southeast Asian island's total export revenue of $1.3 billion comes from America.

According to Dharmawardhane, tailoring was a natural export for a country where so many people still sew. "In the olden days, everyone had a Singer, hand operated and then pedal. And we have fine tailors too."

But all those efforts don't make this teardrop-island country just south of India any bigger. Most people can't locate Sri Lanka on a map even when you tell them its old British name was Ceylon. But, they usually know that Ceylon tea is the world's finest and the island is the original source of many of the world's precious gems. (New York's American Museum of Natural History's "Star of India" is a 563.35-karat blue sapphire from Sri Lanka.)

Most people have heard about the bloody conflict between Tamil separatists in the north and this country's Sinhala majority. Although there is a wide discrepancy in the number of casualties since this civil unrest began in 1983, Sri Lankan government sources report that this "sad conflict" has resulted in more than 50,000 deaths.

"Most of the conflict is confined to the north and most tourist sites are in the southern part of the country," says this veteran diplomat. "In the past fighting in Northern Ireland didn't keep you from going to London, but if something happens in Sri Lanka somehow you think you must not go anywhere near.

"In spite of two insurgencies, this ethnic conflict and one attempted coup back in '62, our democracy has remained intact amidst these serious challenges. What is remarkable is the faith our people have in democracy. We always have such a high voter turnout, one time as high as eighty-seven percent." (Last year Sri Lanka celebrated its 50th year as a democratic soverign nation since achieving its independence from the British rule in 1948.)

Of course, Ambassador Dhanapala wants us to look beyond the international headlines and CNN reports to a country of rich and ancient cultural heritage that was a pioneer and is now a leader in Southeast Asia for parliamentary democracy, market economy and gender equality.

Ceylon Youth Attends US Students Forum

JAYANTHA C. B. DHANAPALA, 18-year old student at Trinity College, Kandy, has been selected by a mixed panel of Ceylonese and American judges to represent Ceylon at the 1957 Eleventh Annual New York Herald Tribune Forum for High Schools sponsored by the New York newspaper and Trans World Airlines.

Dhanapala was selected for participation on the basis of an essay written on the theme "The World We Want". His winning entry is reproduced below in full.

Thirty-eight countries have been invited to send delegates to this year's forum to be held in the United States between January and March, 1957.

The forum is a device designed to give a representative group of secondary school students from all parts of the world a chance to make friends with each other, to share the school and home life of American students and to contribute to the host students' knowledge and understanding of other countries.

While in the U.S. the delegates live as temporary members of the family in four different American homes where there are children of the same age, attend school with them and participate in a normal program of school and community activities. Additionally there are numerous opportunities for the delegates, as a group, to share common experiences.

Dhanapala, the tenth child in a family of eleven, had his early education in Kotahena and later at St. Bedes' College in Badulla. His hobbies include Oriental dancing, badminton, reading and drama. He plays rugger and cricket and represented his college at rugger and boxing.

'The World We Want'

By J. C. B. DHANAPALA

IT is fatally easy in an essay of this nature to visualize an Utopia totally removed from the context of modern conditions. Such a tendency must obviously be avoided for the purpose of this essay is to conceive a situation in the world which, in relation to man's past achievements and contemporary developments, will approximate to a practicable state of perfection. It would avoid being unrealistic and impracticable by being moulded by and related to what mankind has already achieved and is in the process of achieving.

The fundamental aspect to consider is the economic. Among the Four Freedoms which President Roosevelt so eloquently emphasized is the freedom from want and the guaranteeing of this freedom is the primary ideal to be achieved. The [illegible] of the primary impulses

willing to be shouted at by those in whose interest it is to shout. In a democracy a great amount of responsibility devolves upon its leaders who should be conscious of it and of a democratic purpose. The desire to attain this democratic goal should animate every individual on whom an equal amount of responsibility devolves. The public must be ever vigilant and alert and this price for the preservation of liberty is not too high.

Linked with the need for an enlightened public opinion is the problem of education. A fundamental obligation of the state is to provide for its citizens an education which will create an enlightened electorate having an understanding of the democratic process and which will promote the tenet of equality of opportunity. Education must be available to all and must of necess-

The New [illegible] Herald Tribune, together with Trans World Airlines, sponsors annually an international [illegible]m for high school students. Ceylon will be represented at the forthcoming forum by Jayantha [illegible] B. Dhanapala (inset) of Trinity College, Kandy.

A vintage newspaper story on 18-year-old Jayantha Dhanapala, who would become an ambassador and an under-secretary-general at the United Nations. Photo courtesy of the Dhanapalas.

"The international media has a responsibility to report events in developing countries more accurately," says the ambassador who almost became a journalist himself. As a teenager he wrote a winning essay that brought him to the United States for the now defunct *New York Herald Tribune*'s World Youth Forum. He was one of thirty-three international students from thirty-three different countries who came for three months to learn about America and each other. "It was all about 'The World We Want,' where multilateral negotiations and superpower nations would help developing countries with science and technology," deemphasizing differences in ideology and the Cold War."

"The principle of national sovereignty is gradually exhausting its usefulness," the then-18-year-old Dhanapala wrote in 1957, "and certain functions of government are clearly international in character, consequently certain deviations ... are necessary in achieving the world we want. For example, the chief food-producing states should give the F.A.O. [Food and Agriculture Organization of the United Nations] executive authority and other aid ... to eliminate hunger and starvation in the world."

I ask the seasoned diplomat who has spent his adult life representing a developing country what he thought of his own call, as a student journalist, for such "supra-national planning" by the United Nations.

During that three months in America, Jayantha Dhanapala lived both with well-to-do Americans and in very modest homes from Wyoming to the Bronx; went to the White House and met President Dwight Eisenhower; listened to then-Senator John Kennedy and Justice Thurgood Marshall; and was entertained by folksinger Pete Seeger and author Sloan Wilson.

Still handsome at age sixty, this native Sri Lankan especially remembers "visiting the 'Jim Crow' state of Virginia, seeing Colonial Williamsburg and Richmond, "where blacks and whites went to different bathrooms."

"I was surprised by the great diversity of America with its great rural stretches, the Amish and the disparity in money." Most of all for this teenager from 10,000 miles away, this international experience was "mind stretching and opened windows."

"It was right after the Suez Canal crisis and we had Israeli and Arab students who wouldn't even talk to each other," he remembers. In the beginning, "everything was based on preconceived ideas and political prejudices." But later, "personal contact overcame all those political differences."

This experience, he says, "converted me from wanting to be a journalist to being interested in international affairs."

According to *The New York Times,* Jayantha Dhanapala was "masterful" as the highly successful "helmsman" of the UN's 1995 conference indefinitely extending the global treaty banning the spread of nuclear weapons. He persuaded, cajoled and convinced 174 nations to sign, "getting the outcome Washington wanted with the fewest possible countries alienated." There was praise throughout the international media, including Barbara Crossette's *New York Times* story and news broadcasts on the BBC and CNN.

Known for his careful diplomacy, especially with developing nations like his own, and his unfailing sense of humor, at the end of the four-week conference juggling national egos and interests, Dhanapala dismissed all the personal praise. "The president of a conference is not a magician who can produce a rabbit out of a hat," he said. "The rabbit has to be in the hat and must want to come out. All we can do is to coax it occasionally."

With this new visibility, Jayantha Dhanapala was on that "radar screen" like never before. He found it "gave me entree" in Washington. But according to sources outside the embassy, it also gave him trouble at home. His foreign minister back home, who had a "star" ambassador in Washington, was not impressed and some said he was jealous of his ambassador's well-publicized success. At the peak of his diplomatic career, Dhanapala would reluctantly start to consider his alternatives.

In hindsight, it seems Jayantha Dhanapala was destined to be a world-class diplomat. After graduating from Peradeniya University in Kandy, he joined the Sri Lankan diplomatic service at the top of his entry class. Over the years he and his wife have served in embassies in London, Beijing, Washington and then New Delhi. He was also in Geneva as Sri Lanka's representative at the United Nations and then from 1987 to 1992, he left the foreign service to direct the UN's Institute for Disarmament Research in Geneva.

Before returning to diplomacy and becoming ambassador here, he was an assistant foreign secretary in Sri Lanka. Along the way, he did advance studies at The American University in Washington, D.C., and the School of Oriental and African Studies at the University of London. He is fluent in French and Chinese, as well as English and his native Sinhala, a modern-day language born from Sanskrit.

Throughout his tours of duty and travel, he was accompanied by his wife and, later, their two children. When I ask Maureen how many times she has moved, she liltingly replies in her soft Sinhala accent, "I haven't counted and I don't want to know. It's never routine, and packing is always something I'm wanting to put off. And I don't want to see those boxes very soon because that will mean I have to unpack!"

She sighs as she finishes filling her last two suitcases, which they will personally carry on their two-week trip en route to Sri Lanka. After all the packing, farewells and late nights at the office in Washington, finally they will get a short holiday together during which Jayantha will give "another speech somewhere along the way" and they will see their son, Sivanka, who works with refugees in Bosnia.

"He has always put himself on the frontline of helping people," this mother says of Sivanka. "Once, when he was living in Cambodia, as the vicious Khmer Rouge came in his front door, he went out the back, barely escaping with his life. … If I had my life to do over again," she admits, "I would like to do this kind of work and I can't deny it or spoil it for him."

Looking back at the Dhanapalas' career on the road, away from their beloved Sri Lanka, raising a young family in both hemispheres, and always entertaining, I ask her if this is what she thought it would be like when she agreed to marry her old childhood friend.

"Oh, I hadn't thought what it would be like being Jayantha's wife," she laughs. "Our families knew each other and we had been children together. It was not arranged; we were both twenty-five and knew each other at the university."

"It's a good way to see the world," she continues, "but a long way to go to find out that everyone is the same, all human beings are the same." And, then she adds, "I guess I thought it would be a marvelous life and that we would have all the comforts all the time. I didn't realize that I would have no time with Jayantha," nor that she would be expected to entertain on a shoestring while rearing little children by herself and always saying good-bye to friends.

"The disadvantage of this kind of life is that although you make good friends, you've got to leave them. But as soon as you see them again, you're friends again. This is reflected in my address book. Only I can read it. I organize it according to our postings."

We interrupt our interview to exchange addresses one more time and now, e-mail and fax numbers and those of our children's. It's almost time to say good-bye, again. As I remember her packing glow-in-the-dark Frisbees, chocolate M&M's, and denim—"anything" to take "home" to Sri Lanka—I ask my old friend what special items she tucks in her luggage.

"I have clothes for my daughter and good cotton sheets, and we always buy chocolates duty-free when we get to Colombo. Today, so much more is available now with the free market and good economy."

Mostly, she looks forward to being nearby to help her busy daughter. "If I am close by I can help her, make life a little easier," says this long-distance mom who admits that she has "heard no talk of grandchildren" but would love to make the thought of being a working mother more possible for her married daughter.

Also in Colombo, there is her four-year-old fox terrier, Dogmatix, who usually "stays so faithfully by my heel I have to learn not to step on her all over again."

Besides friends, I ask her what she will miss here. "Washington is such a beautiful city. I will miss the seasons, the spring flowers, the fall colors, and the easy day-to-day life. If you want groceries, they are just there." She adds that since their first posting here, "Washington has become more cosmopolitan and we've been more adventuresome trying all the different ethnic restaurants. I'll miss that."

We start to say good-bye again. I congratulate them on a career well done. She passes on the praise. "It's all his, Gail. He has worked so hard and done so well. No one helped him. He did it all by himself."

I suggest she did "help" with decades of packing and unpacking, rearing two children into highly competent adults, handling the details for important dinner parties designed to entertain visiting dignitaries from home and impressing other diplomats, world-famous politicians, members of the media and a multitude of local bureaucrats who could make decisions that would effect every citizen of Sri Lanka—and all of this on a meager budget.

Ever the diplomat herself, Maureen thanks me for the kind words but thinks to add another facet to Sri Lanka's charm.

"Jayantha's success is also a great testament to the free education Sri Lanka gives all qualifying students. The education is the foundation, it worked. People get uplifted out of a feudal system and on the road to a democratic life."

"Gail," she says to close, "lots of strength in your elbow." A perfect exit from this strong diplomatic wife. She's wishing me whatever strength I may need to deal with life's unforseen troubles.

Oh, how I wish the world were smaller.

* * *

In April 1997, Jayantha Dhanapala took early retirement from the Sri Lankan Foreign Service. After five months as diplomat-in-residence at the Centre for Non-proliferation Studies of the Monterey Institute of International Studies in California, Ambassador Dhanapala was appointed under-secretary-general for disarmament affairs by UN Secretary-General Kofi Annan and assumed those duties on February 1, 1998.

15

THAILAND: A WORLD-CLASS COUPLE

They are a striking couple. She is blond and fair with a quick smile and joyous laugh. He is dark and handsome with such an air of royalty that you're sure he is.

We first met at Thailand's official birthday celebration commemorating the 50 years His Majesty King Bhumibol Adulyadej Maharaj has reigned over this country of 60 million people. The ambitious event filled the cavernous ballroom in the depths of the JW Marriott Hotel. Richly costumed Thai dancers and young, shy Thai musicians entertained while Thai chefs prepared mouth-watering delicacies and Thai women carved vegetables and fruits into delicious, edible art. It was the most elaborate embassy party of all.

Ambassador Nitya Pibulsonggram looked regal in his tuxedo adorned with rich ribbons and medals, and his wife, Pacharin, the former Bostonian Patricia Osmond, looked at home in a native aqua Thai silk dress also decorated with medals. One by one, they greeted several thousand guests to their huge but beautifully orchestrated feast that took over the ground floor of this huge hotel.

As we stepped onto the long escalator to descend to the ballroom, we were greeted by giant royal Thai crests projected above on the walls of the multistoried reception atrium. Once there, friendly embassy staffers, mostly women dressed in luscious, long, bright silk native dresses, welcomed guests. As we waited as long as half an hour to go through the receiving line, we wound our way through an elaborate display of Thai history and culture. Pictures of His Majesty with American presidents from Truman to Kennedy to Clinton were prominent. In fact, the Smithsonian has a collection of the 2,000 gifts given to American leaders by successive Thai monarchs and a beautiful book, *Treasures of Two Nations,* describes them all.

I was so impressed by the whole evening that I couldn't wait to learn more about this country that used to be called "Siam." Within a few weeks the ambassador's schedule allowed time for our interview.

* * *

As I approach the handsome Thai residence tucked behind busy Massachusetts Avenue on Decatur Street by the Spanish Steps, I feel like I am entering another time when elegance reigned.

Passing through the ornate iron gates and through the brick forecourt where several big diplomatic cars could fit, I am greeted by a cheerful butler and two jumping, barking red toy poodles. In spite of the butler's gentle commands, Remy and Poco take turns jumping into my arms and circling, excitedly, around my feet. I manage to sign the formal guest book before our funny entourage of soft-spoken butler, little noisy dogs and one curious reporter climb the gracious marble staircase with rich red carpet and elaborate iron railings.

I had heard about the Codman-Davis House before. On the National Register of Historic Places, this important example of Neo-Classical Revival style was designed by well-known architect Ogden Codman, whose most important book, *The Decoration of Houses,* was coauthored with equally influential decorator Edith Wharton. Codman decorated rooms in many great homes of famous, wealthy Americans, including Cornelius Vanderbilt II and John D. Rockefeller.

Built in 1907 for Codman's cousin Martha, heiress to a prominent Boston clipper ship family who was known to give magnificient parties here, it was sold to President Herbert Hoover's Secretary of War Dwight F. Davis. (Davis, one of America's finest tennis players, is the namesake for the internationally prized tennis trophy, the Davis Cup.)

It is just before Christmas and the house is spectacularly decorated. I am escorted to the main drawing room, where a magnificent tall evergreen trimmed in gold is holding forth. All of a sudden, the doggies abandon me as they hear the ambassador and his wife approach. They reenter, like little court escorts, barking and circling everyone's feet, announcing their owners' arrival. We all laugh.

As we find our seats, the doggies nestle in between the diplomatic couple on the sofa, and Ambassador Pibulsonggram begins. "We are your 'First Friend' in Asia," he says. "Our formal relationship goes back to 1833. We have fought wars together. Since the turn of this century, we have sent over 100,000 students to study in your country … who have incorporated a lot of American

Thailand Ambassador Nitya Pibulsonggram and his wife, Pacharin Pibulsonggram. Photo by Chalurmchai Mhojadee.

know-how and can-do spirit," says this career diplomat, who himself holds a bachelors degree in government from Dartmouth College and a masters degree in political science from Brown University.

"Our king was born in your country, in Cambridge [Massachusetts]. There is a 'King of Thailand Square' there. Thailand and America are also tied together by trade. Before Asia's economic problems began in 1997, Thailand was your seventeenth trading partner, with 20 billion [dollars] a year, out of a total possibility of one 185 countries. Two million American jobs are tied to your investments in our part of the world," says the proud ambassador, carefully tiptoeing through his country's current economic minefield.

"It is troubling," he admits, talking about the Asian financial crisis that has threatened to rock even America's record-breaking stock markets. "Hopefully it's only a passing thing. Many analysts now say that it could be one of the best things" for the future to help stimulate better structuring of Asian economies.

"Like a small heart attack that you survive?" I ask. He nods his head, happy that I am approaching his all-consuming topic gently. Thailand and the United States have "a mature relationship that only can come from aging together," he adds, "with formal relations for 165 years. Very few countries can compare."

"We have free entry, no visas are required, and very reasonable exchange rates," he summarizes, never missing a chance to promote his country for American trade and tourism.

His wife adds, "Thailand has a rich and ancient culture that is reflected in its cuisine, manners, kindness of the people, textiles, jewelry. These are things that when you see them you know they didn't happen overnight." Thailand (nicknamed the "Land of Smiles") "is a very blessed and lucky country" that "reflects in the people," who are "happy and kind," she concludes passionately. "I wish everyone had a chance to visit."

It's amazing to witness how much these two people from such diverse backgrounds complement each other and how well they promote Thailand, together, so naturally.

Now it's the ambassador's turn. "We would not want people to think we are Anna and the King of Siam," he says, referring to the popular play and movie *The King and I,* which romantically linked an American schoolteacher and the absolute monarch, forever remembered as the late Yul Bryner. "He was a fine actor and a lovely person," the ambassador adds, diplomatically.

"How *did* you meet?" I ask.

They both laugh, knowing that's what so many people wonder when they see this contrasting couple. "I fell in love with her right away," says the ambassador, being the ultimate diplomatic husband, as he looks over at her, adoringly. Then, together they tell me the truth.

"It was not love at first sight," says the ambassador. "We were introduced by mutual friends," explains his wife. Tom Cutter, his fraternity brother at Dartmouth and her childhood school chum from Wayland, Massachusetts, introduced them. Ironically, Tom married a Thai woman and they have three children, one of whom is an export manager living in Thailand.

* * *

"'Nid' [Nitya] is the creme of the crop," says Tom, the ambassador's old Kappa Kappa Kappa fraternity brother, who pauses to tell me on the phone that "Thais always use nicknames."

"There is a lot of politics in Thailand, and being the American ambassador is the top … he is first rate. By choosing Pat, he may have stacked the cards against himself, as far as the foreign service, because initally back when we all got married it [intercultural marriage] was not as widely accepted. Maybe, at first, it made the ladder [to this top post] longer," he reasons, because "Thais are fairly ethnocentric. But Pat's such a great asset; once they knew her perhaps it made it shorter. She speaks Thai better than my wife Sasiree," says "Cutts," the ambassador's nickname for his American buddy. "The challenge isn't race or religion, it's culture," says Cutter, who thinks Pat is a wonderful example of how to mix two very different cultures gracefully.

The two families remain close and sometimes meet at the Cutter house on Cape Cod. But, "We don't get together as often as we'd like because of Nid's schedule. It's three times busier than mine," says this Massachusetts native. Cutter has been their best man twice, at the Pibulsonggrams' wedding and at their 25th anniversary wedding party, reenacted at the Wayside Inn in Sudbury, Massachusetts.

* * *

While her husband listens, I ask Pat Pibulsonggram to take me back to the beginning. Was it always easy for her to feel at home in both cultures?

"I decided it was not a good idea to test the water if I was definitely sure I wanted to swim," she says, explaining that she chose not to visit his homeland before they married here. "I married into a very sophisticated, very worldly family. I didn't have to struggle making myself understood." She does agree it could be a different story if an American were to fall in love with a Thai from a "less traveled family."

Sitting in the glow of their Christmas tree, I ask if the difference in religions was a hurdle. They look at each other, shrugging their shoulders and shaking their heads as if to say, "No."

"I was born and raised a Christian," she begins, "and I consider myself a Christian and a Buddhist." With a glimmer in his eye, the ambassador quickly responds, "And I'm a Buddhist with a Christmas tree!" We all laugh again.

Later, when Pat Pibulsonggram gives me a tour, she shows me the small meditation room in their private quarters where they both pause everyday to keep balance in their lives. The ambassador mentions, proudly, that his wife is also a "practicing healer and teacher" of Reiki, an ancient Asian system of complementary medicine. "I could never make a living with it but I have private clients and travel to teach classes in other cities," she explains.

Speaking of traveling, I ask them if ever get to travel for fun. "We love to ski together," says the ambassador, looking at his wife. "She's such a pretty skier." The Massachusetts native adds, "We used to go one week a year to Aspen or Stowe," before they got so busy in Washington.

Here, the ambassador might play golf, but "I'm lousy," he says with a melodious chuckle. "If your handicap is too high, no one wants to play with you. But if your handicap is too low [and you can beat everyone], that's not very good for a diplomat either." But because these sports take lots of time, this diplomatic couple has taken up roller blading! They also love to spend time on the C&O Canal, near his Georgetown office, and even gave a fundraiser for the historic canal, which Her Royal Highness Princess Chulabhorn of Thailand and First Lady Hillary Clinton attended.

One look at this diplomatic wife's long and varied résumé and you understand why she is so good at so many different aspects of diplomacy. After graduating from Rhode Island School of Design in 1966, she taught art in public school and designed theater costumes and sets during their three years of courtship.

After marrying and moving to Bangkok, she became an advertising executive. Later, she cofounded a manufacturing textile firm that exported women's fashion to American and Caribbean markets and manufactured large fabric wall collages for major hotels. She also founded a boutique and gallery that was Bangkok's first outlet for designers of contemporary clothing and jewelry. After selling her business, she developed beach properties while still keeping her hand in commercial art, designing textiles for top fabric houses like Brunschwig & Fils and Scalamandre.

"I sold my businesses nine or ten years ago," she says. "I couldn't be in business and do this." The ambassador jumps in, reaching for her hand and tilting his head, as he turns to look at her. "She's in charge of all our finances and she does a wonderful job." Then he mentions that "she is resposible for all this," gesturing around the room to emphazise her expertise in interior design. "You must see her painting in the next room." No wonder the Christmas tree looks professionally decorated.

Graciously, he suggests a tour of the house for me and his wife while he goes to the office in Georgetown. As he's about to exit, they invite me to a reception later that week for the Washington Symphony and the concert following, where, Ambassador Pibulsonggram says, "I will take the stage." At that moment, he snaps his heels together and pretends to conduct the orchestra. He laughs and looks at his canine audience barking approval.

* * *

Doggies in tow, we first go to the solarium, which overlooks their handsome slate terrace. But while I'm eyeing the lap-lane pool, she is inspecting her indoor plants and upon seeing a bug, immediately calls on her Radio Shack portaphone for the gardener.

Next, in the formal parlor is her painting, *Bowl of Heaven*, an artistic wash of gold, which she says symbolizes "a bowl of blessings overturned." As we walk around the beautifully decorated residence, she points out all the handsome details of Ogden Codman's restrained style. In their study, I am especially impressed with the large curio cabinet full of their ribbons and medals, many awarded to them by His Majesty. As we continue our tour through the gallery and the meditation room, both of us begin to smell irresistable aromas wafting from the kitchen. Without realizing why, we start talking about food. "I'm a real 'foodie,'" she says, admitting that they love to sample good restaurants and good wines and were recently in a *Wine Spectator* magazine story. Later I learn the ambassador was the main source for a *Washington Post* story about which Virginia wines go best with Thai food. Not an easy match.

* * *

To me, Ambassador Pibulsonggram and his wife are like Thai silk: naturally smooth and elegant yet colorful. When I return for the reception, he speaks off-the-cuff with warmth and humor thanking the corporate sponsors. One of them is Ford. The ambassador makes corporate friends and entertains the rest of the audience when he ends his remarks by impishly singing, "Have you driven a Ford lately?"—a well-known Ford TV jingle. The room bursts out laughing. The party has begun.

* * *

The Pibulsonggrams epitomize modern diplomacy: retaining the grace and style of the past while putting in long hours to check every detail and make the international connections that keep foreign economies afloat in tough times.

"It's not all parties," says this ambassador. "We also have rough jobs like seeking clemency for a Thai on death row in California or handling touchy problems with the more than 80 Thai Buddhist temples across your country."

During our interview, he mentions how much help the 600 American corporations, such as Ford, Coca-Cola and Amoco, have given to Thailand by being "our support group, our fan club. They have been very good to and for us. They are good friends," said the American-schooled diplomat who majored in government but did take Dartmouth's "standard economics" course. "Clearly, I am not an economist," he says somewhat defensively, "but, I'm learning fast."

"It's a rough time for Thailand. … We've had an 8.5 [percent] growth rate for the past 20 years. It's been consistently high," he begins to explain. "Our credit line ran out on us." He adds, constructively, "We need to learn how to effectively compete to catch up with a more modern economy around the world, the higher-end businesses."

* * *

As the Asian financial crisis continued, I realized I needed to update this chapter and my interviews. When I return to the residence, I am surprised how much difference six months has made to this ambassador, his embassy and his country. He and his wife are happy to see me even though they have unhappy news to report.

"We are downsizing; about forty percent [cut in staff]," says the ambassador. "We officially close the embassy at six and turn the air conditioning off, but our smaller staff often works until nine. At least we haven't had to close."

Mrs. Pibulsonggram adds, "We are cutting back socially, not traveling as much. Hopefullly, it's not something you notice up front. For dinners, we used to hire professional wait staff from the White House but now our driver and other staffers are servers. We make our own desserts instead of getting them from Design Cuisine [a caterer] and use less expensive flowers from the garden."

"I work at home in the morning," says the ambassador, who starts his days around 8 A.M. with the BBC and Radio Thailand as he shaves. Over breakfast, he gets "news briefings" from his wife, who prereads for him *The New York Times, The Wall Street Journal, The Washington Post,* and *The Washington Times.*

"We get to bed very late," he says, and because of the big time difference between Washington and Bangkok, "I work 'til one or two in the morning. We have phone, fax, shortwave here just as we have at the office. E-mail has actually increased exposure." With the fall of the Thai bhat to 40 percent of what it used to be, "the workload has increased and yet we have had to close some offices, the Ministry of Industry and the Thai News Service. We downsized Science and Technology, Agriculture and Commerce, and we have a hiring freeze and a 30 percent decrease in housing allowance." I'm sorry to learn that the efficient staffer who has been my liaison will be leaving by the end of the week.

"With this negative growth, it is dour, sour, glum," he says, making a sad face. She tilts her head and reaches out lovingly to pat his hand.

"Two years later [after Thailand devalued its currency], it is a very, very different time for us." he begins. "But we received good advice from our friends abroad: the IMF and your Treasury Secretary Rubin and helpful feedback from the American business community, who continue to have very strong interest in Thailand and its economic development. This is why we are turning around. Indications attest to the stable economy, new investments coming in and not one leaving. We haven't lost one out of 600 companies," he says proudly. "You name them, we have them.

"We listened well and we made the necessary changes," says this Southeast Asian ambassador, who wants to make sure Americans know that his country is a good example of how to adapt to changing circumstances. "The difficult reform package is being implemented, and we're trying to regain the confidence of foreign investors," he adds. "We have put a lot of things in place to provide a firm foundation for growth.

"We have a good labor force and have managed to avoid some of the social problems others in the region have had to confront. We've been able to maintain political and social stability," Ambassador Pibulsonggram explains, adding that his government "is working hard to put in place a social safety net" for the 1.5 to 2 million unemployed Thais.

Still, they try to keep up their social obligations. They invite me to an upcoming dinner party, the next night—a thank-you for "our cultural and protocal friends," Mrs. Pibulsonggram says, adding that she hopes the austerity measures will not be too obvious.

It's late morning now and time for the ambassador to leave for the chancery in Georgetown. We all go down to the front courtyard, excited doggies leading the ambassador's entourage. We shake hands, the ambassador kisses his wife and off he goes, telling Poco and Remy, "Be good." The ambassador's wife and I take the doggies out to the sidewalk, and as I turn to walk to my car, I see her enjoying a few moments of peace walking the dogs.

* * *

When I return for the dinner party, the ambassador and his wife are welcoming guests with drinks on the terrace. Graciously, they make sure we know one another. The doggies are there too, playing coy and vying for attention. Some of the guests are neighbors: Esther Coopersmith, a former U.S. Representative to the United Nations; Stuart Bloch, a real estate developer whose wife was ambassador to Nepal; and socialite/real estate baroness Allison Laland. Two former chiefs of protocol, Selwa Roosevelt of the Reagan and Bush Administrations and Lloyd Hand of the Johnson Administration, are there, along with Patrick Daly, representing the current chief of protocol, Mary Mel French. There are also art historians of Washington's major galleries, a professor of Southeast Asian studies and Senator Bennett Johnston and his wife, friends of Thailand's king and queen. I want to interview everyone here.

When we go into the formal dining room, I am seated next to Lloyd Hand, with whom I have great time comparing notes about diplomacy, in general, and how to eat each fragrant dish before us, in particular. Just after all 22 of us are seated, the ambassador stands to welcome us formally. Without notes, he proceeds around the table and introduces each of us, with precise information and kind stories. We all marvel at his memory.

In response, Senator Johnston stands to toast our hosts with the charming Southern softness of Louisiana. He says that in all their years in Washington, he and his wife, Mary, haven't known anyone who could do a better job, so elegantly, than this diplomatic couple.

Later he tells me, "'Nid' is one of the greatest practioners of the diplomatic arts. You must begin by being warm, bright, knowledgeable. But, you can only learn so much in order to be a great ambassador. You must be someone people like and trust. He can put someone at ease with his immediate warmth which does not threaten. He's not overwhelming, like all those who want to slap you on the back," says this senator who spent 24 years on the Hill. "He is truly interested in everyone he meets and naturally puts everyone at ease."

Senator Johnston, now a private consultant, and his wife have for many years visited Thailand. During his congressional tenure, he was on committees for appropriations, foreign operations and defense, often dealing with Southeast Asian issues.

He can't say enough good things about the Pibulsonggrams. "They work together so seamlessly and complement each other so well. It is hard to imagine one without the other. Each has his or her own expertise and they are so competent that one would threaten someone else but together they make a perfect team.

"They both have exquisite taste," says Johnston. "You can see it in their home and how they entertain. How good an ambassador is is frequently reflected in what their home is like and how they entertain. I can't remember a good ambassador who did not entertain well."

16

Australia: The Ambassador Is a Bachelor—Again!

"The ambassador is a *bachelor.*" That comment alone gets Washington's society mavens salivating. And if the bachelor is attractive, watch out. He's a marked man, a favorite dinner guest, a popular guy.

Australia has had two bachelor ambassadors in a row, both attractive, both married before. And both with an intriguing personal style that Americans expect from the home of "Crocodile Dundee," the Great Barrier Reef and Sydney's unmistakable Opera House. This land down under, site of the 2000 Olympics, always our Pacific partner, is so far away that one-half of the 300 staffers at the embassy are Americans.

Before Bachelor #2 even arrives, I hear the Hollywood version of his curriculum vitae—for more than 20 years, he has been friend and escort to Oscar-winning American actress and controversial author Shirley MacLaine. And, he has never been an ambassador before.

But the Honorable Andrew Sharp Peacock AC is a distinguished Australian politician of 28 years, his Liberal party's longest-serving member of Parliament, twice the opposition leader and the minister of foreign affairs in former Prime Minister Malcolm Fraser's cabinet. He is also the recipient of his country's highest honor, the Companion of the Order of Australia, which puts the prestigious "AC" after his name for the rest of his life.

I tell him, as we sit in his corner office overlooking Scott Circle, that his reputation preceded him to Washington. He smiles and nods, acknowledging his famous friendship.

"Shirley has the searingly admirable quality of saying what she thinks even if some people disagree. ... I've known her a long time," says the 60-year-old, twice-divorced ambassador, who first met 64-year-old MacLaine in 1976 when she was visiting her daughter Sachi in Australia. "We disagree politically and I don't subscribe to everything she says and does" but over the years, "She has stuck it out." He vividly remembers how she "dropped everything" to help him seek medical advice outside Australia for one of his daughters.

Who, Australia's weekly version of our *People* magazine, in their three-page story titled "Peacock's Tale" (April 21, 1997), quoted MacLaine as once saying, "I thought, as long as he's minister for foreign affairs, I might as well give him one [a foreign affair] he'll never forget."

Will they see each other more now that they live in the same country and on the same continent? He shrugs his shoulders and smiles, keeping his private life private.

But this intriguing diplomat who is an avid surfer does admit he "needs more than one surfboard" for his "three places." When I ask where, he answers, "My beach house and my home in Australia and Malibu." Guess who lives in Malibu?

In fact, surfing is only Peacock's seaside pastime; his real passion is owning and racing thoroughbred horses. "My best was Leilani, a filly twenty years ago," says Peacock, who is "so frustrated" finding new names for his horses that he takes any suggestion from his daughters, his staff and MacLaine. "Cosmic Warning" is hers.

"I spend money not on women or booze or cigarettes but on horses," says the gallant Peacock who long ago got the advice, "Never buy anything that has to be fed" but ignored it: "Horses are easier, you can do all sorts of things without asking anybody."

I'm thinking perhaps it's time we stopped talking about horses, and surfing and Shirley, but I am interested with this ambassador's life outside his official duties in Washington.

According to *Who,* Peacock originally turned down what they say is a $120,000 ambassadorship. At 55, he had retired from politics and had started two companies, Pacific Rim and Asia Pacific Holdings, to match American money with Asian businesses. He regularly commuted between New York and Australia with two weeks here and 10 days away. He says he often "spent weekends in Malibu." But, after discussing the diplomatic opportunity with his three grown daughters back in Australia, he decided, "I could have impact on my country's reputation."

He took the job, resigned from his companies and let his American partner take control until his ambassadorship in Washington is over. "I have agreed to stay three years and have an option for a fourth."

"He is suave, good looking and gives a good public image so people somehow tend to brush him off just because he's flamboyant, comes from a moneyed background," says Connie Lawn of Australian Radio News. "But

Ambassador Peacock and U.S. Secretary of State Madeleine Albright descending the stairs of the Sydney Opera House. Photo by Robert Pearce of The Sydney Morning Herald; *courtesy of the Fairfax Photo Library.*

that's a big mistake to underestimate him," says the American who for 30 years has reported from Washington on people and events affecting Australians. "He has enormous command of every detail, knows the most intricate parts of any trade deal," she adds. "He's very admired by Americans and can pick up the phone and talk with anyone in Congress, at the White House including the president himself."

Lawn, now the third longest-serving White House correspondent, thinks "Peacock's the top of the list" of Washington's best ambassadors. "He is an insider who has just the right light touch."

I ask Lawn, who has watched Peacock strut his stuff on Washington's social circuit, about his longtime friendship with MacLaine. "He's flirtatious but he's quite loyal to Shirley MacLaine and always in some way brings her up like 'I'm here with so and so because Shirley's not available' or 'because she's off making a film.' It's definitely still a romance."

Lawn reminds me about Peacock's first news conference here. "It sounded like we were having an affair," she says. "He said, 'Oh, there's Connie Lawn. I've known nobody longer in Washington than Connie Lawn,' as if I were slithering through the ventilators all over town," she says, understandably proud of her longtime friendship with this ambassador.

From the beginning of his life, Andrew Peacock has called more than one continent home. His parents met on a ship bound for San Francisco and married in that favorite American city's famed Grace Cathedral. But they returned to Melbourne to have their only child.

His father's investments in California kept bringing the family back. "I spent a significant part of my formative years in the U.S. and became married in the U.S.," says the Australian, who adds that "barely a year has gone by" that he can remember not traveling to or living in the United States. In fact, he claims, "I know your country better than I know New Zealand!"

He was educated at Melbourne's prestigious Scotch College and received a law degree from the university there. Before he entered Parliament, he not only practiced law but also worked in business.

Today, he sees nothing but the potential of "economic growth and influence" for his underpopulated but resource-rich homeland. "We are clearly a country with an enormous future. Technology being what it is, our arid areas will become fertile ... and population will grow and then Australia will be a major player.

"The only areas of difference [between Australia and America] are our industries are sophomoric while yours are mature, and we'll compete on trade issues." But he thinks any problems with competitive enterprises can be balanced with joint ventures. "The Australians have invested here, more than five billion [dollars]," he adds, citing big mining companies like BHP and CRA.

"We are a good global partner," he states, especially considering his country's "admirable record" on chemical warfare and disarmament. "Australia has been an ally of the United States in every major conflict." He adds, diplomatically, that New Zealand has too, and that, in fact, that they are the only two countries in the world that have been such constant allies.

* * *

My mind flashes back to the most singularly somber moment I've experienced researching this book. I remember the haunting but brilliant sound from a single bugle, like a knife cutting through the air, closing the annual ANZAC (Australian and New Zealand Army Corps) commemorative service at the National Cathedral.

Speaking then from a marble pulpit high above his seated audience, this ambassador reminded the hundreds of gathered guests about the legendary heroism of the volunteer corps, which included his very own grandfather.

Before dawn on April 25, 1915, thousands of young men from these two young countries began landing on the beaches at the Gallipoli Peninsula behind the Turkish front lines and proceeded "into the belly of death," said the ambassador, dramatically quoting Tennyson. "The innocents went to their slaughter," he added, this time taking words written 82 years ago by an Australian colonel, "with horrendous casualties." The allies lost 33,532 troops and had 78,518 wounded.

Amid stirring hymns, Peacock asked the audience never to forget this supreme sacrifice that left many Australian and New Zealand families without their fathers. In fact, New Zealand's then-Ambassador John Wood, who was sitting with then British ambassador, Sir John Kerr, and his wife, Lady Kerr, was one of those who lost his father in Gallipoli.

Throughout the audience, I saw the signature Australian bush hat, upturned on just one side, along with many other starched uniforms. Lots of ladies wore silk dresses, mostly floral, with big straw hats, and young families brought babies in prams and spent the ceremony keeping them quiet.

In somber remembrance, Australians wore twigs of rosemary and New Zealanders placed red paper poppies on their lapels. Both plants grow wild on Gallipoli Peninsula.

In contrast to the solemn scene inside, outside it was a beautiful, crystal-clear day with busloads of tourists from North Carolina and Wisconsin listening curiously to the accents from down under and wondering if "there had been a wedding." This poignant national day was foreign to them.

From the cathedral, many of us walked down Massachusetts Avenue, past the vice president's house and to the garden reception at the New Zealand ambassador's residence, just behind the British compound and adjacent to the highly stylized brick consultate of New Zealand. There, Steinlager and Hawkes Bay wine helped wash down lollipop lamb chops, sausage rolls and meat patties, while humor and good-natured ridicule between "Aussies" and "Kiwis" filled the air. Quite a contrast to the church ceremony before.

Back in one corner of the garden, it was the bugler, not either ambassador, who was receiving the most attention. Retired U.S. Army Band bugler Patrick Mastroleo was holding court while also holding a huge ham sandwich and telling fans how he still practiced two hours a day. He wanted to make sure he was ready for his annual trip from Orange Park, Florida, to stand above the north transept and play the "Last Post." This American master sergeant who stood alone playing "Taps" at the state funerals of Presidents Eisenhower, Truman and Johnson said, "It's not like on a movie set. You can never be emotional or you lose it."

* * *

Back in Ambassador Peacock's office, I ask this seasoned politician to describe the current relationship between Australia and its Pacific neighbor, New Zealand.

Although "New Zealand and Australia were both settled by the British, New Zealand's core element was not chosen by the best of British judges. It was the largest open-air penitentiary in history," says the ambassador whose country was also settled by the imprisoned subjects of Britain's King George.

Plus, "New Zealand feels small," he says, comparing the national consciousness of Australia's closest neighbor to the United States' big but less powerful neighbor to the north. "Canada feels self-conscious. It is not a popular thing for a Canadian to be photographed with an American politician," he says, referring more to the era of Prime Minister Trudeau than now.

Suddenly he turns dead serious and from the look of him you know this ambassador means business. "In my opinion, New Zealand is not playing their role in defense issues." Peacock continues, "They made a big mistake when they left the alliance [ANZUS, the defense alliance created in 1951 among Australia, New Zealand and the United States] and didn't allow nuclear-armed ships so far from the mother country. There is a significant difference between us." The Australian ambassador is referring to New Zealand's 1984 decision not to allow American nuclear warships into their ports. (At that time in New Zealand, there was a very popular movement against such nuclear use.)

Before I leave, I ask Peacock about his daughters. Proudly he tells me his eldest, Carolyn, is a radio producer at the top-rated current affairs show in Adelaide; Ann used to be on TV but is now an executive in Melbourne and about to marry; and his youngest, Jane, is married, living in London and a top horsewoman.

"Raising a family is one of the hardest tasks," offers this father who is often a 17-hour flight away. He hopes he gives them good guidance and examples "to encourage respect."

"My daughters do love and adore their father. They put their father on a pedestal," he says. But he tells them, "I'm not your role model; you are not to follow just what I do."

Then he sits forward and emphatically explains, "A person must evaluate what's important to him, what's his primary interest or you'll get it wrong. Relationships fall down because people assume the aspirations of the other." I can just hear him coaching his daughters long-distance. I remember how he also said earlier, "Periods of separation can help all relationships."

* * *

Peacock's predecessor, career diplomat John McCarthy, now serves his country from Jakarta, Indonesia, Australia's largest South East Asian trading partner before the Asian financial crisis.

He too has strong ties to the United States. He was born here during World War II (his father worked for the Australian Embassy), practiced law in a New York law firm and held three diplomatic assignments in Washington. Ambassador McCarthy's schooling was British: first in a straightlaced boarding school followed by Cambridge for both his MA and LLB (bachelor of laws).

"John McCarthy was solid," says Connie Lawn. "He had an excellent legal background and was a more traditional ambassador, less a public figure like Peacock."

When I ask Lawn, herself a divorced mother, if she had ever dated either of these eligible bachelors, she tells me that McCarthy "came to my house and I took him out in my boat on the lake in my backyard." Says Lawn, the author of *You Wake Me Each Morning,* memoirs about her morning broadcasts to Australia, "We started to have a social relationship but then, I introduced him to a girlfriend."

* * *

Both Ambassador McCarthy and Ambassador Peacock told me that Congress is at the top of their list of daily duties. On the eve of his departure, McCarthy addressed the Australia America Association at a black-tie dinner held in his honor at Georgetown University, which is proud to have the Center for Australian and New Zealand Studies.

"I'm told by an American that working with Congress is like teaching a pig to sing," McCarthy said, smiling and immediately getting everyone's attention in the audience. "You waste your time and you irritate the pig." But then this clever diplomat quickly added, "America is a great country. I mean that, and this is coming from a man who comes from a country where hyperbole is nonexistent!"

Ambassador McCarthy, who has taken his extensive art collection to each new post, whether Vietnam, Mexico or Thailand, is also quite handsome, divorced and the father of two teenage daughters. He was refreshingly candid when I asked him about diplomacy today.

"The Europeans are superb diplomats. They are more concerned about form and process than are many others."

In comparison, he likes the style of American diplomats, who "are not refined figures strutting the drawing rooms of Europe. They don't prance around. It's much more like they are running a big overseas office with meetings all day."

"The Brits have more humor, enormous skill in writing," he adds, saying they are brilliant in choosing the precise words needed. But, "They tolerate eccentrics to a greater degree … the eccentricities get stamped out of an American before he or she gets to the top."

On the other hand, "Americans are very purposeful with some objective in mind when they go into a meeting. They are quite frank, with an ease in communication and a significantly enhanced ability to debate." He thinks "thrashing it out" in Congress gives us a national taste for disagreement.

What's different about being an ambassador in Washington? "The caliber of the debate … people are on top of their subject matter. You can't go to lunch and decide to waffle through it; you can't afford to wing it."

But, according to this career diplomat, the biggest change in diplomacy today is caused by the new communication technology and reduced staffs. To avoid the expense of more full-timers, "They send specialists from home."

And as for international memos, this ambassador thinks there is more "micromanaging" of embassies abroad from the foreign ministry at home.

To end on a light note, I ask him if he has ever eaten in an American Outback Steakhouse. "I think they have excellent food, resembling our pub class at home but they use names I've never heard of!"

And as far as the Olympics in 2000, "Stay at least three weeks," he advises. That way you could do a walk-around in the Outback and scuba around the Great Barrier Reef. "Australia is a great country," he says, flashing a big, welcoming smile.

17

Croatia: Labor of Love

Just look for the statue. Not Winston Churchill near the impressive British enclave. But down Massachusetts Avenue's long majestic hill, over Rock Creek Park and past the Mosque, just before Sheridan Circle on the left there's a striking bronze sculpture—a muscular man with his head deep down in contemplation. That's St. Jerome, the patron saint of the Croatian Province of Franciscan Fathers and the work of Croatia's patriot sculptor Ivan Mestrovic.

Today, the Croatian Embassy is a showcase for its proud country's art and craftsmanship, Croatian loyalty and hard work. After the breakup of Yugoslavia, the newly independent republic purchased the former Austrian chancery in 1993. It seemed ironic because Croatia had once been part of the Austro-Hungarian Empire as well. However, this empty, dilapidated building was now in need of major repairs. Twenty-five ugly window air conditioners pockmarked the handsome façade, and inside "it was dusty, old fashioned and the old telephone system was a museum piece, like something out of World War II," says attorney Kreso Pirsl, the former counselor at the embassy who supervised the transformation.

"First, the Croatian soccer team from Boston came and destroyed the inside walls, you could see from one side to the other," he says, dramatically waving his arms around. After the demolition, "the ambassador wasn't sure what to say!" But the news got out to the Croatian American community, centered in Cleveland, Pittsburgh and New York, and donations started pouring in. Croatian American newspapers urged patriots to buy a "Croatian Brick," the symbol for the embassy's renovation. Eight hundred fifty thousand dollars were collected. "We never had a preset plan or a budget. They'd just always say, 'Don't worry, we'll get the money.'"

Then an extraordinary thing happened. Every weekend, for almost eight months, Croatian American painters, plumbers, carpenters, electricians, heating and air-conditioning engineers and security and communication experts drove down from Cleveland, Pittsburgh and New York to create this new Croatian showplace.

"The enthusiasm and love for their homeland was channeled into this project," says Pirsl. "The war at home united these people; they felt Croatian again." In fact, after this success in Washington, similar embassy projects were undertaken in Canada and Australia, again with the expert help of displaced but loyal Croatians.

The official embassy press release about the renovation says that this outpouring of pride came when Croatia most needed it. Croatia was "trying to recover from 20 billion dollars in war damages" and was "caring for over 500,000 refugees and displaced persons from Bosnia and Herzegovina," it states.

"For nineteen consecutive weekends," Pirsl remembers, "two 65-year-old carpenters drove seven hours every Friday night to arrive here at 7 A.M. on Saturday morning. They were always the first to arrive and the last to leave." Another man commuted from New York for 55 Saturdays and Sundays and "the ambassador ended up calling his wife to thank her because she was complaining" that he was gone too much. "One weekend we had 70 workers here," says Pirsl, who acted as referee when the artisans disagreed. "Croatians may scream at each other but after five minutes you'll see them drink together. We are very temperamental, hot-blooded."

Pirsl was the embassy storyteller to ensure that this new ambassador and his staff, most of whom weren't there in the beginning, appreciate this outpouring of national pride and talent. Hundreds of brass plaques thanking major donors with names like Novak, Vanjak, Bubic, Smolic, Petrak, Jovic, Bucic and Leko greet you at the front door. "These names will be there forever," promises Pirsl. "Some come back who never saw it finished and bring their families. Everyone who bought a brick got a written, personal thank-you from the president of Croatia."

Inside the embassy, wherever you look, Croatian creativity and loving care are obvious. While I wait for the ambassador, First Secretary Marijan Gubic shows me around.

In the main drawing room overlooking the statue out front, he tells me the striped and marbleized walls in the embassy were meticulously hand-painted by these volunteer artisans. Surely it's striped wallpaper, I think, not paint. I have to touch it. One crème-colored stripe is satiny, the next, flat. The lines are perfect. The effect, elegant. I walk on the fancy parquet and marble floors, watching the colored sunlight filter through the Croatian-designed stained glass windows. The fancy moldings and elaborate plasterwork of Croatia's five crests are impressive handiwork too. The furniture is modern Croatian and Biedermeier antiques. Only the sparkling chandeliers are not Croatian; they are Czech, as they are in many other embassies.

I can see the ambassador through the closed glass-paneled doors. He's walking around his Croatian custom-designed rosewood desk making long sweeping gestures up to the ceiling, obviously emphasizing an important point to his guest. He looks more like a basketball player, I think, than an ambassador.

Meanwhile, in the library I browse through the colorful travel brochures of this country's long, sunny coast and its 1,185 islands. "Two thousand and six hundred sunny hours per year," I read, "which makes it one of the sunniest countries in Europe."

I am surrounded by lime-green stripes in this room. Again, I can't resist touching them. The ambassador's secretaries see me and laugh. "Everybody has to touch the stripes to believe it," says the one with the heavier accent.

As the ambassador and I begin to talk, I can't get over how much he looks like an athlete. "Yes," Dr. Miomir Zuzul answers, "I played basketball in high school but I realized I wasn't good enough to go on." I learn later from his teenage daughters that they think "he's going through a middle-age crisis, dressing up like the pros for all sorts of sports—basketball, tennis, golf … even skiing." He admits his favorite American television shows are tennis and NBA basketball, "especially the Chicago Bulls." (Croatian Toni Kukoc plays with the Bulls. Other well-known Croatian players are Dino Rada, Stojko Vrankovic and Zan Tabak. And there's even a statue to Croatian basketball legend Drazen Petrovic in Lausanne, Switzerland's Olympic Park.)

So proud of Croatian athletic prowess, the ambassador and his diplomatic team set up a Croatia House at the Atlanta Olympics. There, they gave out samples of Croatian food and wine, specially designed silk scarves and neckties (a Croatian invention) and souvenir "passports" that highlighted their homeland and their legendary athletes. "For three weeks we had two chefs, one pastry chef and three bartenders," later says the irrepressible Pirsl, "and our great wine!"

Albeit an amateur athlete, when it came to studies the ambassador "fell in love" with Freud and Jung and went on to earn his Ph.D. at the University of Zagreb, becoming a clinical psychologist specializing in conflict resolution and aggressive behavior—a perfect background for a Croatian diplomat. "I think I was lucky that psychology was never seen [by the state] as being very important." Of course, so many other career tracks, diplomacy or politics, would have "required an allegiance to Marxist ideology."

In 1991 when hostilities broke out in Croatia, this distinguished university professor (he was now head of the developmental psychology department and a vice dean of the university) was attending a psychology conference in the United States. He returned home and volunteered for the Croatian army. He joined the Ministry of Defense, working mostly as a psychologist. But after meeting Croatian President Franjo Tudjman, Zuzul became his assistant minister of foreign affairs, then his deputy minister and finally, his national security advisor. Zuzul then spent three years in Geneva as Croatia's ambassador to the United Nations. But it is his job as special envoy, which he has held since 1994, that has put him on the front lines of peace negotiations in Vienna, Paris and Dayton.

"Before I came here as ambassador, I had already met privately with President Clinton about eight times and four or five times with Vice President Gore. I knew almost all the U.S. officials and had all their private numbers." He claims he doesn't "use those numbers because I have no reason to complain." I raise my eyebrows to that statement and he smiles.

But Zuzul does admit to using psychology every day in diplomacy. "I was entering something very new yet it was still communication and still people," he explains. "I had some special skills like negotiation, conflict resolution, and saw other possibilities besides aggression. Whether it's individual people or relationships among countries, it's the same."

However, this father of four admits he'd rather be the mediator than just a participant. "I like to solve something. I have an intrinsic motivation to help, to use my knowledge and experience. In Geneva, it was typical, multilateral discussions among the institutions and the professions. But, here in the U.S., no program is scheduled in advance. As a diplomat, you are more free, have more space, more room for intiatives. As ambassador, I may have instructions but how I follow through is up to me."

So, what is his agenda? "We want as friendly a relationship with the U.S. as possible with no limitations for our friendship. We want to attract private investors; I personally believe in market economy."

Now, I feel I must ask about the Ron Brown tragedy. On April 3, 1996, U.S. Secretary of Commerce Brown led a group of American businessmen to Dubrovnik. Just before they were to land, their U.S. Air Force jet crashed into a Croatian mountain and there were no survivors. When I mention the disaster, Ambassador Zuzul sighs and starts to speak slowly. "It was a big tragedy. I was one of the three main people waiting for them: our prime minister, me, and your American ambassador. At first we had the wrong information, that the plane had fallen into the sea." When he finally got to the crash site the next morning, "already all the bodies had been found by the

Croatian army. It was a horrible picture," he grimaces. "I knew the businessmen. We had met in preparation for the trip."

But as sorry as he is about the tragedy, he emphasizes the crucial importance of that kind of American help. "In the former Croatia, business didn't exist. Without economic development, it's difficult to imagine a stable situation and long-lasting peace."

Ambassador and Mrs. Zuzul have also gone beyond normal diplomacy to form a personal and continuing friendship with Secretary Ron Brown's family in Washington. Prime Minister Zlatko Matesa flew to Washington for Ron Brown's funeral and later honored the late U.S. secretary of commerce with Croatia's highest honor awarded to a foreigner.

Almost any diplomatic discussion of international business soon leads to NATO, the magic acronym and favorite topic of ambassadors, especially those representing newly independent Eastern European countries. The ambassador thinks Croatia is close to becoming a NATO member but emphatically distinguishes his country from Eastern Europe.

"Americans need to learn that Croatia is a very old nation with very old history and very, very old tendency to establish independence as a soverign state. We are not part of the Balkans. Throughout our history, we have been connected to Western civilization. Croatia is Mediterranean." One might say he speaks like a true Dalmatian. (People from Dalmatia, a historic and picturesque region of Croatia on the Adriatic Sea, are known to have a certain pride about their heritage.)

"Everyone is confused and can't distinguish who is who," he elaborates about the formation and dissolution of Yugoslavia. "After World War II, we were forced to enter into a very bad marriage. The original marriage wasn't legal," he continues, explaining why Croatia's "divorce" from the former Yugoslavian partners was "natural."

Besides representing the 4.5 million Croatians at home, he is also concerned about being "a bridge" to the 2.5 million Croatians in America. "This building shows you how they feel about their country," he adds proudly. "The brother of my grandfather came here and San Pedro, California, is full of fishermen and sailors from the Dalmatian Islands." He adds that many Croatians went to work in American steel mills or mines, settling in Chicago, Cleveland, Pittsburgh or Minneapolis. "And, 300,000 emigrated to Australia."

He says he too likes to travel and especially to see the United States while he and his family are here. The summer before Clinton was reelected, he traveled cross-country to both national political conventions with his whole family: his wife, Tatjana Bradvica, and his daughters, Ivana and Tiona, then

14 and 12 years old, and his young sons, Mihovil and Andrija, then 3 and 2 years old.

When they were out on the road in the embassy's big black Chevy van with the ambassador's driver Damir at the wheel, "It was the first two weeks without a tie I could remember." Even with two teenage girls and two young, active boys they covered the Grand Canyon, Yellowstone, the Black Hills and Mt. Rushmore. "We tried to stay in local hotels and eat in regular restaurants to feel the real America. I tried to eat steak in each different part of the country to see how differently it was cooked," he says, laughing.

But the big thrill came when a U.S. park ranger at Yellowstone saw his diplomatic (DPL) license plate and stopped the van. "He asked us where we were from. It turns out he has a grandfather from Croatia." By the time they were finished talking, "there was a long line of cars behind us!"

"Americans are very curious and very friendly," he thinks. With all the different states and different people, Americans have these two characteristics in common, but even more so out West and in the Midwest. "We all have a tendency to forget how big and diverse the U.S. is." I ask him if he served as the chief negotiator in the van. His eyes twinkle as he answers, "You must give a little bit of punishment with a kiss. They must feel loved," declares the professor who says he tries to remember that as a parent he should be emotional first and theoretical second. "It's always a problem whether you are preparing them for the ideal world or the real world."

* * *

Perhaps he would be surprised to know that his girls told me that it is Mommy who is the compromiser. When I first arrive to interview his family, 14-year-old Ivana reports, "As a Ph.D., he was always talking with troubled kids, sorting things out, giving them pep talks." Twelve-year-old Tiona pipes in, "He never does this for us."

We are sitting in the formal living room of the official residence, a new town home in an upscale gated community across from the Georgetown University Medical Center. Long windows let the afternoon light stream in and show the sparkle on the snow patches outside. The setting is formal but this interview causes curiosity and showmanship typical of a growing family. While the girls and I are settled on the same sofa, their two little brothers are zooming in between the chair legs with their matching police cars. Mir, the one-and-a-half-year-old collie, noses in on the action but most of the time acts like her Croatian name, which means "peace and quiet." (The ambassador's other dog, Imota, appropriately an extrememly well-behaved dalmatian, is named for the ambassador's hometown, Imotski, and makes cameo appearances at

Croatian Ambassador Miomir Zuzul wih his wife, Tatjana Bradvica; sons Andrija and Mihovil; and Pope John Paul II. Photo courtesy of L'Osservatore Romano.

embassy parties. This unofficial but endearing canine diplomat is even featured on the back of one of Croatia's glossiest travel brochures.)

I try to continue our interview that began before all the family members decided that this was the afternoon's main event. Tatjana Bradvica juggles her answers between her two roles: ambassador's wife and mother/chief negotiator of the moment. Mrs. Zuzul's English is not as fluent as the girls', but she senses they may be taking advantage of a reporter's ears. Still, she regularly looks to the girls for help in finding the proper words but is often interrupted by the floor action when there's a minor police car smash-up or a little boy, who was so brave a moment ago, now feels trapped behind a ficus tree. It's Mommy to the rescue, then Mommy back to the interview.

We laugh and continue. Tatjana Bradvica tells me she is an economist who used to be a very ambitious manager of an export-import trade association in Cresia.

"We met while we were at the university. He was a psychology professor at the university but I made the money." She laughs. "We had the same interests and he was very tall and romantic." Did he bring her flowers? Now, she really laughs. "No," she says. "He is a Dalmatian and they are like Italian men. They are very proud. They *never* buy flowers!"

The whole family, including the ambassador, has just recently returned from Rome and a private mass with the Pope. As devout Catholics, they are thrilled and want to tell me every detail. It seems that no one slept the night before, the little boys had high temperatures and took turns vomiting before and after the 7:30 morning meeting with the Pope but of all appointments, this was one you don't cancel. (No one ever thought of protecting His Holiness from their germs.) "It was incredible," sighs Mrs. Zuzul. "You know, the older boy is shy but when he saw the Pope, he ran to him and hugged him and the Pope kissed him. I felt something I never felt before; he brings with him a certain kind of peace, a glow. I've met a lot of famous and important people, but the Pope is very different. He asked about our president," she reports, "but nothing about politics." She caresses the framed picture of the Pope kissing her youngest child, two-year-old Andrija, who looks light green to me and a possible flu victim. As the daughter of a Yale nurse and physician, I'm still thinking of the germs surrounding His Holiness as 14-year-old Ivana tells me, "It was so exciting, fantastic. I had this tingly feeling. … I thought I was going to faint."

I ask the girls if they like being an ambassador's daughter. These Georgetown Day School students admit that sometimes it helps their grades when they speak up in history class and "explain the protests in Serbia." But when family arguments arise, these diplomatic daughters say that they try to turn those confrontations with their parents into "debates"—a special skill they say they learned from their father. "We play 'Let's Make a Deal,'" says Ivana.

But there is a downside when Daddy is the ambassador. "We have more freedom in Croatia … and Washington is different than Geneva. There, we went into town more," says Ivana. "And we don't see Dad as much," adds Tiona. "Most often we see him in the car on our way to school. We call that our 'morning briefing.'"

I remember what their mother said when I asked her about the disadvantages. "When he was the special envoy, we really didn't have time together. It was difficult, a tough time. He was half the time in Geneva and half the time in Zagreb or somewhere else around the world. He was gone for months." One time when he did come home unexpectedly, "the girls yelled, 'Daddy's here!' and ran to embrace him. But the youngest went to the phone, picked it up and said, 'Daddy's here, Daddy's here,' he was so used to only hearing his father's voice the phone."

It seems even ambassadors who are also parents can't escape the consequences of child-rearing from afar.

18

Macedonia: With Purple Passion

It's a wonder the new flag isn't purple. Everything else is. Her suit, her scarf, her nails, her eye shadow, even the fresh flowers sitting in front of me in this modest Washington Harbour suite on the Potomac River.

But don't be misled. This lady means business. Ambassador Ljubica Z. Acevska's passion for politics runs just as deep as her passion for purple. This top diplomat for the Republic of Macedonia, single and attractive, wants not to win attention for herself but instead appreciation for her small, Balkan country.

"It has been pure hell. I was totally ignored, isolated," Acevska complains. "I'm not used to being told, 'No.' It's not great for your ego," says the former American who spent years listening to officials in Washington from the administration, the State Department, the National Security Council and Congress all say "No" to recognizing Macedonia as an independent nation. But she finally won. "If you give up, you better not do this job," she says emphatically.

After a national referendum in 1991, Macedonia proclaimed its independence, breaking off from the former Socialist Republic of Yugoslavia. The other former Yugoslave republics—Croatia, Slovenia, Bosnia and Herzegovina—were quickly recognized in 1992 as new independent nations by the United States, according to Acevska, Macedonia's recognition was foiled by the strong American Greek lobby and opposition in the U.S. Congress.

Meanwhile back home, Greece imposed two embargoes (the first during the fall of 1992 and the second from February 1994 to September 1995) blocking any access to Greek ports for landlocked Macedonia. At the same time, UN sanctions against Serbia left Macedonia unable to export through Serbia. Hence, Macedonia was cut off from its two main trade routes.

"The embargoes paralyzed Macedonia but it did not destroy Macedonia as the Greeks thought. It showed the resistance of the Macedonians. It was more expensive but we improved roads and went through Bulgaria and Albania," says the ambassador.

Finally, on April 8, 1993, Macedonia was admitted as a member of the United Nations but only as the "former Yugoslav Republic of Macedonia." Not until February 8, 1994, was Macedonia recognized by the United States as an independent country. "It was my birthday, February 8th; they had to do it," she says cheerfully.

Ironically, through a UN effort already in place, in July 1993 the United States sent 300 American soldiers to help protect a country the United States didn't officially recognize. And more troops are there today. "That proves they [the United States] trusted us," adds Acevska, "even before they recognized us."

"We had to wait almost three and one-half years for diplomatic relations," she explains, "because of the strong Greek lobby in this country. We even had to redesign our flag," she says, pointing to the brand-new bright yellow-and-orange sunburst standing guard beside her desk. "They [Greece] still want us to change our name!" In fact, at the United Nations, monthly negotiating sessions continue between Greece and Macedonia under the watchful eye of former U.S. Secretary of State Cyrus Vance.

Greeks insist the ancient name *Macedonia* is of Greek origin and belongs only to them. They protest that the use of the name *Macedonia* by this former Yugoslavian republic could lead to territorial claims on the Greek border province, Aegean Macedonia.

"Ridiculous!" Ambassador Acevska pronounces. "We have absolutely no intention of taking over any additional territory. Macedonia is not an expansionist country. Our foreign policy is to have good relations with all our neighbors."

To make matters even worse, other neighbors—Serbia, Bulgaria, Albania and even Turkey—are also threatening a tug-of-war over this poor but strategically located former Yugoslavian republic. Serbian nationalists periodically parade through their own capital, Belgrade, shouting, "Macedonia should be Serbian!" According to this ambassador, only 2 percent of her country's population is Serbian, 4.5 percent is Turkish, almost 23 percent is "enthnically Albanian" and less than 1 percent is Bulgarian. Of the 2 million people, 1.3 million are "Macedonians" who call themselves Orthodox Christians.

Present-day Macedonia lies at the crossroads of ancient trade routes that have connected Europe, Asia and Africa for thousands of years and has often been a battlefield. The vast Ancient Macedonia of Alexander the Great (who was "Macedonian, not Greek," says the ambassador) became part of the Roman Empire in the second century B.C. Macedonia had been alternately ruled by Bulgarians, Byzantians and Serbs until the end of the 14th century, when the Turks invaded and began 500 years of Ottoman domination. Serbia, Greece and Bulgaria all laid claim to Macedonia after defeating the Turks but finally agreed to divide the area among themselves, with the current territory coming under Serb rule. When Yugoslavia was created after World War II, Serbian Macedonia became a separate republic of greater Yugoslavia.

"Macedonia is the only former Yugoslavian republic that declared its independence peacefully," she states. "We have avoided war, established competent leadership and are resolving our conflicts with Greece via political dialogue rather than through the barrel of a gun, as is typical in that region."

The ambassador is proud of her good relationship with the former Greek ambassador here in Washington. "He's a fine ambassador. It's important that the diplomats here have a good rapport so that the countries might." Acevska is particulary pleased that former Greek Ambassador Loucas Tsilas not only attended Macedonia's annual national day celebrating its independence but congratulated Acevska in person. But then, that's diplomacy. "I am flattered that Greece, with its ten million people, membership in the European Union, NATO, and a well-known ancient reputation, is scared of us.

"Only Greece was against the Republic of Macedonia being known as the Republic of Macedonia. Can everyone else be wrong and Greece be right?" she asks rhetorically. "Greeks have problems with all their neighbors. ... Privately, individuals agree with me, even some Greeks, but not publicly," she explains. "Everyone wants to accommodate Greece so they don't have to deal with them." Says Acevska, "As one ambassador told me recently, 'Ambassador, my first wife was Greek, you don't have to tell me about Greeks!'"

Ambassador Acevska walks a verbal tightrope because in diplomacy, "One word can ruin everything. And we are playing with fire. Everything is very volatile in the Balkans. Anything can set things off and all will go up in flames," says the dramatic ambassador. Munich-based Radio Free Europe has broadcast that "Macedonia could cause a greater threat to peace in the Balkans than anything else."

So why voluntarily sit in such an international hot seat? "I had no intention of becoming an ambassador," says this former American who had to give up her U.S. citizenship to become Macedonia's very first ambassador in the world and *still* the only female ambassador that represents her country. "I agreed to help in the beginning just to set up the office but I'm still here," she says, laughing.

But, not only has she had to fight for her own country's recognition, but she herself has had to battle daily to be taken seriously as an ambassador. "I

Macedonian Ambassador Ljubica Acevska, a former American citizen, between her Macedonia-born father Zivko Acevski (right) and Macedonian President Kiro Gligorov (left). Photo courtesy of Ambassador Acevska.

feel sometimes like I should wear a sash like Miss America saying 'I'm the ambassador,'" she laughs good-naturedly. Even as she stood greeting guests for Macedonia's national-day reception held in the Mayflower Hotel's historic balconied ballroom, she remembers, "People would just walk right past me and I'd hear them say, 'Gee, I guess the ambassador can't make it.' At the national political conventions, one ambassador who saw me in San Diego but didn't say anything, then saw me again in Chicago and finally admitted, 'So you are the ambassador. I thought you were only the wife of another ambassador.'

"Ninety percent of the time, people just don't believe that I'm an ambassador. And women are just as bad as men. And age doesn't seem to make any difference. Our mentality hasn't caught up with our reality." We still don't expect an ambassador to be a woman, especially an attractive, young, single woman. Even at Blair House, the official White House guest house across the street from 1600 Pennsylvania Avenue, Acevska says she was greeted before a function with, "So, are you an ambassador or just a wife?"

* * *

Although her life started in the Macedonian village of Selo Capari, she emigrated to the United States with her parents when she was only nine years old. They settled in Mansfield, Ohio, a small steel town where her great-grandfather had settled in 1917 and her grandfather in 1940.

"It was a drastic move for me. We came from a very small primitive village. Everything was new to me; it was the first time I ever saw my grandfather. It was a new language, a new life."

She vividly remembers her first day of school when everyone else was speaking English. "I was supposed to go into fourth grade, but they held me back. My teacher, Vivian VanCura, is retired now but wrote me a wonderful letter after I became ambassador. She said that, even at that time, she knew I had exceptional qualities.

"I come from very humble beginnings," she starts. "My grandfather opened a little restaurant called Chris's Cafe in 1956. My father and uncle, brother and cousin still run it. The menu is more American now, but they have Macedonian specials like goulash with chunks of chicken or beef and mixed vegetables or zelnik, traditional vegetable pie with leeks or pumpkin."

She shows me the picture of her parents and President Clinton when she finally went to present her credentials on February 6, 1996, at the White House. "They were ecstatic," she beams. "They never thought they'd be the parents of an ambassador."

She continues to weave the story of her unusual yet successful life. After graduating in international studies from Ohio State University, she taught graduate students international management and Eastern European politics and economics. She did research for her favorite professor's book, *The Other Europe,* covering the complex history and nationalist issues of Eastern Europe from 1919 to 1945. She came to Washington in 1983 to work in international development as a trade consultant for Gulf Enterprises. She supervised U.S.-based companies' Middle Eastern trade transactions and was responsible for developing international strategies for global companies whose business focused on West Africa, the Persian Gulf, the former Soviet Union and Eastern Europe.

This is when even her apartment walls were purple. She invested in art, handsome furnishings, a stylish wardrobe and drove a smooth Jaguar XJS. Her studies paid off. She made a six-figure salary and business executives, mostly men, listened intently to her advice.

Then, without Josep Broz Tito and the glue of a one-party communist state to hold it together, Yugoslavia started to disintegrate. In 1991, when Macedonia declared its independence, Ljubica Acevska just happened to mention to another Macedonian that the struggling republic should open an office in Washington to help formalize relations. Shortly after that, she was summoned to Macedonia to meet President Kiro Gligorov.

"Psychologically, it was very intimidating," she still recalls. "The day before the meeting I tried to cancel it. I was already there. I thought, who am I to do this?"

As the meeting began, "It was formal and tense," she remembers. "It was the very first time I had ever met President Gligorov. I had a Macedonian journalist with me, translating for me since my Macedonian was so primitive." There she was, an American woman, telling this famous Macedonian leader she revered and his six top advisors, "'This is what you should do.' Finally, I just said, 'Let me speak in Macedonian.' We had such rapport. I said I believed in him and his vision and that I'd like to help."

A few days later he surprised her and asked her to be Macedonia's very first diplomat. She didn't accept at first. "I didn't realize what was going on," she explains. "He had such faith in me. After all, he chose me over so many others. People he knew since they were babies and he picked me."

She came home, gave up her six-figure salary and started on her quest for full recognition for the new Republic of Macedonia. Little did she know it would be such a long and arduous job. At first, she still worked from her old office, ironically only three blocks away from Clinton's Oval Office. But there would be more than four years of hard negotiating before she ever was able to see the president and present her credentials, the first official step of any ambassador.

"It was so frustrating for me," Acevska sadly remembers. "People would say, 'I didn't see you last night' and I'd call State Department and protest. I was invited to Nixon's funeral and then uninvited," she adds. "It was depressing. All those missed opportunities. I felt like I wasn't totally fulfilling my duty.

"It took a lot of explaining. It was so hard for the people in Macedonia to understand this. I felt bad for these people. They were pursuing democracy and yet the greatest democracy in the world wouldn't establish a relationship with them."

Without official recognition, as far as the United States was concerned, she had the status of a lobbyist and therefore had to register every newspaper interview and every State Department visit with the U.S. Department of Justice. She had no embassy, no official residence and no diplomatic status.

During the same time, she was driving around Washington in her white Jaguar and dipping into her savings. (Macedonia gave her only $2,500 a month for expenses.) "It was quite a period," she laughs, "very paradoxical ... presenting the wrong image." She pauses. "But then, maybe not. I'm proof of the potential: Macedonians who make it." I thought about her coveted Medalist Award from the Alumni Association of Ohio State University, the university's highest award for its graduates.

Now that she is an ambassador she claims, "Of course, I do not plan to do this the rest of my life." She laughs. "I have this discussion with the president about leaving all the time. He ignores it totally. I tell him I need 'hardship pay,' and he just laughs. He's fantastic. That's probably why I put up with all this b.s."

* * *

Alone in her living room early one rainy Tuesday evening, we laugh and drink orange juice instead of the Macedonian wine of which she boasts because she's tired and still has another official function that night. She explains how her personal life must wait. "I simply don't have time."

No, she doesn't usually bother to take an escort. Nor does she enjoy casual dating. "It's hard for me," she explains, "to show up with someone once and someone else the next time. I like a more serious relationship." What kind of man would interest her? "First, he'd have to be successful himself," she quickly answers. That's as far as she allows her romantic side to interfere with the interview. "Sometimes I work around the clock, through weekends. Their favorite time to call the U.S. from Macedonia is 5 A.M. here."

"I have always put work first and the more successful I am, the harder I work." She admits to being an overachiever and she's not sure "how to stop working." After this, "maybe a job at the United Nations," she ponders, "as a commissioner or under-secretary working on humanitarian issues, improving mankind." She adds thoughtfully, "I like to visit nursing homes." Even though her parents are only in their early 60s now, "I like that link to the past."

We start to talk about her upcoming trip. "Oh," she sighs, "I hate to pack. As much as I travel, I still don't know how to travel," admits the popular speaker who always packs her purple jogging suit but rarely gets to hike or use the hotel's treadmill. She suspects she spends half her time out of the office, often out of town, speaking on college campuses, to think tanks, business groups, leadership conferences and at all meetings concerning the Balkans.

"The greatest tragedy is if the U.S. doesn't help the new democracies. We've had to change our whole system. Until 'yesterday,' we had paid health, guaranteed salaries. Even with the Greek embargo we've had a transformation to a market economy and, except for Greece, we are stronger [economically] than all our neighbors.

"We have many Greek businesses already. Greeks are investing in our high-grade tobacco." And there are Greek banks and lots of Greek pastry shops in Skopje, Macedonia's capital. "Our wine is better but the Greeks do have better pastry," she admits with a hearty laugh.

Now it's nearing time for me to go, and her evening is just starting. She has no help at home unless she entertains, and then she cooks gravce tavce (baked beans in a clay pot) or thick fried potatoes with lamb. The delicious maznik (feta rolled in phyllo dough) she served me came from her mother's kitchen.

The ambassador just got back from speaking at Kenyon College in Ohio, where she answered questions on Macedonia's role in the international arena and the presence of U.S. troops. "I always take lots of maps and other materials," she explains, because "so few people know anything about Macedonia. We have magnificent lakes, gentle mountains, medicinal springs, archaeological sites." How many times she must say the same things over and over again.

She shows me how she has decorated the residence with some "ultra-modern things from my 'former life.'" The Japanese art hanging over the fireplace is a gift from a friend. In her wood-paneled den, which she calls her "Macedonian Room," she shows me dolls and rugs and clay pots from her ancient culture. But next to her big chair are the latest copies of *Vogue, W* and *Harper's Bazaar,* and a purple-and-white afghan her mother knit for her.

Next, we go to the terraced garden, where on weekends, "I love to get dirt under my nails. I hate housework; I don't touch anything inside. But if the weather is nice, I'm always working in my garden or on the patio," she says, mentioning that her neighbors, the Ukrainian ambassador and his wife, are surprised to see her out there on her hands and knees. She is especially proud of her "purple roses"—"lavenda" she thinks they are called—and her purple pansies.

In the kitchen, everything's white except for purple touches of grape-colored napkins and canisters. She disappears and returns with a miniature silver shopping bag. She takes a purple cocktail napkin and lovingly wraps a jar of homemade ivar, a Macedonian red pepper sauce her mother made, and gives it to me.

We descend the front stairs together. The big, bright Macedonian flag hangs proudly over the entrance to the new residence. I drive away wondering how she does it, day after day, and alone. Five years on the front line without a vacation and still she can laugh about it.

* * *

More than two years later, after seeing each other at dozens of embassy parties and even taking a three-hour walk together one day along Georgetown's C&O Canal, we are sitting down together again, this time over lunch at the Four Seasons Hotel. When I arrive she is already seated. But I can't miss her. She's wearing a bright yellow suit with a deep purple blouse, purple pin and a big summer hat. She laughs when I accuse her of "switching colors." And she accuses me of not really writing a book, just interviewing ambassadors the rest of my life.

We decide that today's meeting should be a celebration. "Yes, yes," she quickly says, her particular way of agreeing just as you finish. I ask her, after accomplishing so much, if she's ready to move on. After all, she now has a staff of seven, including a new deputy, a wonderful old building to renovate into a real embassy, and everyone in town knows her and Macedonia. And, by the looks we're getting in this power dining room, anyone who doesn't already know her, thinks they should.

"I've had to work twice as hard," she says, shaking her long brown curled hair away from her face. "Now everybody's jealous," she says, laughing about how other ambassadors wish for her success rate. "The U.S. is our number-one ally, number two is Germany with economic support. We have great relations with Greece and concrete economic growth."

She stops eating her salmon long enough to tick off an impressive list of "American companies doing business with Macedonia: McDonald's, Coke, RJR Tobacco—we are still a big producer, textiles for Liz Claiborne, Macy's, K-Mart, TJ Max, and we export lots of lamb to Israel and our wine to Europe. Plus, we produce a lot of woolens, men's and boys' suits."

In the beginning, "We started from scratch ... always hitting brick walls. Now we have accessibility and contacts. I'm always asked, 'How have you been able to get U.S. troops to Macedonia?' and I answer, 'Skillful negotiation.' A lot has changed. I'm even letting go [of control]," she exclaims, "now that I have a deputy," and "I'm learning how to play golf!" I tell her that calls for a toast. "Yes, yes!" she agrees.

But this ambassador isn't finished yet. American troops are still needed in her homeland and Greece is still demanding a different name for her country.

"I am not a patient person," she explains. "I have had to have a goal in sight." Besides getting to keep the name *Macedonia,* Ambassador Acevska's "ultimate goal is more U.S. investments, more tourism, and President Clinton going to Macedonia."

Otherwise, nothing's changed. Now that she has a deputy, "when we go to meetings, everyone says, 'Hello, Mr. Ambassador,'" and no one believed she was the ambassador, dressed in fatigues and high heels, when she accompanied her defense minister on maneuvers in upstate New York. Yet, she wishes she had more hobbies and still believes in Macedonian President Kiro Gligorov.

"I believe in his vision and he believes in me. We believe in making a difference. He says there is no one to replace me but everyone, except the president and the prime minister, wants to represent Macedonia in Washington now."

19

SPAIN: "NO HORSE, NO JOHN WAYNE"

I first saw the Spanish ambassador and his wife at the Chinese national day celebration. Separating us was a long, long "assembly line" buffet table laden with dozens of aluminum roaster pans full of Chinese favorites. Amidst the mayhem of several hundred people reaching over one another to fill their plates, I watched this striking diplomatic couple glide through the huge room, seemingly unencumbered by the thick crowd. They are always very noticeable, because she is much taller than he is. I had heard that she was a descendent of an American diplomatic dynasty, a former international debutante and a cover girl. She looks the part.

A few weeks later at the Meridian Ball when I had the chance to ask Ambassador Antonio de Oyarzabal for an interview, he told me surprisingly, "I am shy and I don't do interviews." Then he added the real reason: "It never turns out like you think it will, so I don't do that anymore." Of course, that made me all the more determined to win and keep his trust.

My research assistant, Stephanie Kaplan, and I started calling the embassy again but just got the usual responses: "The ambassador is overbooked," "the ambassador is out of town" and "the ambassador is just too busy right now to add anything else." All probably true and words we had heard over and over again in many different accents at many different embassies over the past few years. But this time, we were not going to give up.

I had always thought theirs would be an interesting story. He, the son of a Spanish diplomat and himself a young lawyer and junior foreign service officer in Madrid, falls in love and marries. She, the tall, elegant debutante daughter of the American ambassador to Spain who herself was such a sensation that *Life* magazine featured her on its cover. And as if this weren't enough, she is from one of this country's leading political families, the Lodges of Massachusetts, who count six U.S. senators on their family tree.

Beatriz Oyarzabal's uncle, Henry Cabot Lodge, was one of America's best-known diplomats. During the mid-1960s, he was U.S. ambassador to South Vietnam, and in 1969 he was chief negotiator of the Vietnam Peace Talks in Paris. Earlier in his political career when he lost his Senate seat to future President John F. Kennedy—the eldest son of another famous political family—President Eisenhower appointed Lodge permanent U.S. representative to the United Nations. In 1960 he ran unsuccessfully for vice president with Richard Nixon on the Republican ticket, losing again to his old Massachusetts rival, Kennedy.

Another Henry Cabot Lodge, the grandfather of this ambassador to Vietnam and the great-great-uncle of Beatriz Oyarzabal, was the longtime Republican U.S. senator from Massachusetts who, following World War I, successfully rallied congressional opposition to the League of Nations. He served as the powerful chairman of the foreign relations committee and was a leading isolationist of the period.

To me, this Spanish–American match seemed like a diplomatic fairy tale. It reminded me of two other beautiful and tall American blondes, Grace Kelly and Queen Noor, both of whom fell for shorter but powerful foreign men. An international mix of the colorful conquistador with the cool patrician of privileged New England was too tempting to miss. I couldn't wait to find out the rest of the story.

When I saw them both a week later at the Papal Embassy, I grabbed the opportunity. This time I approached Mrs. Oyarzabal. She was standing next to her husband, who was just winding up a conversation on his other side. I introduced myself and told her about my book. "I would love to include Spain," I said just as he finished talking. "But, your husband," I added, moving my eyes to his, "says he is too shy."

She laughed—all handsome, long, lean six feet, one inch of her—and said, "Antonio, let's do it. It sounds like fun." Realizing, perhaps, that there was no graceful way out, he smiled and nodded, "Yes." "Call Diane at the embassy," she said quickly. "She will fix everything."

* * *

Diane Flamini has been the Spanish Embassy's social secretary for nine years and for three ambassadors. She and I had talked back in 1996 when I started my research for this book.

At that time, I was trying to catch the former Spanish Ambassador Jaime de Ojeda for an interview before he retired and left Washington. He had already been ambassador for six years. Once before in the 1960s, De Ojeda was in the United States as a young diplomat during the height of the Cold War. Then, the United States had four strategic military bases on Spanish soil and he had the defense detail.

As ambassador, de Ojeda was a colorful eccentric who was not afraid to speak out on the way things used to be and still should be in Washington's diplomatic circles. Just before he left as ambassador, he fearlessly complained to a *New York Times* reporter, Elaine Sciolino, in a May 19, 1996, story, "No one wants to go to balls anymore," and "everyone is dieting now and nobody wants to drink anymore."

On a more serious note, he explained to Sciolino that Washington's top-ranking diplomats find it almost impossible to get access to Congress and the administration but that if they did, "they [U.S. politicians] could learn a lot." He also told Sciolino, "Naturally, diplomats are very unhappy, because we feel as if we're living in Jurassic Park," suggesting that Washington ambassadors feel like dinosaurs, "administering these empty palaces."

* * *

The Spanish residence is one of those handsome old "palaces" with its own ornate ballroom and spacious indoor tiled patio built around a circular fountain. My "window" for interviews was already closed but I decided that if I got on the Oyarzabals' schedule, I must "make" the time.

As much trouble as we had scheduling the two Oyarzabals for an interview, we finally settled for a quick interview with Ambassador Oyarzabal at the chancery and tea at the residence with his wife, Beatriz, on the same day. He was leaving for Madrid immediately after our interview but somehow, "We will make it work," Diane told me. I was impressed that he was keeping his word even with such a hectic international calendar.

* * *

A Spanish policeman in a green uniform meets me in the chancery lobby but quickly goes back to joking in Spanish with two workers as I wait impatiently for a receptionist who never comes. The clock is ticking away and so is my short interview.

After reaching over the empty desk three times and calling the invisible embassy phone operator, I finally get Diane and she comes to my rescue. Although we have never seen each other in person over the past three years, we have spoken often on the phone and, oddly, this feels like a reunion.

Spanish Ambassador Antonio de Oyarzabal and Mrs. Oyarzabal in front of a tapestry woven in the 18th-century factory, Real Fabrica de Tapicaes. Photo courtesy of Mrs. Oyarzabal.

When I realize that the ambassador is still in another meeting and more of our precious interview minutes are evaporating, I ask Diane if she can meet afterward to answer any remaining questions. There isn't anything else I can do but streamline my questions and enjoy the view down Pennsylvania Avenue from his eighth-floor perch across Washington Circle from George Washington University.

At least when his door opens, this ultimate diplomat wants every moment to count. "Spain has changed dramatically," he begins, quickly explaining his country's former identity crisis. "We have accepted that Europe was our original destiny." After three decades with Franco at the helm and as dictator, Ambassador Oyarzabal concedes that Spain identified itself with Latin America and was a "marginal country of a Europe that had done quite a bit of revolutionary changes in their own internal structure. We had not." For years Spain was considered an "outsider." Not until the mid-1980s was

Spain a member of the European Economic Community, NATO or the Council of Europe—"the organizations that had changed the face of Europe." He adds, "So the moment that Franco died, we had to put our house in order."

"I took my part in this generational challenge," says this son of a distinguished Spanish ambassador who, at the time, was working in the prime minister's office. "Just by sheer luck we were there in charge of things when Franco died. We were forty, forty-five [years old], ready to take over and we were the first generation that had not suffered the trauma of the civil war and had been able to travel and compare notes," he explains.

"So we did not get along with our elders. [We were] a generation of people putting into question everything that we had heard our elders insist. When Franco died, our generation took over." But it wasn't easy. According to this ambassador, at that time it was popular for everyone to say, "Spain is different," meaning, "that the Spaniards were not prepared for a democracy." But there were elections and the younger generation prevailed. "We wanted to be as close to Europe as possible.

"The military was the most decisive element," he says, and the fact that they participated in creating the new democracy was amazing because "the army had been brainwashed for many years." In 1978 the new constitution was approved with all sides agreeing, "including those who were at that time considered enemies.

"It was exciting. Imagine what it was for the army on the first day of the new parliament," he says. There, in one day, the army was meeting with many groups that had been hiding from the law for years, including the Communist Party. "The Spanish army had always had this idea that their role in the world was to prevent Spain from falling into the hands of the natural enemy, which was communism."

"The military was in an incredible position of witnessing a communist leader, La Pasionaria, Dolores Ibarruri, the longtime communist and civil war veteran, chairing the new parliament, under the crown." According to Oyarzabal, the communists and the socialists had to accept that the monarchy had returned, peacefully, and that Spain was once again a monarchy. "A contradiction in terms," he agrees, but "there was a capitalist country well-established" and "there were rights for everybody, including the church."

"Today, we are comfortably installed in Europe." And although Spain may have "arrived late to the party," he says that for the first time, Spain has been accepted "with honors at the beginning of the next big step in Europe—the economic and monetary union." He concludes, "The approval of the European Union made a miracle for Spain—our critics disappeared into thin air."

Modern Spain is very proud of its progress. "We have a country that is growing at 3.8 percent now, inflation below 2 percent, deficit below 2 percent," he states. Spain's economy, according to Oyarzabal, "is booming because, among other things, we have learned the art of discipline" for slow but steady growth. He considers "the change in attitude, the change in mentality of the trade unions" to be a "miracle." He explains, "They have been detaching themselves from the old political links that they had and now we have modernized and efficient trade unions."

Seventy percent of Spain's trade is with Europe. "We are the fourth producer and forth exporter of cars in the world, international brands like VWs, Renaults, General Motors cars, Fords. Our main income is tourism—45 million tourists per year."

Although Spain trades with Europe, it invests in Latin America—"20 billion dollars' worth with great success," adds this ambassador. "We are very interested in the stability of Brazil, not only because of Brazil itself, but because of the domino effect on the other Latin American countries. We are very involved in creating stability with Latin America."

Ambassador Oyarzabal wants to explain, first, how Spain successfully reinvented itself, deserving role-model status for other evolving economies. Now he is about to tell me his real passion—his own personal reason to be Spain's ambassador to the United States.

"We still have a lot of historic challenges to win here. Politically, the situation [of U.S.-Spain relations] is very, very good. We have close relations. But even though only 4.5 percent of our trade goes to the States, we have mainly a cultural and historical challenge."

When I ask him to explain, he is delighted. "I think you [Americans] don't know what Spain did because we [early Spaniards in North America] have been sort of left aside," says this Spanish ambassador whose American wife comes from an old New England family. "My activity [job] is mainly to explain that Spain was part of the identity of this country [the United States]. The southern United States is typically of Spanish origin. We have not been, perhaps, treated fairly; historically, we were perhaps the nemesis. The historical doctrine is still floating around portraying the [negative] image of the conquistadors, of what Spain did in South America."

"We [the Spaniards] were perhaps the victims of a cultural clash between two cultures—the Latin Mediterranean and the Anglo-Saxon. They clashed here in the United States. We [the Spaniards] didn't get the best of it and history has been written accordingly."

Glancing at his watch, he starts to gather up his trip papers, then locks his desk and motions for me to join him as he walks to the elevator. He graciously apologizes, saying that he must be in Barcelona for tomorrow's biannual U.S.-Spain Council meeting and that planes don't wait anymore for ambassadors.

Later, I realize that his timing is perfect, just a few concluding moments to set up his favorite line to make sure I never forget Spain's contributions to the United States. "The horse arrived in the United States by the hands of the Spanish," he begins. "Imagine the importance of the horse in the history of this country [the United States]. I always say, 'No horse, no John Wayne!'"

As he opens his door, top embassy staffers start to appear, vying for a moment of his time before the elevator arrives. But it is Diane, speaking fluent Spanish, who checks the last detail with him as she leans into the elevator. Then she waves and says, "Okay, bon voyage" as the doors close and he disappears.

"Okay, bon voyage?" I say, dizzy from our fast-paced conversation jumping from English to Spanish and now French. We laugh together and she ushers me into their handsome conference room where we sit at the corner of a big table, catching our breath from the last hour's frantic pace. We sit here for more than an hour talking about everything and everyone, even the ambassador's whimsical tie collection. Without knowing it, we sit and chat right through lunch.

Immediately, I realize that Diane is much more than the ambassador's social secretary. She is his friend and has known both of the Oyarzabals since they were married. Diane was also an American teenager in Madrid (her father was head of Gulf Oil there) when her friend "Bea" (Beatriz Anna Cabot Lodge) met the future diplomat who would become her husband. But it took the ambassador six years to woo her. "Ask Bea," she advises. "She'll love to tell you the details."

Today, Beatriz Oyarzabal and Diane are still "close friends" even though they are in an interesting working relationship where they each take turns telling each other what needs to be done. Without question, Diane has the ear of the ambassador and his best interest at heart. When they are alone, she always calls the Ambassador simply, "Antonio." "He calls me 'Dianilla,' 'Little Diane' or 'Diana-Chan,' which is a Japanese greeting, since he was four years in Tokyo."

I tell her how impressed I am that when he is catching a plane, he still takes the time to talk to me, making sure I understand why Americans should not just accept but appreciate what the Spanish explorers and traders did for this country. "He is a dying breed of ambassadors," she says proudly. "He's a very good speaker, never uses notes. But, for those of us who hear him speak all the time, we tell him that he's repeating the same speech over and over again. Of course, the audiences don't care; it's the first time they're hearing it!"

"You know," she says, "the ambassador was orphaned at eight?" I look at Diane incredulously. This ambassador who is so polished, so thoughtful, so much the example of "proper upbringing," is an orphan? I just can't believe it. "His father was a very distinguished diplomat. His mother and father were taking a train from Berlin to Paris to return to Madrid. And, on the same train was the German high command and the French resistance blew it up. He was brought up by his aunts and went to boarding school at Le Rosey in Switzerland."

By contrast, the ambassador is a very hands-on father of a big and hyperactive family. "You'll see," she says, referring to my upcoming afternoon interview with the ambassador's wife. "There is always something going on. They are endearingly discombobulated. Bea refers to them as, 'my crazy family,' but I'll just say that you'll have a entertaining time at tea."

"You know they have six children, the oldest is 36 and the youngest are twin boys going to college here and there is one grandchild!" Diane explains, "Each child looks exactly like one parent or the other," adding, "tall like their mother or more like Antonio—three blondes and three brunettes." Only Tammy, or Matilda, who works for a law firm here, looks like both of them.

Not quite ready to totally leave the subject of the ambassador, I ask this senior aide if Oyarzabal has a Latin temper. What does this man of Basque heritage do when he gets angry? "The ambassador is a saint. He rarely gets mad but he can be quite an explosive father." I am surprised with her candor and remind myself to check what information is for "background" and what I can quote.

When I mention that I thought the Lodges were devout New England Protestants she answers, "Oh, Bea is a 'born again Catholic.' She converted herself to Catholicism when she was 17 before she even met the ambassador. Very devout, she goes to mass every day and is very active with her religion."

Diane goes on to say that, even though Bea is the wife of an ambassador, she is the kind of mother who "takes in" her children's friends and "every stray child who wants to learn Spanish." Especially now that all their children are living away from home, this is her way to fill their empty nest."

Bea, born in London, was "the darling of her parents," according to Diane. Her father, John Lodge, was a Hollywood actor. Her mother was a dancer; her sister Lily runs a New York actors' studio. After Hollywood, John Lodge became a politician and was the governor of Connecticut. When he lost his bid for the U.S. Senate, President Dwight Eisenhower appointed him ambassador to Madrid.

I look at my watch and I'm shocked. Diane and I have talked for over an hour and if I'm not careful, I will be late for tea. Now, I can't wait to meet this American woman who calls Spain home but still carries an American passport, who raised six children but "borrows" more and who wears Oscar de la Renta originals but always checks the racks at Filene's Basement.

* * *

Diane had told me exactly what to do. Because of the deteriorating neighborhood, the embassy was forced to install a black iron fence around the white stone mansion but I was welcomed to push the call button and park inside, under the portico. I'm early for tea as requested by Mrs. Oyarzabal so she can go shopping with their daughter Tammy.

The butler meets me at the front door and ushers me into the grand entrance hall where life-size formal portraits of deposed Spanish King Alfonso XIII and his wife, Queen Victoria Eugenia, greet me. Portraits of other Spanish royals are here, but my favorite is the oval-shaped painting of the coat of arms of King Charles III, which belonged to the Spanish legation in Philadelphia in 1798. Don Diego Gardoqui, who became a personal friend of George Washington, headed the mission. Even the rug is regal; the design is modern but it was woven in the Royal Factory of Tapestries (Real Fabrica de Tapices) in Madrid. Spain's palaces are filled with rugs and tapestries woven by this 18th-century factory.

As we enter the main sitting room, another life-size portrait, this one of Beatriz as a young beauty and her dog, hangs over the massive fireplace. Family pictures in silver frames vie for my attention, but the big wooden-framed cover of *Life* magazine, July 9, 1956, over in the far corner wins my eye. "An American Beauty and Diplomatic Daughter in a Spanish Debut," reads the banner above the glamorous picture of a handsome pageboy blonde looking coyly over her ribboned shoulder.

The butler has disappeared to get me tea and I can't resist looking for the fountain; I've been hearing it since I arrived and the relaxing waterfall has me transported to the Iberian Peninsula. Twenty minutes later, Beatriz Oyarzabal enters with a great flourish, her little dachshund, Benson, "trumpeting" her arrival as he circles in excitement. She finishes directing an aide in Spanish before she dramatically apologizes to me in English. She is as lean as she is tall, wearing a narrow, short leather skirt. At 60, she's still got it.

I ask how she and her husband met. Turns out it was not love at first sight at all. "Another Antonio who was Portuguese introduced us," she begins the complicated but colorful story of their six-year on-and-off courtship. It seems their first dinner together was anything but romantic and she left shortly thereafter for boarding school in Barcelona. "He wrote to me all that year and asked to see me when I came home. But the night that we were supposed to go out," she makes a grimace, "someone else called me and I really wanted to go out with him. So, I told Antonio I was sick. He saw me leaving with this other young man and wrote me a note saying, 'If you don't want to see me, just tell me. Don't lie to me.'" The story goes on and on. But mainly he won her heart after he returned from law school all trim and polished. "He conquered me by his tremendous elegance; he was very much a gentleman, he respected me."

Just then, I hear rustling and several voices speaking Spanish, and in walks the ambassador! "My plane was delayed so I am taking a later plane," he announces, kissing his wife quickly and crossing the room to sit down next to me. "But I don't think I finished answering some of the things you asked me," he says as he starts exactly where he left off in his office four hours ago. Mrs. Oyarzabal leaves the room, making sure that he has something to eat and drink.

"My main concern here is to correct this wrong perception that people have of the role of Spain. [We're] handicapped by not having a correcting element in American society. We have never had a big ethnic community in the United States like the Italians, the Irish, the Greeks, the Danes, the Germans—they are all a strong presence in America."

Mrs. Oyarzabal sits down again when the phone rings across the large room and she's up again to answer. She's talking in Spanish and the ambassador and I are still speaking in English.

"Antonio," she says, nodding to me an apology for interrupting, "it's all about your flights. Come and talk with them," she explains as she holds the phone out to him. We wait and listen to his staccato conversation. Then Mrs. Oyarzabal comes back to sit with me, and we begin again. However, when I suggest that their marriage is a mixture of their two cultures, he responds first, having just hung up the phone and crossing back to join us. "People here in America, they ask her, 'Where are you from?' So that means she has an accent in all languages!" We all laugh.

Several more times in the next few minutes the phone rings and she answers in Spanish while the ambassador and I continue our conversation on the other side of the room. At least one call is about her family estate in Marbella, which they are regretfully selling. "The taxes are just too much," says the diplomatic wife who, as a U.S. citizen, still has to pay American income and property taxes.

I ask what the ambassador, the embassy and Spain are doing to change this old conquistador image in 1998, exactly a century since the Spanish-

American War. "We are making a big effort in education of quality. Over three years, we have two thousand official teachers of the public system in Spain coming here to teach. We have sixteen to eighteen agreements already with American public schools—here in D.C. recently, New York, Connecticut, and Miami. We have four hundred fifty to six hundred teachers here this year."

Now, he must go. While we are talking, Mrs. Oyarzabal slips out again in the direction of the kitchen. Alone, I glance at my watch and realize I should have already left to be on time for another interview, with the new ambassador of Luxembourg. Mrs. Oyarzabal reappears and realizes her husband has left. She calls out, "Antonio, you aren't leaving without saying 'Good-bye' are you?" Now, from the other room, he answers in Spanish and she, satisfied, comes to sit next to me again. When I mention that I thought she was going to go shopping with her daughter, she says, "Oh, we went shopping yesterday. She's already in Spain today. I have time to show you around now. You know we redid the embassy when we came; it was so dilapidated."

I ask her about the three diplomatic men in her life: her father, her uncle and her husband. "My uncle was caring, loving, kind, elegant and incredibly intelligent. He was lots of fun and a great humanitarian." She continues: "I'm very proud of my heritage. I'm very proud of my family and what my family achieved, the tremendous patriots that they were. Both my father and my uncle gave themselves entirely to their country and I'm very proud of that."

Earlier she had told me, "My husband has no hang-ups from being an orphan. Of course, when we started having so many children he asked, 'What are we doing?'" Now, in comparison with her father, she thinks her husband "is very easy to live with, very patient, has a lot of inner peace. He's a lot easier to live with than my father, who was very high-strung, a genius but difficult, strict. I was fearful of him."

I try to piece our interview back together. What does she call "home"? "When I got married, my father knew the minister of foreign affairs and by my father's request, I was the first foreign wife allowed to keep my nationality. Since I haven't lived here since I was 16, I don't identify myself as an American. But I do identify with Spain especially. I love it dearly. You know, when my father was ambassador it was 1955 under Franco. It was very dark and they were very poor, just coming out of a civil war. Now, it's so exciting: Spain is so prosperous, they are part of the EU, and in all sorts of ways the economy has expanded and improved."

In closing, I ask her if being the ambassador's wife in Washington is different than she had expected. "It's more demanding than I thought," she answers. "Here, you expect an embassy to play a major role and that's hard to convey to the government. Our allowance isn't that great and sometimes we have to say, 'No.' I've never been so involved in fundraising of so many charities. This is a tremendous opportunity to meet people at all these marvelous parties. And the traveling part; I didn't know the U.S. was so big," says this striking American woman.

I am now writing and walking as she gives me a quick tour of the refurbished ballroom, draped in red silk with antique Spanish tapestries. "We have a big family room upstairs; Antonio has his desk there and often works while I read. We have lots of phone calls and faxes from the children but no e-mail yet," says this devoted mother of six who likes to hear her children's voices too much to consider e-mail.

When we say good-bye, I get my first glimpse of the rush-hour traffic. I'm afraid to look at my watch. As I drive past the front door, I wind down my window to wave and she says, "Nice car." This American woman, born in London, raised in Connecticut, introduced to "society" in Paris, schooled in Barcelona and Madrid, but married in Morristown, New Jersey, is all about style.

20

LAST DANCE: NEW PARTNERS

Just as my final deadline approached, I discovered several newly arrived ambassadors who had wonderful stories to tell. Since diplomacy in Washington is an ever-changing dance (during my more than three years of interviewing, Israel had three different ambassadors), why not "break in" on some diplomatic dancers who are just too interesting to leave out.

CYPRUS: MORNING COFFEE WITH E-MAIL

I have always been intrigued by those countries that are not exactly friendly with another and, in fact, are not even on speaking terms but may be neighbors on Embassy Row. For example, Turkey, which refuses to recognize the legitimacy of the internationally recognized Government of Cyprus, is only a quick walk around Sheridan Circle from the Embassy of Cyprus. But because Turkey does not recognize the Cypriot government, some Turkish ambassadors won't even speak to their Cypriot colleagues, even if they end up at the same party. The island of Cyprus has remained divided since 1974, when Turkish troops invaded and occupied the northern half.

When I heard the new Cypriot ambassador was a woman—a highly unusual appointment for this part of the Mediterranean—I wanted to find out more. Dr. Erato Kozakou-Marcoullis and I first met at her front door. There she was in colorful native dress greeting guests for Cyprus's national day after only being in Washington one month.

Later, when I mention how much I enjoyed the Cypriot specialties, she apologized for having to use a local Cypriot caterer. "Whenever I can I will cook myself. In Stockholm (her immediate past post), I personally cooked—with my Filipino housekeeper—the food and desserts for four hundred people.

Cyprus Ambassador Erato Kozakou-Marcoullis and her DCM Andreas Kakouris and Mrs. Kakouris. Photo by Larry Luxner.

We made six hundred sweets of three different kinds—that's eighteen hundred pieces! I enjoy cooking," she says, beaming. "We are a small country but we have a long history and tradition. And, I want to keep our roots and transmit everything to the younger generation."

* * *

When I see Ambassador Kozakou-Marcoullis at the embassy later, she is dressed in a red-and-black business suit, Chanel style, and is just as warm and gracious, even on the subject of Turkey.

"I am an optimist," she says, hoping "to welcome the new millennium with the solution. I think it would be a shame if we bring this unsolved problem—with such tragic consequences [into the new century]." She hopes the potential for Cyprus's EU membership serves as a catalyst, adding an urgency and focus to solve the bloody division.

"It needs a lot of effort and determination, but it can be done. Let's see: Ten years ago there was the Cold War, two Germanys, the Soviet Union, Apartheid in South Africa. We had so many ongoing conflicts that have now found their way to a solution. If you talked at that time about these dramatic changes that transformed Europe and beyond, they would have said that you're crazy. That is why I am personally optimistic. I believe in our people: the Greek-Cypriots and the Turkish-Cypriots deserve a better future." I am struck by her demeanor—how she is calm and passionate at the same time.

Although Ambassador Kozakou-Marcoullis agrees that it may be "especially unusual" to have a woman from her part of the world in this top post, she thinks she has "a great advantage in diplomacy," because women are positive thinkers, work without frustration, have calm characters and "understanding how people feel."

But she agrees that "a woman in such a demanding job needs a lot of support and I have it." She is in constant touch with her son, Panos, who is a political science major in Ann Arbor, Michigan, and her husband, George, who is a physician in Cyprus. "Every morning we exchange e-mails. We copy everything to our son and he copies everything to us. So, it's my morning coffee and e-mail."

"My son introduced me to e-mail. He came to Sweden a year and a half ago and brought me a laptop. I didn't know how to type; it changed our life completely." Now she spends any free time she has surfing the Web to find her way around Washington's power maze. "It's a wonderful tool of learning, with such easy access," says this lawyer with a Ph.D. in political science and sociology.

As a mother, she sees the conflict at home from her son's perspective. "My vision is to have this island—with such long history, tragic most of the time, rich as far as culture—reunited so we can work, live and cooperate together. My son is 21 years old and he has never met with Turkish Cypriots a few meters away! That's tragic, a shame, no excuse," says this ambassador whose own mother was born in Russia.

This optimistic ambassador hopes that maybe through some alternative approach she can make some human connection. It has happened that way before she confides in me. "Women make a difference," she vows. "Women come to conclusions faster together; we have so many common denominators."

In Sweden, her former post (where she was also accredited to Finland, Norway, Denmark, Iceland, Estonia, Latvia and Lithuania), she traveled constantly but still found her group of 14 female ambassadors, out of a total of 90 in Stockholm, a constant "support system." She adds, "In Sweden, it was easier because 50 percent of the government is women." Here, she is determined to help Washington's top female diplomats—usually around a dozen out of approximately 170 foreign ambassadors—to meet regularly.

When I ask her what keeps her going, so far away from her family and in an uphill diplomatic battle, she has a ready answer. "It's a mission, not a job—there is a difference. Otherwise, I probably couldn't do it. Maybe, because we have a cause, a goal. If it were just a profession, probably I would have decided not to do it."

She thanks me for coming and holds her arms out to hug me goodbye—-an unusual ending for a formal first interview. Then, she asks me where

I buy my clothes, and we end up planning to go shopping together someday. When I ask if she'd like to come to my next party, she smiles and suggests, "You're going to invite the Turkish ambassador, aren't you?"

ICELAND: READY TO CELEBRATE

This ambassador and his wife—from a cold, physically isolated island—are so likeable, fun, and interesting that once you meet them you will never feel the same way about Iceland again.

Ambassador Jon Baldvin Hannibalsson, a Fulbright Scholar, has been a deep-sea trawler fisherman, a high school teacher, a journalist, a college president and, for much of his life, a politician who served as Iceland's minister of foreign affairs under two different prime ministers.

"I am not a diplomat," says this son of a politician, "I retired into diplomacy and I find it so civilized in comparison to the wild life of political jungle where you are fighting for survival, day-to-day." He gives me an impish wink and picks up his glass. We are sitting in their living room, fat candles flicker in their fireplace and good wine lightens our mood at the end of a busy day.

Iceland's first lady in Washington is Bryndis Schram, an author, actress, linguist, former TV anchor, beauty queen (Miss Iceland at age 17) and once Iceland's prima ballerina whose sense of style is indisputable.

Together, they are like fireworks going off at close range. You feel the electricity. Quick wit and deep devotion to their country make this conversation like a Victor Borge concert: underlying seriousness with light-hearted repartee.

"Our mission here is to introduce our country so Americans get to know us," she says of her island nation, often called "a stepping stone to Europe."

"We are worn-out warriors, Iceland and her four Nordic neighbors—all democratic and independent—but we are happy warriors," he adds with a twist. "Incidentally, *Happy Warriors* happens to be the name of a hilarious historical novel of war and conquest by our Icelandic Nobel laureate, Halldor Laxness. He makes great fun of our *big* warriors, our *big* heroes."

Many in this city's diplomatic circles knew of this ambassador before he ever arrived in Washington. Ambassador Hannibalsson was an early champion for NATO's restoration of independence to the Baltic States, and he was the first foreign minister in the world to recognize Croatia as a sovereign nation in 1991. "It was the same day as the Pope's recognition," proudly says Croatian Ambassador Miomir Zuzul. "The United States was four days later."

As different as Ambassador Hannibalsson and his wife are from each other, together they are entertaining, clever and *never* boring. And, they are adamant about making one thing perfectly clear: It is Leif Eriksson, not Chris-

Icelandic Ambassador Jon Hannibalsson and his wife, Bryndis Schram, with her Icelandic cousins at Islendingadagur (The day of the Icelanders). The world's oldest parliament building is pictured in the background. Photo courtesy of Bryndis Schram.

topher Columbus, who discovered America. In 1964, the U.S. Congress acknowledged this fact and proclaimed every October 9 "Leif Eriksson Day." The year 2000 is a wonderful excuse to celebrate the 1,000th anniversary of that first Viking voyage and make their point clear, once and for all.

The Smithsonian Institution is creating a unique millennial exhibition entitled "West-Viking: The North Atlantic Saga," which is scheduled to open April 15, 2000, and is endorsed by the White House Millennium Council. And this ambassadorial home will be party central.

"We have the oldest relationship with North America; we were the first Europeans to reach your shores 1,000 years ago—500 years before Columbus!" he says with appropriate bravado. "We have hard evidence," he adds.

"And," she begins, "the most recent scholarship proves that the expedition was co-led by an Icelandic lady, Gudridur Thorbjarnardottir, probably the greatest female explorer in history, who, in the early eleventh century, became the mother of the first child of European descent born on the American continent."

"And," he adds proudly, "the Canadian Museum of Civilization in Ottawa has decided to erect a statue in her memory for our 1,000th anniversary."

Moving on to more personal matters, I ask them how their marriage has lasted so well for 40 years. After all, she has had so many different careers all these years while he has been a major politician. Plus, they are the parents of four children and grandparents of five.

"Being married to a politician messes up everything," she says immediately. "The way I survived is just by doing my things. I went on as if I was

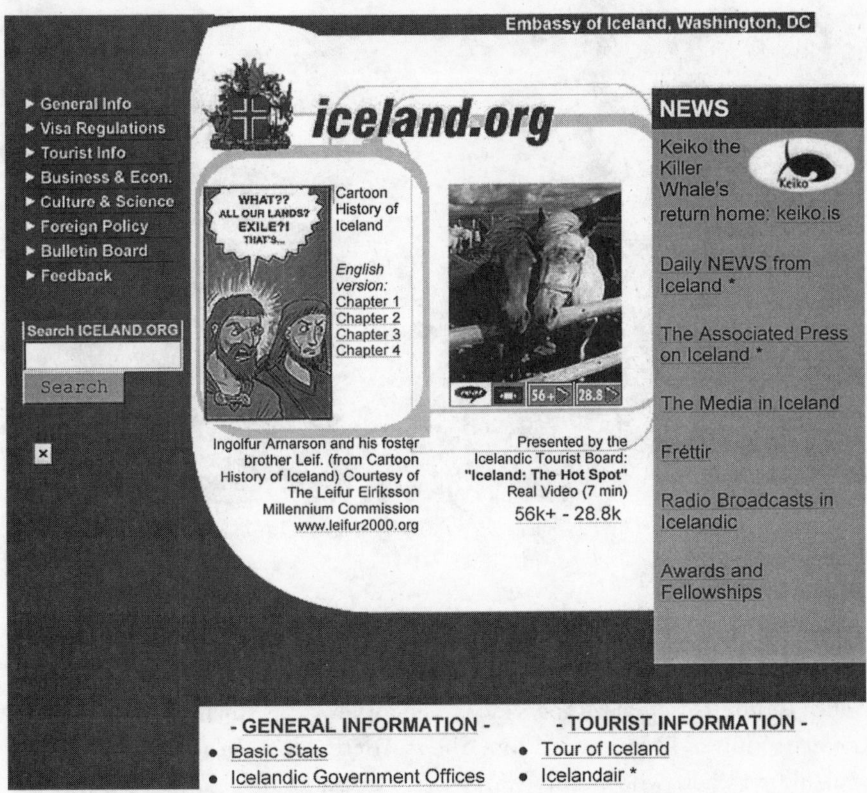

The Embassy of Iceland's website homepage, the first embassy website. Original artwork by Webmaster and designer Stefan Gudjohnsen of GlobeScope.

alone. So many women get angry at their husbands for not helping with the children and that arguing can just be so tiring. So, I just acted on my own, taking care of my work and the children."

Now I'm curious how they met. This time, Ambassador Hannibalsson fields the question. He leans back and, mocking a serious pose, says, "I first saw her from behind." His eyebrows go sky-high and we all laugh. They both jump in to explain that he sat two rows behind her in school when they were both 15 and became good friends. Two summers later, when she was just 17 years old, she entered and won the "Miss Iceland" title and went off to Long Beach, California, to compete in the "Miss World" beauty pageant. He strongly disapproved of what he calls "her misdemeanor." That summer, when he was doing hard construction work on the telegraph line, "I first heard about it [her entrance into a beauty contest]. I remember walking to the nearest village, about a two-hour walk away, to send her a telegram. It said, 'Shame on you.' We didn't talk to each other for a year."

Didn't I say they weren't boring?

Luxembourg Ambassador Arlette Conzemius Paccoud and her family in their neighborhood. Photo courtesy of Ambassador Paccoud.

LUXEMBOURG: DANCING DOUBLE TIME

The new ambassador to the United States from the Grand Duchy of Luxembourg is the first female ambassador in history for this small European country steeped in old-world tradition. She is Arlette Conzemius Paccoud, a 42-year-old mother, who modestly says, "The fact that I come from a small country allowed me to become an ambassador at my age."

Her highly successful diplomatic career has been much watched since, at age 37, she represented Luxembourg to the Council of Europe, a group of 40 countries that monitors human rights, democracy and the rule of law. She served as deputy chief of mission during her first posting to Washington from 1989 to 1993.

"Now Luxembourg has ambassadors who are women at the United Nations and in China," Ambassador Paccoud says as a matter of fact. "But since I had the rank of ambassador in Strasbourg at the Council of Europe, I alone was the only woman for five years. Frankly, it was my turn. No one put me ahead of anyone else," says this petite woman. "You always have people who are envious when you have such a nice posting like Washington." Recently, through her own foreign service grapevine, she heard that a colleague in another foreign post complained, "It's only women who get the nice appointments now."

Ambassador Paccoud, who calls herself a feminist and supports women's issues, thinks it's time to "repair the imbalance." She explains, "Worldwide we need more women in all sectors—We represent 50 percent of mankind, why not?" She also thinks "it is important for women to be responsible and help each other."

It is at the end of a normal workday as we sit in her spacious, dark-paneled, high-ceilinged office in the particularly handsome mansion on Massachusetts Avenue, which Luxembourg purchased years ago to be its embassy and residence. She has graciously agreed to talk with me before her evening events begin.

"Now we have a residence, a family home in Spring Valley, which was bought several years ago when another ambassador came with his two sons. The house is not prestigious but we do have a small backyard and a swimming pool. Here, we are right on this busy street," says the grateful mother who is happy she has a quiet neighborhood for her family.

Like other working parents, Ambassador Paccoud says, "It's a challenge to keep up both lives, because it is true you can never stop being a mother or having a household. But I have learned to delegate quite a few of my duties."

In order to help her take full advantage of her career possibilities, her husband, Thierry Paccoud, chose to be a consultant in international development aid and assistance and to maintain a home office. His independent work arrangement gives this young family what they need most: flexibility in his schedule and mobility to move with his wife and children (Antoine, age 14, and Olivier, age 11) anywhere in the world. In addition, the Paccouds have "an au pair, who is more than a traditional nanny," to help with the boys' homework, grocery shopping and driving, while a housekeeper does most of the cooking.

During the week, Ambassador Paccoud finds it often impossible, like this night, to get home for dinner or even before her sons' bedtime. "But Sundays are the days we are always together, only the family. Not even the boys' friends. We go hiking and spend the day outside as much as we can."

No matter how late the prior evening goes, this busy mom "always gets up with them at 7:30 or 8 before school but can't drive them to school "because it's in the opposite direction." She "fights her feelings of guilt" but says, "I try to remember that for them *this* is normal." Born herself in Kinshasa, when it was the former Belgian Congo, Ambassador Paccoud says, "I was used to living abroad since I was in nursery school. It was 'normal' for me too." She is happy her sons are proud of their mother, the ambassador. "They were with me when I presented my credentials—and they are proud of themselves." But she admits the family has had to make one minor concession: "Sadly, we have no pets."

This graduate of the Fletcher School of Law and Diplomacy is proud to represent her tiny but important EU country (less than 1,000 square miles, bordering Belgium on the west, Germany on the east and France on the South) in the heart of Western Europe. As ambassador, "the biggest problem is that we have to find ways to get some interest in Luxembourg," she says frankly. "The U.S. and Luxembourg traditionally have been allies and friends. But Congress is more difficult because they go by their interests."

Speaking of Congress, I ask her to comment on President Clinton's nomination of James C. Hormel for U.S. Ambassador to Luxembourg and the Senate Foreign Relations Committee's refusal to vote before the deadline, therefore killing Mr. Hormel's chances. A former University of Chicago Law School dean, an heir to the Hormel meat-packing fortune and a San Francisco philanthropist, Hormel is openly homosexual.

"We're not discussing the substance of the matter," she says diplomatically. "When the U.S. government asked for an *agrement,* for us it was not an issue. We do all we can to not discriminate on any basis." I am impressed with her straightforward answer.

When I ask about her goals here as ambassador, she gives an honest response. "I have to have realistic ambitions," she says, admitting that her job is mostly promoting her country, "in the best way that I can on the cultural scene and economically."

Ambassador Paccoud still runs into Americans who say, "Luxembourg, where is that, in Germany?" So she doesn't worry about spending much time within the diplomatic community like she might in another world capital. "Here, it is just the opposite: the objective is to meet as many Americans as you can and not to stick with your diplomatic colleagues.

"I know we are a small country," she says, "but Luxembourg is a country that has, in a way, a bigger importance than the size would let you think." Ambassador Paccoud is proud that her country, the size of Rhode Island, was a founding member of the European Union and NATO. "We had only to gain by joining the European Union. We had no other option. How could we survive? We need the markets; we need all the advantages of the bigger union."

Her secretary interrupts to say she has less than ten minutes to get to the Kennedy Center for her event: a foreign film festival featuring a Luxembourg film. We get up immediately and quickly gather our belongings, putting on our coats and gloves as we continue to chat while descending the grand staircase together.

"Whenever I can, I try to combine my interests and find an excuse to go to a gallery, museum, concert or some cultural event." I smile, knowing that she is doing just that tonight.

Her driver is waiting as we step outside and shake hands. "I wish you were coming with me," she says. "That way, we could keep talking." The car door closes, but before her big, shiny black sedan melts into the evening traffic, I see her turn and wave through the back window.

Ecuadorian Ambassador Ivonne A-Baki and her award-winning painting, "Beyond the Veil." Photo by Gail Scott.

ECUADOR: CREATING IMAGES

An artist, Ecuadorian Ambassador Ivonne A-Baki is as passionate about her country as she is about her paintings. She thinks art and diplomacy are much alike. "Through art, you work with feelings and through diplomacy, you work with words, the art of speaking. I think the brain, heart and hand should be working together," she says, explaining how she tries to achieve success, diplomatically.

Although she has never been an ambassador before, she has been a major peace negotiator for her country and an honorary consul general. "My husband is Lebanese and during the war I lived there, and our children were born there. That's why I care so much for peace. I am against wars. They can't do anything except kill everything. Violence can only generate violence.

"Often in extreme political movements, the real problem is oppression," says this experienced negotiator. "You have to include the people, listen to the people. There is never just one single solution. You have to find out what they really want, like when a child really wants something. It doesn't matter how many people they kill. They just say, 'Come and see us and bring CNN.' They want the world's attention above all else."

But in regular negotiations, "We have to have to find something that is good for everyone, some balance." In reference to the recent settlement of her country's almost 60-year border dispute with Peru, she says, "When we have agreements between countries, nothing is 100 percent right but we always try to go for a 'win-win result.'"

Ambassador A-Baki may be passionate about peace, but she herself is a bombshell. Dressed in an open-collared shirt and a gray pantsuit, her short jacket and stretch pants reveal her toned figure. This mother and grandmother moves like the trained dancer she is, whether sitting down in a chair, leaning over the front of her massive desk to catch the phone or showing me her huge paintings on all four walls. From her long, flowing auburn hair to her gray high heels, this woman is striking. She shows her emotions, gestures widely and speaks and moves with great energy.

Later, she admits to me that she not only took ballet from the time she was very young but still works out with weights, uses a Stairmaster and goes to aerobic classes.

Throughout our interview, Rimsky-Korsakov's *Scheherazade* is seducing me into thinking I'm someplace else. Together we enjoy the musical interlude in the middle of a hectic day. "I love the music of different countries!" she exclaims.

As an award-winning international artist, Ambassador A-Baki studied art in Paris, Vienna and Berlin and received a bachelors degree in architecture from the Arab University in Beirut. In 1991, she founded the Harvard Foundation for the Arts. "I regularly combine my two worlds, the arts and diplomacy, by organizing monthly cultural and political events at Harvard and here to promote peace in the world," she adds.

"Women know the value of life. Because of this position [being ambassador], I am having to act tough, make tough decisions. But you have to be what you are. I am not a traditional diplomat, I am not going to change. People must accept me the way I am," says this intellectual with a masters degree from Harvard's Kennedy School of Government, where she won a prestigious Mason Fellowship in 1992–93.

"I am a free spirit, always have been and I think there are no limits to what the individual can be and do. I identify myself as an artist," she explains. "But nothing is static and I like challenges and difficulties. I don't need more than three hours sleep, never have.

"I paint at night. That's when I'm creative. I write poetry then too. And after midnight, it's time for me and my daughter, Tatiana," a 24-year-old Harvard graduate who is a writer, and an artist and lives at the residence. Ambassador A-Baki's eldest, 30-year-old Mohammad Manolo, a Princeton undergraduate with a Ph.D. from Yale in mathematical economics, lives in

Manhattan with his wife and two babies, where he works for Merrill Lynch. Her middle child, 28-year-old Faisal Alexander, is a Harvard economist and lives in Ecuador.

"I love living, meeting people, because when I am with people I can see their issues," she says, admitting that being an ambassador has been "an opportunity to put *more discipline* in my life."

Before I leave, Ambassador A-Baki wants to make sure I know what "a very special country" Ecuador is. She calls her homeland "a true paradise" but admits there is still much to do to fight poverty and achieve social and economic development.

"Ecuador is an amazing clean place, no drugs, peaceful people centered and connected with our God," says this woman, who left her South American country at age 15 to visit Lebanon. She returned to the Middle East one year later to marry her current husband, Sami Baki, who along with his family "has always been involved in politics."

"Ecuador has many faces, great music, the best beaches and gorgeous mountains." She makes me hungry describing the luscious exports: bananas (number-one banana exporter), shrimps, mangoes and asparagus, for which her country is known worldwide. "We have the best roses—the best quality. Because of our location on the equator, we have the most light and the stems are straighter and thicker."

"I love Ecuador," this dramatic woman says, eyes flashing. "I think it is the best country in the world." She smiles and adds, "I also belong here."

Epilogue

Three years ago when I started my research for this book, Japan and the Pacific Rim countries were riding the tidal wave of economic prosperity, Madeleine Albright was herself an ambassador and Secretary of Commerce Ron Brown was helping to invent commercial diplomacy. Russia's fledgling market economy was on the path to liberalization and most of us had never heard of Monica Lewinsky. Not one Washington embassy had a website, few embassies took security seriously and diplomatic license plates in Washington usually meant you didn't get punished.

As I write this now, the Asian financial crisis needs a new name as it infects economies worldwide and as Americans watch their foreign investments with a cautious new attitude. Madeleine Albright, now this country's first female secretary of state, continues to talk tough, wear brooches that signal her mood to world leaders and serve as an inspiration to the growing number of top women diplomats worldwide, including Washington's female ambassadors. The tragic death of Secretary of Commerce Ron Brown and more than a dozen prominent American business leaders helped dramatize how today's diplomacy is often about trade. And, Russia is anything but a successful economic model of capitalism. In the meantime, President Clinton still tries to talk his way out of his national embarrassment.

Today, more than 100 of Washington's approximately 170 embassies proudly boast websites, embassy security is no joke following the Japanese Embassy hostage crisis in Peru and when a Georgian diplomat was handed over by his own country to American courts and convicted of killing a Washington-area woman while intoxicated and speeding, the Washington diplomatic corps was abruptly reminded that diplomatic immunity is not tantamount to civic irresponsibility.

A lot has happened in three years that has dramatically affected diplomacy here and abroad. In fact, often I've felt like I was covering a moving target. As a former TV anchorwoman who began in radio, I regularly found myself wanting to do daily updates. At times, it has been a struggle to keep my words and the quotes I chose meaningful in today's world of fast-paced diplomacy.

Over and over again, I actually heard ambassadors give a big sigh of relief when I told them I wasn't there just to get a "pull quote" on their crisis du jour. In fact, I was personally and professionally pleased that so many of the ambassadors and their spouses and the embassy diplomats and staff members trusted me enough to go "off the record" and invite me to return for more casual times together.

I have been extremely careful not to quote anyone unfairly, considering that many of today's diplomats have not had a lot of experience with Western media. To avoid any "international incidents," almost all of the interviews were taped by me and often by the embassies themselves.

I began my research not knowing how this book would start and end and which ambassadors would be our guest storytellers. But I did know that the world and diplomacy had completely transformed since the end of the Cold War with the popularity of CNN and the instantaneous dissemination of news around the globe, and that cyberspace communication would make protected e-mail the diplomatic pouch of the millennium.

Where once there was the giant and scary Soviet Union that reached from the eastern edge of the Bering Straits to the Baltic Sea, there are now 15 different countries with 15 separate governments represented in Washington by 15 unique ambassadors in 15 distinct embassies. And since the demise of the Soviet Union, the former Yugoslavia has disintegrated into a handful of new nations that still are struggling, but nevertheless evolving.

Being the ambassador of one of these brand new Balkan countries wasn't always easy. I will never forget Slovenia's very first ambassador, Dr. Ernest Petric, telling me how discouraging it was when he first arrived in 1991 with his wife and young daughter.

"I needed to set up an embassy and a residence. We were living in a hotel and my daughter cried every day, because she couldn't go to school," remembers this distinguished lawyer and university professor. "We found a house and my daughter was all excited," he recounts. "But when I told the real estate agent that I was the Slovenia Ambassador and that I would pay in cash, they didn't trust me. No one had ever heard of Slovenia."

Five years later in 1997, when he returned to his young country, this extremely hard-working and passionate ambassador had been vindicated.

Slovenia was being featured in American television ads as a foreign country that deserved the attention of sophisticated American investors.

Only Germany had officially merged two countries into one and is, in fact, still struggling to accommodate the disparities between the former West and East Germany. I understood the tension having seen firsthand, as a teenager, the infamous Berlin Wall and the stark realities for East Berliners.

Talking with former East German Christiane Hohmann, the first female diplomat to serve in Washington as part of the new *united* German diplomatic corps, I realized the obligation she felt to perform *beyond* expectations so that no one would ever say, "Oh, she's *just* an East German."

So I knew the diplomatic dance floor was more crowded than ever, and I expected more competition among ambassadors vying for attention. I even predicted more "grand-standing" by a few impatient or aristocratic or just plain arrogant members of the diplomatic corps.

I understood and was not surprised by certain embassies' lack of cooperation due to small, overwhelmed staffs or unfamiliarity with Western media. For example, in response to the original letter that I sent to all ambassadors (and their press counselors/attachés), one small country called to ask, "How much does it cost to be in your book?" That question, asked innocently, probably was a direct result of being bombarded with requests from well-connected lobbyists and slick public relations firms who required big retainers, promising all kinds of access and visibility.

Often overenthusiastic embassy "gatekeepers" were just protecting their ambassador's calendar and privacy from me. I was delighted when two proactive, enlightened ambassadors made it a point to call me themselves in response to my query. Several others quickly wrote back, offering their assistance, understanding that my request for information and an interview was an opportunity for their country.

Still others "officially" agreed to be interviewed but never found the time. One ambassador, whom I finally won over with the persuasion of his savvy American wife, tried to excuse himself by saying, "I'm too shy."

Of course, one of the most interesting things about spending three years doing such a project is to contrast and compare the differences among the ambassadors and their embassies and even the differences between two ambassadors from the same country. Israel's Itamar Rabinovich was a thoughtful academic who was one of the country's top negotiators; his wife was a research scientist who went to laboratories of the National Institute of Health every day, having little time to entertain. Rabinovich's successor, Ambassador Eliahu Ben-Elissar, was an outspoken, feisty politician whose wife, Nitya, was a dramatic storyteller and spent her days with Israeli charities. She initiated ecumenical Bible studies at the Israeli residence but loved to "run away" to Washington's museums and cultural events.

Even the two British ambassadors had very different styles. Sir John Kerr, KCMG, and Lady Kerr were the expected, proper British diplomats who together welcomed me graciously to a cup of tea and a warm fireside chat at the residence. In comparison, Sir Christopher Meyer, KCMG, and Lady Meyer, younger and in their first year of marriage, met me much more casually and spoke more candidly. She, dressed in khaki slacks and a black pullover, was nursing a bad ankle, the result of a mishap during an embassy tennis tournament. He, at the office in shirt sleeves and his signature bright-colored socks, was the only ambassador I met who wore a picture ID hanging on a chain around his neck.

From how the phone is answered (some embassies play native music while you wait "on hold") to whether you must submit questions in advance, ambassadors and their spouses display a myriad of personal styles.

But what I didn't expect were the staffers who knew better but were repeatedly unresponsive or "too busy" to get the proper word to their ambassador. If you are one of those ambassadors, I'm sorry we didn't get to hear your story. Or, if you are the diplomat or staffer who tried to convince your ambassador to "dance" with me but didn't succeed, thank you for trying.

When I began, Warren Christopher was the secretary of state and the late Ron Brown was leading the Commerce Department. I knew "public" and "commercial" diplomacy were redefining this age-old profession, but those changes became even more dramatic when Madeleine Albright became secretary of state and Ron Brown's widely reported and tragic death emphasized his worldwide mission.

To commemorate the late commerce secretary's work and to further promote "commercial diplomacy," his family and friends have established the Ronald H. Brown Foundation, which is based in Washington and headed by his son, Michael.

As a former broadcaster and media coach, I understand how any successful ambassador must be comfortable speaking English almost to the point of being glib. However, longtime Latvian Ambassador Ojars Kalnins, now dean of the European corps and a former Chicago advertising and marketing executive, is especially equipped to take full advantage of any spotlight. To prove how important "public" diplomacy has become and how crucial media relations are for a Washington ambassador, several major embassies are headed by former government spokespersons: the British and the German embassies to name just two.

Which reminds me how and when the Monica Lewinsky–President Clinton scandal finally seeped into polite diplomatic conversation. At the

September 1998 Ambassador's Ball, held for the last 20 years as a black-tie benefit for the National Multiple Sclerosis Society, even ambassadors, who all curry favor with President Clinton, went "public" with their opinions.

It all started when Ambassador Kalnins was quoted by James Morrison in *The Washington Times* as saying: "In reflecting on President Clinton's present crisis, I think it is important to put it into a broader perspective. President Clinton has been an effective leader in the international arena and a good, reliable friend and partner to many countries around the world. However, the future of President Clinton is up to the American people. They must decide whether they want him to continue to lead or not. In most foreign capitals, the story now isn't so much what the President did, but what the American people will do in response."

Another unexpected transition took place during the writing of this book and reflects the latest development in the communication revolution in our society and in the world—the World Wide Web. When I began, not one embassy had a website, and we were rushing to the rescue with a top-heavy directory. Now, a growing number of embassies have customized cyber billboards. Whether you want to simply get a visa or do business and live abroad, these new embassy portals are open 24 hours a day, seven days a week.

In fact, today the world is virtually on *one* time. At least, the world of diplomacy is. CNN and other worldwide news outlets have forced Washington's diplomats to be on a 24-hour schedule. I remember how the wife of the Egyptian ambassador sleeps with earplugs and an eye mask to hide from all-night CNN and the fax machine in their bedroom.

As a result of the takeover of Japan's embassy in Peru and the bombings of American embassies in Kenya and Tanzania, embassy security in Washington has become much tighter. When visiting an embassy, always take proper ID with you and expect to be delayed at the door. Although I was never searched, several embassies walked me through the x-ray devices and asked to look in my briefcase. As expected, the Israelis are the most zealous and their chancery felt most like a fortification. They have two checkpoints now and always have "extra eyes" on the street.

When discussing yet another pending crisis in Iraq, U.S. Defense Secretary William Cohen was asked how long diplomacy would continue as a means of resolution before the United States unleashed its military might. In response, Secretary Cohen commented that "diplomacy should have every opportunity to dance. But at some point, a dance has a beginning and an end."

And so it goes for this dance. I have enjoyed every step.

Glossary

Diplomacy, like many other fields, has its own language and "insider's talk." For example, a "secretary" in diplomacy may be someone who does secretarial work, such as the ambassador's personal secretary, but it also may mean a diplomatic position of career rank within the embassy such as the first or second secretary, with first secretary having a higher position. Knowing the language of diplomacy is the first step toward joining the *diplomatic dance.*

Agrément: Request for approval of an ambassador by the host country.

Ambassador, E. and P.: Ambassador Extraordinary and Plenipotentiary.

Attaché: A member of the embassy staff often assigned to a specific duty such as the press attachè or defense attachè.

Casual Dress: Not black-tie. In embassy circles, this refers to business attire.

Chancery: The embassy office; often a separate building.

Charges D'Affaires: A member of the embassy staff (usually the deputy chief of mission) who temporarily assumes control of the mission in the event that the ambassador travels outside the post country; literally "in charge of affairs" in the ambassador's absence.

Chief of Protocol: Highest ranking American official in charge of "national etiquette" and housed in the U.S. State Department's Office of Protocol. Usually a presidential political apointee.

Commercial Diplomacy: Negotiation in the pursuit of business and financial interests regarding the commercial relationships between nations.

Consul: Designated head of consulate.

Consulate (Consular Posts): Embassy office(s) not in the capital city of the host country that provides services such as visas and travel information.

Counselor: High-ranking member of an embassy staff.

Credentials: Letters of accreditation that an ambassador presents to the head of state of the host country. Upon presentation of credentials, an ambassador's term officially commences.

Deputy Chief of Mission (DCM): The second-ranking individual in an embassy, second only to the ambassador. When the ambassador travels outside the country, the DCM most often becomes the charges d'affaires.

Dean of the Diplomatic Corps: The ambassador who has served at a post for the longest *consecutive* period of time.

Diplomat: Governmental envoy who represents his or her country's interests and may conduct international negotiations in a foreign country; either often a career diplomat or political appointee.

Diplomacy: The art and practice of international negotiation.

Diplomatic Immunity: The general principle of international law that waives the right of the host government to prosecute criminal offenses committed by diplomats in their host country. Protection under the law can be waived in the event that the head of state of the sending country revokes immunity and condones the diplomat's indictment.

Diplomatic Pouch: A secure envelope used to transport documents between an embassy and the sending country; often contains classified materials.

Dossier: A compilation of documents.

DPL Tags: Diplomatic license plates assigned to the vehicles of all foreign diplomats residing in the United States.

Embassy: The official location of a foreign mission, usually in a building or office, in the capital city of each nation. According to international law, an embassy is considered sovereign territory of the sending nation.

Envoy: A governmental emissary sent on a mission abroad in order to negotiate, arbitrate or represent the views of the sending country (e.g., former President Jimmy Carter and former senator Bob Dole have been "special envoys" to international hot spots).

European Union: Formerly known as the European Community (EC), an economic organization of European states established in 1957 for the purpose of enhancing trade and lowering barriers to trade among the member countries.

Economic and Monetary Union (EMU): An economic community that establishes a common currency, the euro, and harmonizes fiscal policies for the participating European nations.

The Group of Eight (G8): The assembly of eight industrialized nations that meet at annual summits for the purpose of addressing prevalent political and economic issues that affect both domestic and international realms. G8 members are: France, Britain, the United States, Germany, Japan, Italy, Canada and, most recently, Russia. Prior to Russia's addition in 1998, the seven participating nations were labeled the G7, or Group of Seven.

Legation: A foreign mission that is not considered a full embassy.

Meritocracy: A promotion system based upon merit, performance and ability without regard to race, religion, gender or class; epitomized by the Singapore culture.

Minister: Embassy staffer that has the high rank of minister.

Minister-Counselor: Embassy staffer who has the rank of minister but only deals with consular matters.

Ministry: Government department and/or building in which such a government department is located (e.g., the foreign ministry).

National Day: A day of national celebration that varies from country to country. Usually takes place on the occasion of a nation's independence, a royal birthday, or significant anniversaries. Foreign missions often host large gatherings at the embassy in celebration of their respective national days (e.g., the Fourth of July in the United States).

North American Treaty Organization (NATO): A collective security alliance, established by the Atlantic Pact in 1949 after World War II, between the United States, Canada, Belgium, Britain, Denmark, France, Germany, Greece, Italy, Iceland, Luxembourg, the Netherlands, Norway, Portugal and Turkey.

Organization of American States (OAS): Established in 1948 in order to coordinate the political, economic and military activities of the participating states in North and South America, including the United States and several Latin American, South American and Caribbean nations.

Protocol: The rules and proper etiquette governing the conduct of diplomatic relations as well as official government and business functions.

Sauna Diplomacy: Diplomatic meetings conducted in a sauna in an effort to rapidly induce compromise due to the brief duration one can remain in a sauna; a method especially employed by the Finns.

Secretary: An embassy staff member; not to be confused with the position of receptionist or the high-ranking American cabinet officials. Embassy secretaries are often ranked by seniority (i.e. first secretary, second secretary, etc., with the first secretary being the highest rank).

Vice-Dean: The second-most senior ambassador to serve at a single post.

Visa: Written permission to enter and travel within the territory of a country. The ambassador and their staff, as representatives of their country, issue visas that can be obtained by contacting the appropriate embassy. Visas are often not necessary between friendly nations.

Appendix 1

EMBASSY DIRECTORY

The following directory is as complete and accurate as possible at the time of this book's publication. Embassies are continually adding new websites, and changes occur every day in Washington's Embassy Row.

AFGHANISTAN

Embassy of the Republic of Afghanistan (Embassy ceased operations August 28, 1997 [2341 Wyoming Avenue NW, Washington, DC 20008].)

Capital: Kabul. National Day: August 19. Currency: Afghani. Language: Pashtu, Dari Persian (both official), Turkic. Religion: Sunni Muslim (84%), Shia Muslim (15%). Location: Southwest Asia. Neighbors: Pakistan (E, S), Iran (W), Turkmenistan, Uzbekistan, Tajikistan (N), China (NE). Government: In transition.

ALBANIA

Embassy of the Republic of Albania: 2100 S Street NW, Washington, DC 20005.

Phone: (202) 223-4942. Fax: (202) 628-7342. E-mail: albaniaemb@aol.com.

Capital: Tirana. National Day: November 28. Currency: Lek. Language: Albanian, Greek. Religion: Muslim (70%), Albanian Orthodox (20%), Roman Catholic (10%). Location: Southeastern Europe. Neighbors: Macedonia (E), Adriatic and Ionic Seas (W), Yugoslavia (N), Greece (S). Government: Multiparty system, emerging democracy.

ALGERIA

Embassy of the Democratic & Popular Republic of Algeria: 2118 Kalorama Road NW, Washington, DC 20008.

Phone: (202) 265-2800. Fax: (202) 667-2174. *Website: http://www.algeriaun.org/msiepage. E-mail: embalgus@cais.com.

Capital: Algiers. National Day: November 1. Currency: Dinar. Language: Arabic (official), French, Berber dialect. Religion: Sunni Muslim (99%) state religion. Location: Northwestern coast of Africa. Neighbors: Tunisia, Libya (E), Morocco (W), Mauritania, Mali, Niger (S), Libya, Tunisia (E). Government: Republic.

---

* = website is not embassy-based

ANDORRA

Consulate of the Principality of Andorra: Two United Nations Plaza, 25th Floor, New York, NY 10017.

Phone: (212) 750-8064. Fax: (212) 750-6630.

Capital: Andorra la Vella. National Day: September 8. Currency: French franc, Spanish peseta. Language: Catalan (official), French, Castilian. Religion: Roman Catholic. Location: Southwestern Europe, in Pyrenees Mountains. Neighbors: France (N, E), Spain (S, W). Government: Parliamentary democracy.

ANGOLA

Embassy of the Republic of Angola: 1615 M Street NW, Suite 900, Washington, DC 20036.

Phone: (202) 785-1156. Fax: (202) 785-1258. Website: http://www.angola.org.

Capital: Luanda. National Day: November 11. Currency: Kwanza. Language: Portuguese (official), Bantu. Religion: Roman Catholic (38%), Protestant (15%), indigenous (47%). Location: Southwestern Africa. Neighbors: Zambia (E), Congo (formerly Zaire) (NE), Namibia (S). Government: Multiparty democracy (transitional).

ANTIGUA AND BARBUDA

Embassy of Antigua and Barbuda: 3216 New Mexico Avenue NW, Washington, DC 20016.

Phone: (202) 362-5122. Fax: (202) 362-5225. *Website: http://www.membeeeuu.-mrecic.gov.ar.

Capital: Saint John's. National Day: November 1. Currency: East Caribbean dollar. Language: English (official), local dialects. Religion: Anglican (predominant), Protestant sects, Roman Catholic. Location: Eastern Caribbean Sea. Neighbors: Saint Kitts and Nevis (W), Guadeloupe (Fr.) (S). Government: Parliamentary democracy.

ARGENTINA

Embassy of the Argentine Republic: 1600 New Hampshire Avenue NW, Washington, DC 20009.

Phone: (202) 238-6400. Fax: (202) 238-6471. Website: http://www.emu=eeeuu.-mrecis.gov.ar.

Capital: Buenos Aires. National Day: May 25. Currency: Peso. Language: Spanish (official), English, Italian. Religion: Roman Catholic (90%). Location: South America. Neighbors: Chile (W), Bolivia, Paraguay (N), Brazil, Uruguay (NE). Government: Republic.

ARMENIA

Embassy of the Republic of Armenia: 2225 R Street NW, Washington, DC 20008.

Phone: (202) 319-1976. Fax: (202) 319-2982. Website: http://www.armeniaemb.org.

Capital: Yerevan. National Day: September 21. Currency: Dram. Language: Armenian (official). Religion: Armenian Orthodox (94%). Location: Southwestern Asia. Neighbors: Azerbaijan (E), Turkey (W), Georgia (N), Iran (S). Government: Presidential republic.

AUSTRALIA

Embassy of Australia: 1601 Massachusetts Avenue NW, Washington, DC 20036.
Phone: (202) 797-3000. Fax: (202) 797-3168. Website: http://www.austemb.org.
Capital: Canberra. National Day: January 26. Currency: Australian dollar. Language: English (official), indigenous. Religion: Anglican (26%), Roman Catholic (26%), other Christian (24%). Location: Southeast Asia. Neighbors: Indian Ocean (S, W), Pacific Ocean (E); nearest states are Indonesia, Papua New Guinea (N), Soloman Islands, Fiji, New Zealand (E). Government: Federal parliament.

AUSTRIA

Embassy of Austria: 3524 International Court NW, Washington, DC 20008.
Phone: (202) 895-6700. Fax: (202) 895-6750. *Website: http://www.austria.org.
Capital: Vienna. National Day: October 26. Currency: Schilling. Language: German (official), Slovene, Croatian, Hungarian. Religion: Roman Catholic (85%), Protestant (6%). Location: South central Europe. Neighbors: Slovakia, Hungary (E), Liechtenstein, Switzerland (W), Germany, Czech Republic (N), Italy, Slovenia (S). Government: Federal republic.

AZERBAIJAN

Embassy of the Republic of Azerbaijan (temporary): 927 15th Street NW, Suite 700, Washington, DC 20005.
Phone: (202) 842-0001. Fax: (202) 842-0004. Website: http://www.azembassy.com.
Capital: Baku. National Day: May 28. Currency: Manat. Language: Azeri (official), Turkish, Russian, Armenian. Religion: Shia Muslim (70%), Sunni Muslim (17%), Russian Orthodox (5.6%), Armenian Orthodox (2%). Location: Southwestern Asia. Neighbors: Caspian Sea (E), Georgia, Russia (N), Armenia (W), Iran (S). Government: Constitutional republic.

BAHAMAS

Embassy of the Commonwealth of The Bahamas: 2220 Massachusetts Avenue NW, Washington, DC 20008.
Phone: (202) 319-2660. Fax: (202) 319-2668. E-mail: bahemb@aol.com.
Capital: Nassau. National Day: July 10. Currency: Bahamian dollar. Language: English (official), Creole. Religion: Baptist (29%), Anglican (23%), Roman Catholic (22%), other Christian. Location: Archipelago of islands off the eastern coast of Florida. Neighbors: Nearest countries are the United States (W), Cuba (S). Government: Independent state within Commonwealth of Nations.

BAHRAIN

Embassy of the State of Bahrain: 3502 International Drive NW, Washington, DC 20008.

Phone: (202) 342-0741. Fax: (202) 362-2192. Website: http://www.usembassy.com.bh.

Capital: Manama. National Day: December 16. Currency: Dinar. Language: Arabic (official), English, Farsi. Religion: Shia Muslim (70%), Sunni Muslim (30%). Location: Southwestern Asia. Neighbors: Saudi Arabia (W), Qatar (E). Government: Monarchy.

BANGLADESH

Embassy of the People's Republic of Bangladesh: 2201 Wisconsin Avenue NW, Suite 300, Washington, DC 20007.

Phone: (202) 342-8372. Fax: (202) 333-4971.

Capital: Dhaka. National Day: March 26. Currency: Taka. Language: Bangla (official), English. Religion: Muslim (83%), Hindu (16%). Location: South Asia. Neighbors: India (W, N, E), Myanmar (formerly Burma) (SE). Government: Parliamentary democracy.

BARBADOS

Embassy of Barbados: 2144 Wyoming Avenue NW, Washington, DC 20008.

Phone: (202) 939-9200. Fax: (202) 332-7467. E-mail: barbados@oas.org.

Capital: Bridgetown. National Day: November 30. Currency: Barbadian dollar. Language: English (official). Religion: Protestant (67%), Roman Catholic (29%). Location: Atlantic Ocean. Neighbors: Nearest are Saint Lucia, Saint Vincent, the Grenadines (W). Government: Parliamentary democracy; Queen Elizabeth II is chief of state.

BELARUS

Embassy of the Republic of Belarus: 1619 New Hampshire Avenue NW, Washington, DC 20009.

Phone: (202) 986-1604. Fax: (202) 986-1805.

Capital: Minsk. National Day: July 27. Currency: Belarussian ruble. Language: Belarussian (official), Russian. Religion: Eastern Orthodox (60%). Location: Northeastern Europe. Neighbors: Latvia, Lithuania (N), Ukraine (S), Russia (E), Poland (W). Government: Republic.

BELGIUM

Embassy of Belgium: 3330 Garfield Street NW, Washington, DC 20008.

Phone: (202) 333-6900. Fax: (202) 333-3079. Website: http://www.diplobel.org/usa.

Capital: Brussels. National Day: July 21. Currency: Belgian franc. Language: Dutch (Flemish), French, German. Religion: Roman Catholic (75%), Protestant and other (25%). Location: Northwestern Europe on the North Sea. Neighbors:

Netherlands (N), Luxembourg, Germany (E), France (S), North Sea (W). Government: Constitutional monarchy.

BELIZE

Embassy of Belize: 2535 Massachusetts Avenue NW, Washington, DC 20008.

Phone: (202) 332-9636. Fax: (202) 332-6888.

Capital: Belmopan. National Day: September 21. Currency: Dollar. Language: English (official), Spanish, Maya, Garifuna (Caribbean). Religion: Roman Catholic (62%), Protestant (30%). Location: Eastern coast of Central America. Neighbors: Mexico (N), Guatemala (W, S). Government: Parliamentary democracy.

BENIN

Embassy of the Republic of Benin: 2737 Cathedral Avenue NW, Washington, DC 20008.

Phone: (202) 232-6656. Fax: (202) 265-1996.

Capital: Porto Novo. National Day: August 1. Currency: CFA franc. Language: French (official), Fon, Yoruba. Religion: Indigenous (70%), Muslim (15%), Christian (15%). Location: Western Africa on Gulf of Guinea. Neighbors: Togo (W), Burkina Faso, Niger (N), Nigeria (E). Government: Republic.

BHUTAN

Consulate General of the Kingdom of Bhutan: Two United Nations Plaza, 27th Floor, New York, NY 10017.

Phone: (212) 826-1919. Fax: (212) 826-2998. Website: http://www.bhutan/info/org.

Capital: Thimphu. National Day: December 17. Currency: Ngultrum. Language: Dzongkha (official), Tibetan and Nepalese dialects. Religion: Lamaistic Buddhist (75%) (state religion), Hindu (25%). Location: South Asia, eastern Himalayas. Neighbors: India (W, S), China (N). Government: Monarchy.

BOLIVIA

Embassy of the Republic of Bolivia: 3014 Massachusetts Avenue NW, Washington, DC 20008.

Phone: (202) 483-4410. Fax: (202) 328-3712. E-mail: bolembus@erols.com.

Capital: La Paz (administrative), Sucre (judicial). National Day: August 6. Currency: Boliviano. Language: Spanish, Quechua, Aymara (all official). Religion: Roman Catholic (95%), Protestant. Location: West central South America. Neighbors: Peru, Chile (W), Argentina, Paraguay (S), Brazil (E, N). Government: Republic.

BOSNIA AND HERZEGOVINA

Embassy of the Republic of Bosnia and Herzegovina: 2109 E Street NW, Washington, DC 20037.

Phone: (202) 337-1500. Fax: (202) 337-1502. Website: http://www.bosnianembassy.org.

Capital: Sarajevo (Bosnia), Mostar (Herzegovina). National Day: NA. Currency: Yugoslav New Dinar. Language: Serbo-Croatian (official). Religion: Slavic Muslim (44%), Orthodox (31%), Catholic (15%), Protestant (4%), other (6%). Location: Southeastern Europe. Neighbors: Croatia (N, W), Yugoslavia (S, E), Adriatic Sea (SW). Government: Democratic republic (emerging).

BOTSWANA

Embassy of the Republic of Botswana: 1531–1533 New Hampshire Avenue NW, Washington, DC 20036.

Phone: (202) 244-4990. Fax: (202) 244-4164.

Capital: Gaborone. National Day: September 30. Currency: Pula. Language: English (official), Setswana. Religion: Indigenous (50%), Christian (50%). Location: Southern Africa. Neighbors: Namibia (N, W), South Africa (S), Zimbabwe (NE); Botswana claims border with Zambia (N). Government: Parliamentary republic.

BRAZIL

Brazilian Embassy: 3006 Massachusetts Avenue NW, Washington, DC 20008.

Phone: (202) 238-2700. Fax: (202) 238-2827. Website: http://www.brasilemb.org.

Capital: Brasilia. National Day: September 7. Currency: Real. Language: Portuguese (official), Spanish, English, French. Religion: Roman Catholic (70%). Location: Eastern South America. Neighbors: French Guiana, Suriname, Guyana, Venezuela (N), Colombia, Peru, Bolivia, Paraguay, Argentina (W), Uruguay (S). Government: Federal republic.

BRUNEI

Embassy of the State of Brunei Darussalam: 2600 Virginia Avenue NW, Suite 300, Washington, DC 20037.

Phone: (202) 342-0159. Fax: (202) 342-0158. E-mail: tupong@erols.com.

Capital: Bandar Seri Begawan. National Day: February 23. Currency: Dollar. Language: Malay (official), English, Chinese. Religion: Muslim (63%), Buddhist (14%), Christian (8%). Location: Southeast Asia. Neighbors: Malaysia (E, S, W). Government: Independent sultanate.

BULGARIA

Embassy of the Republic of Bulgaria: 1621 22nd Street NW, Washington, DC 20008.

Phone: (202) 387-7969. Fax: (202) 234-7973. Website: http://www.bulgaria.com/embassy/wdc. E-mail: bulgaus@access.digex.net.

Capital: Sofia. National Day: March 3. Currency: Lev. Language: Bulgarian (official), Turkish. Religion: Eastern Orthodox (90%), Judaic, Armeno-Georgian,

Muslim (3%), Catholic, Protestant. Location: Southeast Europe, Balkan Peninsula. Neighbors: Romania (N), Black Sea (E), Turkey, Greece (S), Macedonia, Yugoslavia (W). Government: Republic.

BURKINA FASO

Embassy of Burkina Faso: 2340 Massachusetts Avenue NW, Washington, DC 20008.
Phone: (202) 332-5577. Fax: (202) 667-1882.
Capital: Ouagadougou. National Day: December 11. Currency: CFA franc. Language: French (official), indigenous. Religion: Muslim (50%), Roman Catholic (10%), indigenous (40%). Location: West Africa, south of the Sahara. Neighbors: Mali (NW), Niger (NE), Benin, Togo, Ghana, Cote d'Ivoire (S). Government: Republic.

BURUNDI

Embassy of the Republic of Burundi: 2233 Wisconsin Avenue NW, Suite 212, Washington, DC 20007.
Phone: (202) 342-2574. Fax: (202) 342-2578. E-mail: burundiembassy@erols.com.
Capital: Bujumbura. National Day: July 1. Currency: Franc. Language: Kirundi, French (both official), Swahili. Religion: Roman Catholic (62%), indigenous (32%), Protestant (5%). Location: Central Africa. Neighbors: Rwanda (N), Congo (formerly Zaire) (W), Tanzania (E, S). Government: Transitional.

CAMBODIA

Embassy of Royal Cambodia: 4500 16th Street NW, Washington, DC 20011.
Phone: (202) 726-7742. Fax: (202) 726-8381. E-mail: cambodia@embassy.org. Website: http://www.embassy.org/cambodia.
Capital: Phnom Penh. National Day: November 9. Currency: Riel. Language: Khmer (official), French. Religion: Theravada Buddhist (95%). Location: Southeast Asia. Neighbors: Thailand (W, N), Laos (NE), Vietnam (E). Government: Constitutional monarchy.

CAMEROON

Embassy of the Republic of Cameroon: 2349 Massachusetts Avenue NW, Washington, DC 20008.
Phone: (202) 265-8790. Fax: (202) 387-3826.
Capital: Yaounde. National Day: May 20. Currency: CFA franc. Language: English, French (both official), indigenous. Religion: Indigenous (51%), Christian (33%), Muslim (16%). Location: Between west and central Africa. Neighbors: Nigeria (NW), Chad, Central African Republic (E), Congo, Gabon, Equatorial Guinea (S). Government: Republic.

CANADA

Embassy of Canada: 501 Pennsylvania Avenue NW, Washington, DC 20001.

Phone: (202) 682-1740. Fax: (202) 682-7726. Website: http://www.cdn-embwashdc.org.

Capital: Ottawa. National Day: July 1. Currency: Dollar. Language: English, French (both official). Religion: Roman Catholic (46%), United Church (12%), Anglican (8%). Location: Northern North America. Neighbors: Arctic Ocean (N), Greenland (NE), Atlantic Ocean (E), United States (S), Pacific Ocean (W). Government: Confederation with parliamentary democracy.

CAPE VERDE

Embassy of the Republic of Cape Verde: 3415 Massachusetts Avenue NW, Washington, DC 20007.

Phone: (202) 965-6820. Fax: (202) 965-1207. Website: http://www.capeverde-usembassy.org.

Capital: Praia. National Day: July 5. Currency: Cape Verdian escudos. Language: Portuguese (official), Crioulo. Religion: Roman Catholic fused with indigenous beliefs. Location: Atlantic Ocean, off west tip of Africa. Neighbors: Nearest are Mauritania, Senegal (E). Government: Republic.

CENTRAL AFRICAN REPUBLIC

Embassy of Central African Republic: 1618 22nd Street NW, Washington, DC 20008.

Phone: (202) 483-7800. Fax: (202) 332-9893.

Capital: Bangui. National Day: December 1. Currency: CFA franc. Language: French (official), Sangho (national), Arabic, Hausa, Swahili. Religion: Protestant (25%), Roman Catholic (25%), indigenous (24%), Muslim (15%). Location: Central Africa. Neighbors: Chad (N), Cameroon (W), Congo Republic, Congo (formerly Zaire) (S), Sudan (E). Government: Republic.

CHAD

Embassy of the Republic of Chad: 2002 R Street NW, Washington, DC 20009.

Phone: (202) 462-4009. Fax: (202) 265-1937. Website: http://www.chadembassy.org.

Capital: N'Djamena. National Day: August 11. Currency: CFA franc. Language: French, Arabic (both official), Sara, Sango, more than 100 others. Religion: Muslim (50%), Christian (25%), indigenous (25%). Location: Central North Africa. Neighbors: Libya (N), Niger, Nigeria, Cameroon (W), Central African Republic (S), Sudan (E). Government: Republic.

CHILE

Embassy of Chile: 1732 Massachusetts Avenue NW, Washington, DC 20036.

Phone: (202) 785-1746. Fax: (202) 887-5579. Website: http://www.chile-usa.org.

Capital: Santiago. National Day: September 18. Currency: Peso. Language: Spanish (official). Religion: Roman Catholic (89%), Protestant (11%). Location: South America. Neighbors: Peru (N), Bolivia (NE), Argentina (E). Government: Republic.

CHINA

Embassy of the People's Republic of China: 2300 Connecticut Avenue NW, Washington, DC 20008.
Phone: (202) 328-2500. Fax: (202) 328-2582. Website: http://www.china-embassy.org.
Capital: Beijing. National Day: October 1. Currency: Renminbi (Yuan). Language: Mandarin (official), Yue, Wu, Hakka, Xiang, Gan, Minbei, Minnan. Religion: Atheist (official), Buddhist, Taoist, some Muslim, Christian. Location: East Asia. Neighbors: Mongolia (N), Russia (NE, NW), Afghanistan, Pakistan, Tajikistan, Kazakhstan (W), India, Nepal, Bhutan, Myanmar, Laos, Vietnam (S), North Korea (NE). Government: Communist.

COLOMBIA

Embassy of Colombia: 2118 Leroy Place NW, Washington, DC 20008.
Phone: (202) 387-8338. Fax: (202) 232-8643. Website: http://www.colombiaemb.org.
Capital: Bogota. National Day: July 20. Currency: Peso. Language: Spanish (official). Religion: Roman Catholic (95%). Location: Northwestern South America. Neighbors: Panama (NW), Ecuador, Peru (S), Brazil, Venezuela (E). Government: Republic.

COMOROS

Embassy of the Federal and Islamic Republic of the Comoros; (temporary) care of the Permanent Mission of the Federal and Islamic Republic of the Comoros to the United Nations: 336 E. 45th Street, 2nd Floor, New York, NY 10017.
Phone: (212) 349-2030. Fax: (212) 619-5832.
Capital: Moroni. National Day: July 6. Currency: Franc. Language: Arabic, French, Comoran (all official). Religion: Sunni Muslim (86%), Roman Catholic (14%). Location: Three islands—Grande Comore (Njazidja), Anjouan (Nzwani), and Moheli (Mwali)—in the Mozambique Channel between northwestern Madagascar and southeastern Africa. Neighbors: Nearest are Mozambique (W), Madagascar (E). Government: In transition.

CONGO (FORMERLY ZAIRE)

Embassy of the Democratic Republic of Congo: 1800 New Hampshire Avenue NW, Washington, DC 20009.
Phone: (202) 234-7690. Fax: (202) 237-0748.
Capital: Kinshasa. National Day: June 30. Currency: Congolese franc. Language: French (official), more than 400 dialects. Religion: Christian (70%), Muslim

(10%), Kimbanguist (10%). Location: Central Africa. Neighbors: Republic of the Congo (W), Central African Republic, Sudan (N), Uganda, Rwanda, Burundi, Tanzania (E), Zambia, Angola (S). Government: Republic with strong presidential authority (in transition).

CONGO REPUBLIC

Embassy of the Republic of the Congo: 4891 Colorado Avenue NW, Washington, DC 20011.

Phone: (202) 726-5500. Fax: (202) 726-1860.

Capital: Brazzaville. National Day: August 15. Currency: CFA franc. Language: French (official), Lingala, Kikongo, other indigenous. Religion: Christian—mostly Roman Catholic (50%), indigenous (48%), Muslim (2%). Location: West central Africa. Neighbors: Gabon, Cameroon (W), Central African Republic (N), Congo (formerly Zaire) (E), Angola (SW). Government: Republic.

COSTA RICA

Embassy of Costa Rica: 2114 S Street NW, Washington, DC 20008.

Phone: (202) 234-2945. Fax: (202) 265-4795. E-mail: embcr@erols.com. Website: http://www.costarica.com.

Capital: San Jose. National Day: September 15. Currency: Colon. Language: Spanish (official). Religion: Roman Catholic (95%). Location: Central America. Neighbors: Nicaragua (N), Panama (S). Government: Republic.

COTE D'IVOIRE (IVORY COAST)

Embassy of the Republic of the Ivory Coast 2424 Massachusetts Avenue NW, Washington, DC 20008.

Phone: (202) 797-0300. Fax: (202) 462-9444.

Capital: Yamoussoukra (official), Abidjan (de facto). National Day: August 7. Currency: CFA franc. Language: French (official), Akan, Moshi-Dagomba, Ewe, Ga. Religion: Indigenous (38%), Muslim (30%), Christian (24%). Location: Southern coast of West Africa. Neighbors: Burkina Faso (N), Togo (E). Government: Republic.

CROATIA

Embassy of the Republic of Croatia: 2343 Massachusetts Avenue NW, Washington, DC 20008.

Phone: (202) 588-5899. Fax: (202) 588-8936. Website: http://www.croatiaemb.org.

Capital: Zagreb. National Day: May 30. Currency: Kuna. Language: Croatian (official). Religion: Roman Catholic (76%), Orthodox (11%). Location: Southeastern Europe, Balkan Peninsula. Neighbors: Slovenia, Hungary (N), Bosnia, Yugoslavia (E). Government: Parliamentary democracy.

CUBA

Cuban Interests Section: 2630 16th Street NW, Washington, DC 20009.

Phone: (202) 797-8518. Fax: (202) 797-8521. E-mail: cubaseccion@prodigy.net. Website: http://www.cubaseccion@iqc.apc.org.

Capital: Havana. National Day: January 1. Currency: Cuban peso. Language: Spanish (official). Religion: Roman Catholic (85%) prior to Castro. Location: In the Caribbean, westernmost of West Indies. Neighbors: Bahamas, United States (N), Mexico (W), Jamaica (S), Haiti (E). Government: Communist.

CYPRUS

Embassy of the Republic of Cyprus: 2211 R Street NW, Washington, DC 20008.

Phone: (202) 462-5772. Fax: (202) 483-6710. *Website: http://www.undp.org/missions/cyprus.

Capital: Nicosia. National Day: October 1. Currency: Pound. Language: Greek, Turkish (both official). Religion: Greek Orthodox (78%), Muslim (18%). Location: Eastern Mediterranean island. Neighbors: Turkey (N), Lebanon, Syria (E). Government: Republic.

CZECH REPUBLIC

Embassy of the Czech Republic: 3900 Spring of Freedom Street NW, Washington, DC 20008.

Phone: (202) 363-6315. Fax: (202) 966-8540. E-mail: 72360.544@compuserve.com.

Capital: Prague. National Days: May 8, October 28. Currency: Koruna. Language: Czech (official), Slovak. Religion: Atheist (39.8%), Roman Catholic (39.2%), Protestant (4.6%), Orthodox (3%). Location: East central Europe. Neighbors: Poland (N), Germany (N, W), Austria (S), Slovakia (E, SE). Government: Republic.

DENMARK

Royal Danish Embassy: 3200 Whitehaven Street NW, Washington, DC 20008.

Phone: (202) 234-4300. Fax: (202) 328-1470. E-mail: ambadane@erols.com. Website: http://www.denmarkemb.org.

Capital: Copenhagen. National Day: April 16. Currency: Krone. Language: Danish (official), Faroese. Religion: Evangelical Lutheran (91%). Location: North Europe, separating North and Baltic Seas. Neighbors: Germany (S), Norway (NW), Sweden (NE). Government: Constitutional monarchy.

DJIBOUTI

Embassy of the Republic of Djibouti: 1156 15th Street NW, Suite 515, Washington, DC 20008.

Phone: (202) 331-0270. Fax: (202) 331-0302. E-mail: usdjibouti@aol.com.

Capital: Djibouti City. National Day: June 27. Currency: Djibouti franc. Language:

French, Arabic, Afar, Somali. Religion: Muslim (94%), Christian (6%). Location: East coast of Africa. Neighbors: Ethiopia (W, SW), Eritrea (NW), Somalia (SE). Government: Republic.

DOMINICA

Embassy of the Commonwealth of Dominica: 3216 New Mexico Avenue NW, Washington, DC 20016.

Phone: (202) 364-6781. Fax: (202) 364-6791.

Capital: Roseau. National Day: November 3. Currency: East Caribbean dollar. Language: English (official), French patois. Religion: Roman Catholic (77%), Protestant (15%). Location: Eastern Caribbean, most northerly Windward Island. Neighbors: Guadeloupe (N), Martinique (S). Government: Parliamentary democracy.

DOMINICAN REPUBLIC

Embassy of the Dominican Republic: 1715 22nd Street NW, Washington, DC 20008.

Phone: (202) 332-6280. Fax: (202) 265-8057. Website: http://www.domrep.org.

Capital: Santo Domingo. National Day: February 27. Currency: Peso. Language: Spanish (official). Religion: Roman Catholic (95%). Location: West Indies, sharing island of Hispaniola with Haiti. Neighbors: Haiti (W), Puerto Rico (U.S.) (E). Government: Republic.

ECUADOR

Embassy of Ecuador: 2535 15th Street NW, Washington, DC 20009.

Phone: (202) 234-7200. Fax: (202) 667-3482. Website: http://www.ecuador.org/-embassy.htm

Capital: Quito. National Day: August 10. Currency: Sucre. Language: Spanish (official), Quechuan. Religion: Roman Catholic (95%). Location: Northwestern South America. Neighbors: Colombia (N), Peru (E, S). Government: Republic.

EGYPT

Embassy of the Arab Republic of Egypt: 3521 International Court NW, Washington, DC 20008.

Phone: (202) 895-5400. Fax: (202) 244-5131. Website: http://www.sis.gov.eg.

Capital: Cairo. National Day: July 23. Currency: Egyptian pound. Language: Arabic, English, French. Religion: Muslim (94%), Coptic Christian and other (6%). Location: Northeastern corner of Africa. Neighbors: Libya (W), Sudan (S), Israel (E). Government: Republic.

EL SALVADOR

Embassy of El Salvador: 2308 California Street NW, Washington, DC 20008.

Phone: (202) 265-9671. Fax: (202) 234-3834. Website: http://www.elsalvador.org.

Capital: San Salvador. National Day: September 15. Currency: Colon. Language:

Spanish (official). Religion: Roman Catholic (75%), many Protestant groups. Location: Central America. Neighbors: Guatemala (W), Honduras (N). Government: Republic.

EQUATORIAL GUINEA

Embassy of the Republic of Equatorial Guinea: 1511 K Street NW, Suite 405, Washington, DC 20005.

Phone: (202) 296-4195. Fax: (202) 393-0348.

Capital: Malabo. National Day: October 12. Currency: CFA franc. Language: Spanish (official), Fang, Bubi. Religion: Predominantly Roman Catholic. Location: Biolo Island off coast of West Africa in Gulf of Guinea, and Rio Muni, mainland enclave. Neighbors: Gabon (S), Cameroon (E, N). Government: Republic.

ERITREA

Embassy of the State of Eritrea: 1708 New Hampshire Avenue NW, Washington, DC 20009.

Phone: (202) 319-1991. Fax: (202) 319-1304. E-mail: veronica@embassyeritrea.org.

Capital: Asmara. National Day: May 24. Currency: Birr. Language: Tigrinya, Tigre. Religion: Evenly split, Muslim and Christian. Location: Southwestern coast of East Africa, bordering the Red Sea. Neighbors: Ethiopia (S), Djibouti (SE), Sudan (W). Government: In transition.

ESTONIA

Embassy of Estonia: 2131 Massachusetts Avenue NW, Washington, DC 20008.

Phone: (202) 588-0101. Fax: (202) 588-0108. Website: http://www.estemb.org.

Capital: Tallinn. National Day: February 24. Currency: Kroon. Language: Estonian (official), Latvian, Lithuanian, Russian. Religion: Lutheran, Orthodox. Location: Eastern Europe, bordering the Baltic Sea and Gulf of Finland. Neighbors: Russia (E), Latvia (S). Government: Republic.

ETHIOPIA

Embassy of Ethiopia: 2134 Kalorama Road NW, Washington, DC 20008.

Phone: (202) 234-2281. Fax: (202) 328-7950. Website: http://www.nicom.com/~ethiopia.

Capital: Addis Ababa. National Day: May 28. Currency: Birr. Language: Amharic, English (both official), Tigrinya, Orominga. Religion: Muslim (45–50%), Ethiopian Orthodox (35–40%), animist (12%). Location: East Africa. Neighbors: Sudan (W), Kenya (S), Somalia, Djibouti (E), Eritrea (N). Government: Federal republic.

FIJI

Embassy of the Republic of Fiji: 2233 Wisconsin Avenue NW, Suite 240, Washington, DC 20007.

Phone: (202) 337-8320. Fax: (202) 337-1996. E-mail: fijiemb@earthlink.net.

Capital: Suva. National Day: October 10. Currency: Fiji dollar. Language: English (official), Fijian, Hindustani. Religion: Christian (52%), Hindu (38%), Muslim (8%). Location: Western South Pacific Ocean. Neighbors: Nearest are Vanuatu (W), Tonga (E). Government: Republic.

FINLAND

Embassy of Finland: 3301 Massachusetts Avenue NW, Washington, DC 20008.

Phone: (202) 298-5800. Fax: (202) 298-6030. Website: http://www.finland.org.

Capital: Helsinki. National Day: December 6. Language: Finnish, Swedish (both official). Religion: Evangelical Lutheran (89%). Location: Northern Europe. Neighbors: Norway (N), Sweden (W), Russia (E). Government: Constitutional republic.

FRANCE

Embassy of France: 4101 Reservoir Road NW, Washington, DC 20007.

Phone: (202) 944-6000. Fax: (202) 944-6166. Website: http://www.info-france-usa.org.

Capital: Paris. National Day: July 14. Currency: Franc. Language: French (official), Breton, Alsatian German, Flemish, Italian, Basque, Catalon. Religion: Roman Catholic (90%). Location: Western Europe, between Atlantic Ocean and Mediterranean Sea. Neighbors: Spain (S), Italy, Switzerland, Germany (E), Luxembourg, Belgium (N). Government: Republic.

GABON

Embassy of the Gabonese Republic: 2034 20th Street NW, Suite 200, Washington, DC 20009.

Phone: (202) 797-1000. Fax: (202) 332-0668.

Capital: Libreville. National Day: March 12. Currency: CFA franc. Language: French (official), Bantu dialects. Religion: Mostly Christian, some Muslim and animist. Location: West central Africa, bordering Atlantic Ocean. Neighbors: Equatorial Guinea and Cameroon (N), Congo (E, S). Government: Republic.

THE GAMBIA

Embassy of The Gambia: 1155 15th Street NW, Suite 1000, Washington, DC 20005.

Phone: (202) 785-1399. Fax: (202) 785-1430. Website: http://www.gambia.com.

Capital: Banjul. National Day: February 18. Currency: Dalasi. Language: English (official), Mandinka, Wolof. Religion: Muslim (90%), Christian (9%). Location: Western tip of Africa, bordering Atlantic Ocean. Neighbors: Surrounded on three sides by Senegal. Government: Republic.

GEORGIA

Embassy of the Republic of Georgia: 1511 K Street NW, Suite 424, Washington, DC 20005.

Phone: (202) 393-5959. Fax: (202) 393-6060. Website: http://www.steele.com/-embgeorgia.

Capital: Tbilisi. Currency: Lari. Language: Georgian (official), Russian. Religion: Georgian Orthodox (65%), Muslim (11%), Russian Orthodox (10%). Location: Southwestern Asia, bordering Black Sea. Neighbors: Russia (N, NE), Turkey, Armenia (S), Azerbaijan (SE). Government: Republic.

GERMANY

Embassy of the Federal Republic of Germany: 4645 Reservoir Road NW, Washington, DC 20007.

Phone: (202) 298-4000. Fax: (202) 298-4249. Website: http://www.germany-info.org.

Capital: Berlin. National Day: October 3. Currency: Deutsche Mark. Language: German (official). Religion: Protestant (45%), Roman Catholic (37%). Location: Central Europe. Neighbors: Denmark (N), Netherlands, Belgium, Luxembourg, France (W), Switzerland, Austria (S), Czech Republic, Poland (E). Government: Federal republic.

GHANA

Embassy of Ghana: 3512 International Drive NW, Washington, DC 20008.

Phone: (202) 686-4520. Fax: (202) 686-4527. Website: http://www.ghana-embassy.org.

Capital: Accra. National Day: March 6. Currency: Cedi. Language: English (official), Akan, Moshi-Dagomba, Ewe, Ga. Religion: Indigenous (38%), Muslim (30%), Christian (24%). Location: South coast of West Africa. Neighbors: Cote d'Ivoire (W), Burkina Faso (N), Togo (E). Government: Republic.

GREECE

Embassy of Greece: 2221 Massachusetts Avenue NW, Washington, DC 20008.

Phone: (202) 939-5800. Fax: (202) 939-5824. Website: http://www.greekembassy.org.

Capital: Athens. National Day: March 25. Currency: Drachma. Language: Greek (official), English, French. Religion: Greek Orthodox (98%) (official). Location: Southern end of Balkan Peninsula in southeastern Europe. Neighbors: Albania, Macedonia, Bulgaria (N), Turkey (E). Government: Parliamentary republic.

GRENADA

Embassy of Grenada: 1701 New Hampshire Avenue NW, Washington, DC 20009.

Phone: (202) 265-2561. Fax: (202) 265-2468.

Capital: Saint George's. National Day: February 7. Currency: East Caribbean dollar. Language: English (official), French patois. Religion: Roman Catholic (53%), Protestant (38%). Location: Caribbean Ocean, 90 miles north of Venezuela. Neighbors: Venezuela, Trinidad and Tobago (S), St. Vincent and the Grenadines (N). Government: Parliamentary democracy.

GUATEMALA

Embassy of Guatemala: 2220 R Street NW, Washington, DC 20008.

Phone: (202) 745-4952. Fax: (202) 745-1908. E-mail: embaguat@sysnet.net.

Capital: Guatemala City. National Day: September 15. Currency: Quetzal. Language: Spanish (official), Mayan dialects. Religion: Mostly Roman Catholic, some Protestant, indigenous. Location: Central America. Neighbors: Mexico (N, W), El Salvador (S), Honduras, Belize (E). Government: Republic.

GUINEA

Embassy of the Republic of Guinea: 2112 Leroy Place NW, Washington, DC 20008.

Phone: (202) 483-9420. Fax: (202) 483-8688.

Capital: Conakry. National Day: October 2. Currency: Franc. Language: French (official), Peuhl, Malinke, Soussou. Religion: Muslim (85%), Christian (8%). Location: West Africa, bordering Atlantic Ocean. Neighbors: Guinea-Bissau, Senegal, Mali (N), Cote d'Ivoire (E), Liberia (S). Government: Republic.

GUINEA-BISSAU

Embassy of the Republic of Guinea-Bissau: 1511 K Street NW, Suite 519, Washington, DC 20005.

Fax: (202) 347-3954.

Capital: Bissau. National Day: September 24. Currency: CFA franc. Language: Portuguese (official), Criolo, indigenous. Religion: Indigenous (65%), Muslim (30%), Christian (5%). Location: West Africa, bordering Atlantic Ocean. Neighbors: Senegal (N), Guinea (E, S). Government: Republic.

GUYANA

Embassy of Guyana: 2490 Tracy Place NW, Washington, DC 20008.

Phone: (202) 265-6900. Fax: (202) 232-1297. E-mail: embassy@hotmail.com.

Capital: Georgetown. National Day: February 23. Currency: Dollar. Language: English (official), Amerindian dialects. Religion: Christian (57%), Hindu (33%), Muslim (9%). Location: North coast of South America. Neighbors: Venezuela (W), Brazil (S), Suriname (E). Government: Republic.

HAITI

Embassy of the Republic of Haiti: 2311 Massachusetts Avenue NW, Washington, DC 20008.

Phone: (202) 332-4090. Fax: (202) 745-7215. Website: http://www.haiti.org/embassy.

Capital: Port-au-Prince. National Day: January 1. Currency: Gourde. Language: Haitian Creole, French (both official). Religion: Roman Catholic (80%), Protestant (16%), voodoo widely practiced. Location: In Caribbean, occupies western third of Island of Hispaniola. Neighbors: Dominican Republic (E), Cuba (W). Government: Republic.

THE HOLY SEE (VATICAN CITY)

Apostolic Nunciature: 3339 Massachusetts Avenue NW, Washington, DC 20008.

Phone: (202) 333-7121. Fax: (202) 337-4036. Website: http://www.vatican.va.

Capital: NA. National Day: October 22. Currency: Vatican lira, Italian lira. Language: Latin (official), Italian. Religion: Roman Catholic. Location: In Rome, Italy. Neighbors: Surrounded by Italy. Government: Papal commission.

HONDURAS

Embassy of Honduras: 3007 Tilden Street NW, Suite 4M, Washington, DC 20008.

Phone: (202) 966-7702. Fax: (202) 966-9751. E-mail: embhonduras@netcom. Website: http://www.embhondu@ix.netcom.com.

Capital: Tegucigalpa. National Day: September 15. Currency: Lempira. Language: Spanish (official). Religion: Roman Catholic (97%). Location: Central America. Neighbors: Guatemala (W), El Salvador, Nicaragua (S). Government: Republic.

HUNGARY

Embassy of the Republic of Hungary: 3910 Shoemaker Street NW, Washington, DC 20008.

Phone: (202) 966-7726. Fax: (202) 686-6412. Website: http://www.hungaryemb.org/.

Capital: Budapest. National Day: August 20. Currency: Forint. Language: Hungarian (Magyar) (official). Religion: Roman Catholic (67.5%), Calvinist (20%), Lutheran (5%). Location: East central Europe. Neighbors: Slovakia, Ukraine (N), Austria (W), Slovenia, Yugoslavia, Croatia (S), Romania (E). Government: Parliamentary democracy.

ICELAND

Embassy of the Republic of Iceland: 1156 15th Street NW, Suite 1200, Washington, DC 20005.

Phone: (202) 265-6653. Fax: (202) 265-6656. Website: http://www.iceland.org.

Capital: Reykjavik. National Day: June 17. Currency: Krona. Language: Islenska (official). Religion: Evangelical Lutheran (96%). Location: North Atlantic Ocean. Neighbors: Greenland (W). Government: Constitutional republic.

INDIA

Embassy of India: 2107 Massachusetts Avenue NW, Washington, DC 20008.

Phone: (202) 939-7000. Fax: (202) 483-3972. Website: http://www.indianembassy.org.

Capital: New Delhi. National Day: January 26. Currency: Rupee. Language: Hindi (official), English (associate official), 17 regional. Religion: Hindu (80%), Muslim (14%), Christian (2%), Sikh (2%). Location: Occupies most of the Indian subcontinent in South Asia. Neighbors: Pakistan (W), China, Nepal, Bhutan (N), Myanmar, Bangladesh (E). Government: Federal republic.

INDONESIA

Embassy of the Republic of Indonesia: 2020 Massachusetts Avenue NW, Washington, DC 20036.

Phone: (202) 775-5200. Fax: (202) 775-5365. E-mail: www.indonsia@dgs.dgsys.com.

Capital: Jakarta. National Day: August 17. Currency: Rupiah. Language: Bahasa Indonesian (Malay), English, Dutch. Religion: Muslim (87%), Protestant Javanese (6%). Location: Archipelago, Southeast Asia. Neighbors: Malaysia (N), Papua New Guinea (E). Government: Republic.

IRAN

Iranian Interests Section: 2209 Wisconsin Avenue NW, Washington, DC 20007.

Phone: (202) 965-4990 (answering service only).

Capital: Tehran. Currency: Rial. Language: Persian (Farsi) (official), Turkic, Kurdish, Luri. Religion: Shia Muslim (89%), Sunni Muslim (10%). Location: Between the Middle East and South Asia. Neighbors: Turkey, Iraq (W), Armenia, Azerbaijan, Turkmenistan (N), Afghanistan, Pakistan (E). Government: Islamic republic.

IRAQ

Iraqi Interest Section: 1801 P Street NW, Washington, DC 20036.

Phone: (202) 483-7500. Fax: (202) 462-5066.

Capital: Baghdad. Currency: Dinar. Language: Arabic (official), Kurdish. Religion: Shia Muslim (60–65%), Sunni Muslim (32–37%). Location: Middle East. Neighbors: Jordan, Syria (W), Turkey (N), Iran (E), Kuwait, Saudi Arabia (S). Government: Republic.

IRELAND

Embassy of Ireland: 2234 Massachusetts Avenue NW, Washington, DC 20008.

Phone: (202) 462-3939. Fax: (202) 232-5993. Website: http://www.irelandemb.org.

Capital: Dublin. National Day: March 17. Currency: Pound. Language: English predominates, Irish (Gaelic) spoken by minority (both official). Religion: Roman

Catholic (93%), Anglican (3%). Location: Atlantic Ocean west of Great Britain. Neighbors: United Kingdom (Northern Ireland) (E). Government: Parliamentary republic.

ISRAEL

Embassy of Israel: 3514 International Drive NW, Washington, DC 20008.
Phone: (202) 364-5500. Fax: (202) 364-5249. Website: http://www.israelemb.org.
Capital: Jerusalem (Israeli capital), Tel Aviv (U.S. embassy). National Day: April 24. Currency: New Shekel. Language: Hebrew (official), Arabic, English. Religion: Jewish (82%), Muslim (14%), Christian (4%). Location: Middle East. Neighbors: Lebanon (N), Syria, Jordan, Palestinian National Authority (E), Egypt (W). Government: Parliamentary democracy.

ITALY

Embassy of Italy: 1601 Fuller Street NW, Washington, DC 20009.
Phone: (202) 328-5500. Fax: (202) 483-2187. Website: http://www.italyemb.org.
Capital: Rome. National Day: June 2. Currency: Lira. Language: Italian (official), German, French, Slovene. Religion: Roman Catholic (98%). Location: Southern Europe, jutting into Mediterranean Sea. Neighbors: France (W), Switzerland, Austria (N), Slovenia (E). Government: Republic.

JAMAICA

Embassy of Jamaica: 1520 New Hampshire Avenue NW, Washington, DC 20036.
Phone: (202) 452-0660. Fax: (202) 452-0081. E-mail: emjam@sysnet.net. Website: http://www.jiswashington.gov.
Capital: Kingston. National Day: August 5. Currency: Dollar. Language: English (official), Jamaican Creole. Religion: Protestant (56%), Roman Catholic (5%), spiritual cults and other (39%). Location: West Indies. Neighbors: Nearest are Cuba (N), Haiti (E). Government: Parliamentary democracy.

JAPAN

Embassy of Japan: 2520 Massachusetts Avenue NW, Washington, DC 20008.
Phone: (202) 238-6700. Fax: (202) 328-2187. Website: http://www.embjapan.org.
Capital: Tokyo. National Day: December 23. Currency: Yen. Language: Japanese. Religion: Buddhist, Shintoist shared by large majority. Location: Archipelago off east coast of Asia. Neighbors: Russia (N), South Korea (W). Government: Parliamentary democracy.

JORDAN

Embassy of the Hashemite Kingdom of Jordan: 3504 International Drive NW, Washington, DC 20008.

Phone: (202) 966-2664. Fax: (202) 966-3110. Website: http://www.jordanembassyus.org.

Capital: Amman. National Day: May 5. Currency: Dinar. Language: Arabic (official). Religion: Sunni Muslim (92%), Christian (8%). Location: Middle East. Neighbors: Israel (W), Saudi Arabia (S), Iraq (E), Syria (N). Government: Constitutional monarchy.

KAZAKHSTAN

Embassy of the Republic of Kazakhstan (temporary): 3421 Massachusetts Avenue NW, Washington, DC 20007.

Phone: (202) 232-5488. Fax: (202) 333-4509. E-mail: kazak@inter.net.

Capital: Astana. National Day: October 5. Currency: Tenge. Language: Kazakh, Russian. Religion: Muslim (47%), Russian Orthodox (44%). Location: Central Asia. Neighbors: Russia (N), China (E), Kyrgyzstan, Uzbekistan, Turkmenistan (S). Government: Republic.

KENYA

Embassy of the Republic of Kenya: 2249 R Street NW, Washington, DC 20008.

Phone: (202) 387-6101. Fax: (202) 462-3829. Website: http://www.embassyofkenya.com.

Capital: Nairobi. National Day: December 12. Currency: Shilling. Language: Swahili, English (both official), indigenous. Religion: Protestant (38%), Roman Catholic (28%), indigenous (26%). Location: East Africa, bordering Indian Ocean. Neighbors: Uganda (W), Tanzania (S), Somalia (E), Ethiopia (N), Sudan (NW). Government: Republic.

KUWAIT

Embassy of the State of Kuwait: 2940 Tilden Street NW, Washington, DC 20008.

Phone: (202) 966-0702. Fax: (202) 966-0517. *Website: http://www.kuwait.-info.nw.dc.us.

Capital: Kuwait City. National Day: February 25. Currency: Dinar. Language: Arabic (official). Religion: Muslim (85%). Location: Northern Middle East. Neighbors: Iraq (N), Saudi Arabia (S). Government: Constitutional monarchy.

KYRGYZSTAN

Embassy of the Kyrgyz Republic: 1732 Wisconsin Avenue NW, Washington, DC 20007.

Phone: (202) 338-5141. Fax: (202) 338-5139. Website: http://www.kyrgyzstan.org.

Capital: Bishbeck. National Day: August 31. Currency: Som. Language: Kyrgyz, Russian. Religion: Sunni Muslim (75%), Russian Orthodox (20%). Location: Central Asia. Neighbors: Kazakhstan (N), China (E), Uzbekistan (W), Tajikistan (S). Government: Republic.

LAOS

Embassy of the Lao People's Democratic Republic: 2222 S Street NW, Washington, DC 20008.

Phone: (202) 332-6416. Fax: (202) 332-4923. Website: http://www.laoembassy.com.

Capital: Vietiane. National Day: December 2. Currency: Kip. Language: Lao, French, English. Religion: Buddhist (60%), animist and other (40%). Location: Southeast Asia. Neighbors: Myanmar, China (N), Thailand (W), Vietnam (E), Cambodia (S). Government: Communist.

LATVIA

Embassy of Latvia: 4325 17th Street NW, Washington, DC 20011.

Phone: (202) 726-8213. Fax: (202) 726-6785. Website: http://www.ambergateway.com.

Capital: Riga. National Day: November 18. Currency: Lat. Language: Latvian (official), Lithuanian, Russian. Religion: Lutheran, Roman Catholic, Russian Orthodox. Location: East Europe, bordering Baltic Sea. Neighbors: Estonia (N), Lithuania, Belarus (S), Russia (E). Government: Republic.

LEBANON

Embassy of Lebanon: 2560 28th Street NW, Washington, DC 20008.

Phone: (202) 939-6300. Fax: (202) 939-6324. E-mail: emblebanon@aol.com. Website: http://www.emboflebanon.org.

Capital: Beirut. National Day: November 22. Currency: Pound. Language: Arabic, French (both official). Religion: Muslim (70%), Christian (30%). Location: Middle East, east end of Mediterranean Sea. Neighbors: Syria (E), Israel (S). Government: Republic.

LESOTHO

Embassy of the Kingdom of Lesotho: 2511 Massachusetts Avenue NW, Washington, DC 20008.

Phone: (202) 797-5533. Fax: (202) 234-6815. E-mail: lesotho@afrika.com.

Capital: Maseru. National Day: October 4. Currency: Loti. Language: English, Sesotho. Religion: Christian (80%), indigenous (20%). Location: Southern Africa. Neighbors: Surrounded by South Africa. Government: Modified constitutional monarchy.

LIBERIA

Embassy of the Republic of Liberia: 5201 16th Street NW, Washington, DC 20011.

Phone: (202) 723-0437. Fax: (202) 723-0436. Website: http://www.liberiaemb.org.

Capital: Monrovia. National Day: July 26. Currency: Dollar. Language: English (official), indigenous. Religion: Indigenous (70%), Muslim (20%), Christian (10%).

Location: Southwestern coast of Africa. Neighbors: Sierra Leone (W), Guinea (N), Cote d'Ivoire (E). Government: Republic.

LITHUANIA

Embassy of the Republic of Lithuania: 2622 16th Street NW, Washington, DC 20009.

Phone: (202) 234-5860. Fax: (202) 328-0466. Website: http://www.ltembassyus.org.

Capital: Vilnius. National Day: February 16. Currency: Litas. Language: Lithuanian (official), Polish, Russian. Religion: Mostly Roman Catholic. Location: East Europe on southeastern coast of the Baltic Sea. Neighbors: Latvia (N), Belarus (E, S), Poland, Russia (W). Government: Republic.

LUXEMBOURG

Embassy of the Grand Duchy of Luxembourg: 2200 Massachusetts Avenue NW, Washington, DC 20008.

Phone: (202) 265-4171. Fax: (202) 328-8270. E-mail: ambalux@earthlink.net.

Capital: Luxembourg. National Day: June 23. Currency: Franc. Language: French, German, Luxembourgisch. Religion: Roman Catholic (97%). Location: Western Europe. Neighbors: Belgium (W), France (S), Germany (E). Government: Constitutional monarchy.

MACEDONIA

Embassy of the Former Yugoslav Republic of Macedonia: 3050 K Street, NW, Suite 210, Washington, DC 20007.

Phone: (202) 337-3063. Fax: (202) 337-3093. E-mail: Rmacedonia@aol.com.

Capital: Skopje. National Day: September 8. Currency: Denar. Language: Macedonian (official), Albainian, Turkish, Serbo-Croatian. Religion: Eastern Orthodox (67%), Muslim (30%). Location: Southern part of Balkan Peninsula. Neighbors: Serbia (N), Bulgaria (E), Greece (S), Albania (W), Yugoslavia (N, NE). Government: Emerging democracy.

MADAGASCAR

Embassy of the Republic of Madagascar: 2374 Massachusetts Avenue NW, Washington, DC 20008.

Phone: (202) 265-5525. Fax: (202) 265-3034. E-mail: malagasy@embassy.org. Website: http://www.embassy.org/madagascar.

Capital: Antananarivo. National Day: June 26. Currency: Malagasy franc. Language: French, Malagasy (both official). Religion: Indigenous (52%), Christian (41%), Muslim (7%). Location: Southeast of Africa. Neighbors: Mozambique (300 miles west). Government: Republic.

MALAWI

Embassy of the Republic of Malawi: 2408 Massachusetts Avenue NW, Washington, DC 20008.

Phone: (202) 797-1007. Fax: (202) 265-0976.

Capital: Lilongwe. National Day: July 6. Currency: Malawian kwacha. Language: English, Chichewa (both official), Tombuka. Religion: Protestant (55%), Roman Catholic (20%), Muslim (20%), indigenous. Location: Landlocked in southern central Africa. Neighbors: Tanzania (N), Mozambique (E, S, SW), Zambia (W), Lake Malawi (E). Government: Multiparty democracy.

MALAYSIA

Embassy of Malaysia: 2401 Massachusetts Avenue NW, Washington, DC 20008.

Phone: (202) 328-2700. Fax: (202) 483-7661. E-mail: embmaldc@erols.com.

Capital: Kuala Lumpur. National Day: August 31. Currency: Malaysian ringgit. Language: Malay (official); English; Chinese dialects, including Mandarin and Hakka; Tamil; numerous tribal dialects. Religion: Muslim (Malay majority and Chinese); Buddhist or Confusianist (Indians); Hindu, Christian. Location: Eleven states are Peninsular Malaysia located in Southeast Asia; two, Sabah and Sarawak, located off the northern coast of Borneo. Neighbors: Peninsular Malaysia—Thailand (N), South China Sea (E), Singapore (S), Sumatra (Indonesian island) (W); Sabah and Sarawak—South China Sea (NW), Sulu Sea (NE), Celebes Sea (E), Indonesia (S). Government: Constitutional monarchy.

MALI

Embassy of the Republic of Mali: 2130 R Street NW, Washington, DC 20008.

Phone: (202) 332-2249. Fax: (202) 332-6603. Website: http://www.maliembassy-usa.org.

Capital: Bamako. National Day: September 22. Currency: CFA franc. Language: French (official), Bambara, many indigenous. Religion: Muslim (90%), indigenous (9%). Location: West Africa. Neighbors: Mauritania, Senegal (W), Guinea, Cote d'Ivoire, Burkina Faso (S), Niger (E), Algeria (N). Government: Republic.

MALTA

Embassy of Malta: 2017 Connecticut Avenue NW, Washington, DC 20008.

Phone: (202) 462-3611. Fax: (202) 387-5470. E-mail: maltaembassy@compuserve.com. Website: http://www.magnet.mt.

Capital: Valletta. National Day: September 21. Currency: Lira. Language: Maltese, English (both official). Religion: Roman Catholic (98%). Location: Mediterranean Sea. Neighbors: Nearest is Italy (N). Government: Parliamentary democracy.

MARSHALL ISLANDS

Embassy of the Republic of the Marshall Islands: 2433 Massachusetts Avenue NW, Washington, DC 20008.

Phone: (202) 234-5414. Fax: (202) 232-3236. E-mail: info@rmiembassy.us.org. Website: http://www.rmiembassyus.org.

Capital: Majuro. National Day: May 1. Currency: U.S. dollar. Language: English (official), Marshallese, Japanese. Religion: Protestant (90%). Location: North Pacific Ocean, composed of two 800-mile-long parallel chains of coral atolls. Neighbors: Nearest are Micronesia (W), Nauru, Kiribati (S). Government: Republic.

MAURITANIA

Embassy of the Islamic Republic of Mauritania: 2129 Leroy Place NW, Washington, DC 20008.

Phone: (202) 232-5700. Fax: (202) 319-2623. Website: http://www.embassy.org/mauritania.

Capital: Nouakchott. National Day: November 28. Currency: Ouguiya. Language: Hasaniya Arabic, Wolof (both official). Religion: Sunni Muslim (99%). Location: Northwestern Africa. Neighbors: Morocco (N), Senegal (S), Algeria, Mali (E). Government: Islamic Republic.

MAURITIUS

Embassy of the Republic of Mauritius: 4301 Connecticut Avenue NW, Suite 441, Washington, DC 20006.

Phone: (202) 244-1491. Fax: (202) 966-0983. Website: http://www.mauritius-online.com.

Capital: Port Louis. National Day: March 12. Currency: Mauritian rupee. Language: English (official), Creole, French, Hindi, Urdu, Hakka, Bejpoori. Religion: Majority Roman Catholic, Hindu (52%); Christian (28.3%); Muslim (16.6%); Anglican. Location: Southwest Indian Ocean. Neighbors: Reunion (SW). Government: Parliamentary democracy.

MEXICO

Embassy of Mexico: 1911 Pennslyvania Avenue NW, Washington, DC 20006.

Phone: (202) 728-1600. Fax: (202) 728-1698. E-mail: mexembusa@aol.com. Website: http://www.embassyofmexico.org.

Capital: Mexico City. National Day: September 16. Currency: Peso. Language: Spanish. Religion: Roman Catholic (89%), Protestant (6%). Location: Southernmost part of North America. Neighbors: United States (N), Gulf of Mexico (E), Belize, Guatamala (S), Pacific Ocean (W). Government: Federal republic, under centralized government.

MICRONESIA

Embassy of the Federated States of Micronesia: 1725 N Street NW, Washington, DC 20036.

Phone: (202) 223-4383. Fax: (202) 223-4391. Website: http://www.fsmgov.org.

Capital: Kolonia. National Day: May 10. Currency: U.S. dollar. Language: English (official), Trukese, Pohnpeian, Yapese, Kosraean. Religion: Roman Catholic (53%), Protestant (47%). Location: Archipelago of Caroline Islands. Neighbors: Guam (NW), Marshall Islands (E), Papua New Guinea (S), Philippines (W). Government: Constitutional.

MOLDOVA

Embassy of the Republic of Moldova: 2101 S Street NW, Washington, DC 20008.

Phone: (202) 667-1130. Fax: (202) 667-1204. E-mail: moldova@dgs.dgsys.com.

Capital: Kishina. National Day: August 27. Currency: Leu. Language: Moldovan (official), Russian, Gagauz. Religion: Eastern Orthodox (98.5%), Jewish (1.5%). Location: Southeastern Europe. Neighbors: Ukraine (N, E, S), Romania (W). Government: Republic.

MONGOLIA

Embassy of Mongolia: 2833 M Street NW, Washington, DC 20007.

Phone: (202) 333-7117. Fax: (202) 298-9227. Website: http://www.undp.org/-missions/mongolia/.

Capital: Ulaanbaatar. National Day: July 11. Currency: Tugrik. Language: Khalka Mongolian. Religion: Traditionally Tibetan Buddhist. Location: East Central Asia. Neighbors: Russia (N), China (E, W, S). Government: Republic.

MOROCCO

Embassy of the Kingdom of Morocco: 1601 21st Street NW, Washington, DC 20009.

Phone: (202) 462-7979. Fax: (202) 265-0161. E-mail: embassyusa@trident.net.

Capital: Rabat. National Day: March 3. Currency: Dirham. Language: Arabic (official), Berber. Religion: Sunni Muslim (99%). Location: Northwestern coast of Africa. Neighbors: Algeria (E), Western Sahara (S). Government: Constitutional monarchy.

MOZAMBIQUE

Embassy of the Republic of Mozambique: 1990 M Street NW, Suite 570, Washington, DC 20036.

Phone: (202) 293-7146. Fax: (202) 835-0245. E-mail: embamoc@aol.com. Website: http://www.embamoc-usa.org.

Capital: Maputo. National Day: June 25. Currency: Metical. Language: Portuguese, Makua, Malawi, Shona, Tsonga. Religion: Indigenous (50%), Christian (30%), Muslim (20%). Location: Southeastern Africa. Neighbors: Tanzania (N), Malawi, Zambia, Zimbabwe (W), South Africa, Swaziland (S). Government: Republic.

MYANMAR (FORMERLY BURMA)

Embassy of the Union of Myanmar: 2300 S Street NW, Washington, DC 20008.

Phone: (202) 332-9044. Fax: (202) 332-9046. Website: http://www.myanmar.com.

Capital: Yangon (Rangoon). National Day: January 4. Currency: Kyat. Language: Burmese. Religion: Buddhist (89%), Christian (4%), Muslim (4%). Location: South Asia. Neighbors: Bangladesh, India (W), China, Laos, Thailand (E). Government: Military.

NAMIBIA

Embassy of the Republic of Namibia: 1605 New Hampshire Avenue NW, Washington, DC 20009.

Phone: (202) 986-0540. Fax: (202) 986-0443. E-mail: embnamibia@aol.com.

Capital: Windhoek. National Day: March 21. Currency: Dollar. Language: Afrikaans, English, German, indigenous. Religion: Lutheran (50%), other Christian (30%). Location: Southwestern Africa. Neighbors: Angola (N), Botswana (E), South Africa (S). Government: Republic.

NEPAL

Royal Nepalese Embassy: 2131 Leroy Place, NW, Washington, DC 20008.

Phone: (202) 667-4550. Fax: (202) 667-5534. E-mail: nepali@erols.com.

Capital: Kathmandu. National Day: December 28. Currency: Rupee. Language: Nepali. Religion: Hindu (90%), Buddhist (5%), Muslim (3%). Location: Asia. Neighbors: China (N), India (S). Government: Constitutional monarchy.

NETHERLANDS

Royal Netherlands Embassy: 4200 Linnean Avenue NW, Washington, DC 20008.

Phone: (202) 244-5300. Fax: (202) 362-3430. Website: http://www.netherlands-embassy.org.

Capital: Amsterdam. National Day: April 30. Currency: Guilder. Language: Dutch (official). Religion: Roman Catholic (34%), Protestant (36%), Muslim (3%), unaffiliated. Location: Western Europe. Neighbors: North Sea (N, W), Germany (E), Belgium (S). Government: Constitutional monarchy.

NEW ZEALAND

Embassy of New Zealand: 37 Observatory Circle NW, Washington, DC 20008.

Phone: (202) 328-4800. Fax: (202) 667-5227. Website: http://www.nzemb.org.

Capital: Wellington. National Day: February 6. Currency: Dollar. Language: English, Maori. Religion: Anglican (24%), Presbyterian (18%), Roman Catholic (15%). Location: Southwest Pacific Ocean. Neighbors: Australia (W), Fiji, Tonga (N). Government: Parliamentary democracy.

NICARAGUA

Embassy of Nicaragua: 1627 New Hampshire Avenue NW, Washington, DC, 20009.

Phone: (202) 939-6570. Fax: (202) 939-6545. Website: http://www.embanic-prensa@andyne.net.

Capital: Managua. National Day: September 15. Currency: Cordoba. Language: Spanish (official), English, indigenous minorities. Religion: Roman Catholic (95%). Location: Central American isthmus. Neighbors: Honduras (N), Caribbean Sea (E), Costa Rica (S), Pacific Ocean (W). Government: Republic.

NIGER

Embassy of the Republic of Niger: 2204 R Street NW, Washington, DC 20008.

Phone: (202) 483-4224. Fax: (202) 483-3169. E-mail: nigeremb@erols.com.

Capital: Niamey. National Day: December 18. Currency: CFA franc. Language: French (official), Hausa, Djerma. Religion: Muslim (80%), indigenous (20%), Christian. Location: Landlocked in western Africa. Neighbors: Algeria, Libya (N), Chad (E), Nigeria (S), Benin, Burkina Faso (SW), Mali (W). Government: Republic.

NIGERIA

Embassy of the Federal Republic of Nigeria: 1333 16th Street NW, Washington, DC 20036.

Phone: (202) 822-1539. Fax: (202) 775-1385. Website: http://www.nigeria-government.com.

Capital: Abuja. National Day: October 1. Currency: Naira. Language: English (official), Hausa, Yoruba, Ibo. Religion: Muslim (N) (50%), Christian (S) (40%). Location: Southern coast of West Africa. Neighbors: Benin (W), Niger (N), Chad, Cameroon (E). Government: Republic.

NORWAY

Royal Norwegian Embassy: 2720 34th Street NW, Washington, DC 20008.

Phone: (202) 333-6000. Fax: (202) 337-0870. Website: http://www.norway.org.

Capital: Oslo. National Day: May 17. Currency: Norwegian krone. Language: Norwegian (official). Religion: Evangelical Lutheran (87.8%), Protestant (3.8%). Location: Northern Europe. Neighbors: Norwegian Sea (N, W), Russia, Finland (NE), Sweden (E), North Sea (S, W). Government: Constitutional monarchy.

OMAN

Embassy of the Sultanate of Oman: 2535 Belmont Road NW, Washington, DC 20008.

Phone: (202) 387-1980. Fax: (202) 745-4933.

Capital: Muscat. National Day: November 18. Currency: Rial omani. Language: Arabic (official). Religion: Ibadhi Muslim (75%), other Muslim, Hindu. Location:

Southeastern coast of Arabian Peninsula. Neighbors: United Arab Emirates, Saudi Arabia, Yemen (W). Government: Absolute monarchy.

PAKISTAN

Embassy of Pakistan: 2315 Massachusetts Avenue NW, Washington, DC 20008.

Phone: (202) 939-6205. Fax: (202) 387-0484. Website: http://www.pakistan-embassy.com.

Capital: Islamabad. National Day: March 23. Currency: Rupee. Language: Urdu, English (both official). Religion: Sunni Muslim (77%), Shia Muslim (20%). Location: Southwest Asia. Neighbors: Iran (W), Afghanistan, China (N), India (E). Government: Republic.

PALAU

Embassy of the Republic of Palau: 1150 18th Street NW, Suite 750, Washington, DC 20036.

Phone: (202) 452-6814. Fax: (202) 452-6281.

Capital: Koror. National Day: October 1. Currency: U.S. dollar. Language: English, Palauan (both official), Sonsorolese, Anguar, Japanese, Tobi (all official within certain Palauan states). Religion: Roman Catholic, Protestant, Modekngei. Location: Archipelago in Southeast Asia (W), in Pacific Ocean, 530 miles southeast of Philippines. Neighbors: Micronesia (E), Indonesia (S). Government: Republic.

PANAMA

Embassy of the Republic of Panama: 2862 McGill Terrace NW, Washington, DC 20008.

Phone: (202) 483-1407. Fax: (202) 483-8413. E-mail: rva@panemb.dc.ccmail.-compuserve.com.

Capital: Panama. National Day: November 3. Currency: Balboa. Language: Spanish (official), English. Religion: Roman Catholic (85%), Protestant (15%). Location: Central America. Neighbors: Costa Rica (W), Colombia (E). Government: Constitutional republic.

PAPUA NEW GUINEA

Embassy of Papua New Guinea: 1615 New Hampshire Avenue NW, 3rd Floor, Washington, DC 20009.

Phone: (202) 745-3680. Fax: (202) 745-3679. E-mail: kunduwash@aol.com. Website: http://www.pngembassy.org.

Capital: Port Moresby. National Day: September 16. Currency: Kina. Language: English (official), Tok Pinsin, Motu. Religion: Protestant (44%), Roman Catholic (22%), indigenous (34%). Location: Southeast Asia, occupying east half of island of New Guinea and about 600 nearby islands. Neighbors: Indonesia (W), Australia (S). Government: Parliamentary democracy.

PARAGUAY

Embassy of Paraguay: 2400 Massachusetts Avenue NW, Washington, DC 20008.

Phone: (202) 483-6960. Fax: (202) 234-4508. E-mail: embapar@erols.com.

Capital: Asuncion. National Day: May 14. Currency: Guarani. Language: Spanish, Guarani. Religion: Roman Catholic (66%). Location: South America. Neighbors: Bolivia (N), Argentina (S), Brazil (E). Government: Republic.

PERU

Embassy of Peru: 1700 Massachusetts Avenue NW, Washington, DC 20036.

Phone: (202) 833-9860. Fax: (202) 659-8124. E-mail: lepruwash@aol.com.

Capital: Lima. National Day: July 28. Currency: New sol. Language: Spanish (official), Quechua, Aymara. Religion: Roman Catholic. Location: South America. Neighbors: Ecuador, Colombia (N), Brazil, Bolivia (E), Chile (S). Government: Republic.

PHILIPPINES

Embassy of the Philippines: 1600 Massachusetts Avenue NW, Washington, DC 20036.

Phone: (202) 467-9300. Fax: (202) 328-7614. E-mail: uswashpe@aol.com.

Capital: Manila. National Day: June 12. Currency: Peso. Language: Filipino, English. Religion: Roman Catholic (83%), Protestant (9%), Muslim (5%). Location: Archipelago in Southeast Asia. Neighbors: Malaysia, Indonesia (S), Taiwan (N). Government: Republic.

POLAND

Embassy of the Republic of Poland: 2640 16th Street NW, Washington, DC 20009.

Phone: (202) 234-3800. Fax: (202) 328-6271. Website: http://www.polishworld.com/polemb.

Capital: Warsaw. National Day: May 3. Currency: Zloty. Language: Polish (official). Religion: Roman Catholic (95%). Location: On Baltic Sea, East central Europe. Neighbors: Germany (W), Czech Republic, Slovakia (S), Lithuania, Belarus, Ukraine (E), Russia (N). Government: Republic.

PORTUGAL

Embassy of Portugal: 2125 Kalorama Road NW, Washington, DC 20008.

Phone: (202) 328-8610. Fax: (202) 462-3726.

Capital: Lisbon. National Day: June 10. Currency: Escudo. Language: Portuguese (official). Religion: Roman Catholic (97%). Location: Southwestern extreme of Europe. Neighbors: Spain (N, E). Government: Republic.

QATAR

Embassy of the State of Qatar: 4200 Wisconsin Avenue NW, Suite 200, Washington, DC 20016.

Phone: (202) 274-1600. Fax: (202) 237-0061. E-mail: znaimi.qtr@erols.com.

Capital: Doha. National Day: September 3. Currency: Riyal. Language: Arabic (official), English. Religion: Muslim (95%). Location: Middle East, occupying peninsula on west coast of Persian Gulf. Neighbors: Saudi Arabia (S). Government: Traditional monarchy.

ROMANIA

Embassy of Romania: 1607 23rd Street NW, Washington, DC 20008.

Phone: (202) 332-4846. Fax: (202) 232-4748. Website: http://www.embassy.org/romania.

Capital: Bucharest. National Day: December 1. Currency: Leu. Language: Romanian (official), Hungarian, German. Religion: Romanian Orthodox (70%), Roman Catholic (6%), Protestant (6%). Location: Southeast Europe, bordering Black Sea. Neighbors: Moldova (E), Ukraine (N), Hungary, Yugoslavia (W), Bulgaria (S). Government: Republic.

RUSSIA

Embassy of the Russian Federation: 2650 Wisconsin Avenue NW, Washington, DC 20007.

Phone: (202) 298-5700. Fax: (202) 298-5735. Website: http://www.russianembassy.org.

Capital: Moscow. National Day: June 12. Currency: Ruble. Language: Russian (official), other. Religion: Russian Orthodox, Muslim, other. Location: From East Europe across North Asia to Pacific Ocean. Neighbors: Finland, Norway, Estonia, Latvia, Belarus, Ukraine (W), Georgia, Azerbaijan, Kazakhstan, China, Mongolia (N), Korea (S); Kalingrad exclave bordered by Poland (S), Lithuania (N, E). Government: Republic.

RWANDA

Embassy of the Republic of Rwanda: 1714 New Hampshire Avenue NW, Washington, DC 20009.

Phone: (202) 232-2882. Fax: (202) 232-4544. Website: http://www.rwandemb.org.

Capital: Kigali. National Day: July 1. Currency: Franc. Language: French, Kinyarwanda (both official). Religion: Christian (74%), indigenous (25%), Muslim (1%). Location: East central Africa. Neighbors: Uganda (N), Congo (formerly Zaire) (W), Burundi (S), Tanzania (E). Government: Republic.

SAINT KITTS AND NEVIS

Embassy of Saint Kitts and Nevis: 3216 New Mexico Avenue NW, Washington, DC 20016.

Phone: (202) 686-2636. Fax: (202) 686-5740.

Capital: Basseterre. National Day: September 19. Currency: East Caribbean dollar. Language: English (official). Religion: Protestant (76%), Roman Catholic (11%). Location: East Caribbean Sea. Neighbors: Antigua, Barbuda (E). Government: Constitutional monarchy.

SAINT LUCIA

Embassy of Saint Lucia: 3216 New Mexico Avenue NW, Washington, DC 20016.

Phone: (202) 364-6792. Fax: (202) 364-6728. E-mail: eofsaintlu@aol.com.

Capital: Castries. National Day: February 22. Currency: East Caribbean dollar. Language: English (official), French patois. Religion: Roman Catholic (90%), Protestant (7%). Location: East Caribbean Sea. Neighbors: Martinique (N), St. Vincent (S). Government: Parliamentary democracy.

ST. VINCENT AND THE GRENADINES

Embassy of St. Vincent and the Grenadines: 3216 New Mexico Avenue NW, Washington, DC 20016.

Phone: (202) 364-6730. Fax: (202) 364-6736.

Capital: Kingstown. National Day: October 27. Currency: East Caribbean dollar. Language: English (official), French patois. Religion: Anglican, Methodist, Roman Catholic. Location: East Caribbean Sea. Neighbors: St. Lucia (N), Barbados (E), Grenada (S). Government: Constitutional monarchy.

SAMOA (FORMERLY WESTERN SAMOA)

Embassy of the Independent State of Samoa: 800 2nd Avenue, Suite 400D, New York, NY 10017.

Phone: (212) 599-6196. Fax: (212) 599-0797.

Capital: Apia. National Day: June 1. Currency: Tala. Language: Samoan, English (both official). Religion: Christian (99.7%). Location: South Pacific Ocean. Neighbors: Fiji (SW), Tonga (S). Government: Constitutional monarchy.

SÃO TOMÉ AND PRÍNCIPE

Permanent Mission of São Tomé and Príncipe to the UN: 400 Park Avenue, 7th Floor, New York, NY 10022.

Phone: (212) 317-0533. Fax: (212) 317-0580. E-mail: stpun@undp.org.

Capital: São Tomé. National Day: July 12. Currency: Dobra. Language: Portuguese (official). Religion: Roman Catholic, Protestant. Location: In Gulf of Guinea, 125 miles off central West Africa. Neighbors: Gabon, Equatorial Guinea (E). Government: Republic.

SAUDI ARABIA

Royal Embassy of Saudi Arabia: 601 New Hampshire Avenue NW, Washington, DC 20037.

Phone: (202) 342-3800. Fax: (202) 944-3113. Website: http://www.saudiembassy.net.

Capital: Riyadh. National Day: September 23. Currency: Riyal. Language: Arabic. Religion: Muslim (100%). Location: Arabian Peninsula. Neighbors: Kuwait, Iraq, Jordan (N), Yemen, Oman (S), United Arab Emirates, Qatar (E). Government: Monarchy.

SENEGAL

Embassy of the Republic of Senegal: 2112 Wyoming Avenue NW, Washington, DC 20008.

Phone: (202) 234-0540. Fax: (202) 332-6315.

Capital: Dakar. National Day: April 4. Currency: CFA franc. Language: French (official), Wolof, Pulaar, Diola, Mandingo. Religion: Muslim (92%), indigenous (6%), Christian (2%). Location: West Africa. Neighbors: Mauritania (N), Mali (E), Guinea, Guinea-Bissau (S); surrounds Gambia on three sides. Government: Republic.

SEYCHELLES

Embassy of the Republic of Seychelles: 800 2nd Avenue, Suite 400C, New York, NY 10017.

Phone: (212) 972-1785. Fax: (212) 972-1786. Website: http://www.seychelles-online.com.sc.

Capital: Victoria. National Day: June 18. Currency: Rupee. Language: English, French (both official), Creole. Religion: Roman Catholic (90%), Anglican (8%). Location: Indian Ocean, 700 miles northeast of Madagascar. Neighbors: Nearest are Madagascar (SW), Somalia (NW). Government: Republic.

SIERRA LEONE

Embassy of Sierra Leone: 1701 19th Street NW, Washington, DC 20009.

Phone: (202) 939-9261. Fax: (202) 483-1793.

Capital: Freetown. National Day: April 27. Currency: Leone. Language: English (official), indigenous. Religion: Muslim (60%), indigenous (30%), Christian (10%). Location: West coast of West Africa. Neighbors: Guinea (N, E), Liberia (S). Government: In transition.

SINGAPORE

Embassy of the Republic of Singapore: 3501 International Place NW, Washington, DC 20008.

Phone: (202) 537-3100. Fax: (202) 537-0876. Website: http://www.gov.sg.

Capital: Singapore. National Day: August 9. Currency: Dollar. Language: Chinese, Malay, Tamil, English (all official). Religion: Buddhist, Taoist, Muslim, Christian, Hindu. Location: Off tip of Malayan Peninsula, Southeast Asia. Neighbors: Malaysia (N), Indonesia (S). Government: Republic.

SLOVAKIA

Embassy of the Slovak Republic: 2201 Wisconsin Avenue NW, Suite 250, Washington, DC 20007.

Phone: (202) 965-5161. Fax: (202) 965-5166. Website: http://www.slovakemb.com.

Capital: Bratislava. National Day: September 1. Currency: Koruna. Language: Slovak (official), Hungarian. Religion: Roman Catholic (60%), Protestant (8%). Location: East central Europe. Neighbors: Poland (N), Hungary (S), Austria, Czech Republic (W), Ukraine (E). Government: Republic.

SLOVENIA

Embassy of the Republic of Slovenia: 1525 New Hampshire Avenue NW, Washington, DC 20036.

Phone: (202) 667-5363. Fax: (202) 667-4563. Website: http://www.embassy.org/slovenia.

Capital: Ljubljana. National Day: June 25. Currency: Tolar. Language: Slovenian (official), Serbo-Croatian. Religion: Roman Catholic (96%). Location: Southeast Europe. Neighbors: Italy (W), Austria (N), Hungary (NE), Croatia (SE, S). Government: Republic.

SOLOMAN ISLANDS

Embassy of the Soloman Islands: 800 2nd Street, Suite 400L, New York, NY 10017.

Phone: (212) 599-6193. Fax: (212) 661-8925. Website: http://www.solomans.com.

Capital: Honiara. National Day: July 7. Currency: Dollar. Language: English (official), Melanesian, Papuan, Polynesian languages. Religion: Anglican (34%), Roman Catholic (19%), Baptist (17%), other Christian (26%). Location: Melanesian Archipelago in West Pacific Ocean. Neighbors: Nearest is Papua New Guinea (W). Government: Parliamentary democracy within the Commonwealth of Nations.

SOMALIA

Embassy of the Somali Republic. (Embassy closed operations May 8, 1991.)

SOUTH AFRICA

Embassy of the Republic of South Africa: 3051 Massachusetts Avenue NW, Washington, DC 20008.

Phone: (202) 232-4400. Fax: (202) 265-1607. Website: http://www.southafrica.net.

Capital: Capetown (legislative), Pretoria (executive), Bloemfontein (judicial). National Day: April 27. Currency: Rand. Language: Eleven official languages, including Afrikaans, English, Ndebile, Sotho. Religion: Christian, Hindu, Muslim. Location: Africa. Neighbors: Namibia, Botswana, Zimbabwe (N), Mozambique, Swaziland (E), surrounds Lesotho. Government: Federal republic with bicameral parliament and universal suffrage.

SOUTH KOREA

Embassy of the Republic of Korea: 2450 Massachusetts Avenue NW, Washington, DC 20008.

Phone: (202) 939-5600. Fax: (202) 387-0302. Website: http://www.koreaemb.org.

Capital: Seoul. National Day: August 15. Currency: Won. Language: Korean. Religion: Christian (49%), Buddhist (47%). Location: Northeast Asia. Neighbors: North Korea (N). Government: Republic.

SPAIN

Embassy of Spain: 2375 Pennsylvania Avenue NW, Washington, DC 20037.

Phone: (202) 452-0100. Fax: (202) 833-5670.

Capital: Madrid. National Day: October 12. Currency: Peseta. Language: Castilian Spanish (official), Catalan, Galician, Basque. Religion: Roman Catholic (99%). Location: Southwest Europe. Neighbors: Portugal (W), France (N). Government: Constitutional monarchy.

SRI LANKA

Embassy of the Democratic Socialist Republic of Sri Lanka: 2148 Wyoming Avenue NW, Washington, DC 20008.

Phone: (202) 483-4025. Fax: (202) 232-7181. Website: http://www.slembassy.org.

Capital: Colombo. National Day: February 4. Currency: Rupee. Language: Sinhala, Tamil (both official), English. Religion: Buddhist (69%), Hindu (15%), Christian (8%), Muslim (8%). Location: In Indian Ocean off southeast coast of India. Neighbors: India (NW). Government: Republic.

SUDAN

Embassy of the Republic of the Sudan: 2210 Massachusetts Avenue NW, Washington, DC 20008.

Phone: (202) 338-8565. Fax: (202) 667-2406.

Capital: Khartoum. National Day: January 1. Currency: Pound. Language: Arabic (official), Nubian, Ta Bedawie. Religion: Sunni Muslim (70%), indigenous (25%), Christian (5%). Location: East end of Sahara desert zone. Neighbors: Egypt (N), Libya, Chad, Central African Republic (W), Congo (formerly Zaire), Uganda, Kenya (S), Ethiopia, Eritrea (E). Government: Military.

SURINAME

Embassy of the Republic of Suriname: 4301 Connecticut Avenue NW, Suite 460, Washington, DC 20008.

Phone: (202) 244-7488. Fax: (202) 244-5878. E-mail: embsur@erols.com.

Capital: Paramaribo. National Day: November 25. Currency: Guilder. Language: Dutch (official), Sranang Tongo, English, Hindustani. Religion: Christian (48%), Hindu (27%), Muslim (20%). Location: North shore of South America. Neighbors: Guyana (W), Brazil (S), French Guiana (E). Government: Republic.

SWAZILAND

Embassy of the Kingdom of Swaziland: 3400 International Drive NW, Suite 3M, Washington, DC 20008.

Phone: (202) 362-6683. Fax: (202) 244-8059. E-mail: swaziland@compuserve.com.

Capital: Mbabane. National Day: September 6. Currency: Lilangeni. Language: English, Swazi (both official). Religion: Christian (60%), indigenous (40%). Location: Southern Africa. Neighbors: South Africa (N, W, S), Mozambique (E). Government: Constitutional monarchy.

SWEDEN

Embassy of Sweden: 1501 M Street NW, Washington, DC 20005.

Phone: (202) 467-2600. Fax: (202) 467-2699. Website: http://www.swedenemb.org/.

Capital: Stockholm. National Day: June 6. Currency: Krona. Language: Swedish. Religion: Evangelical Lutheran (94%). Location: Northern Europe, Scandinavian Peninsula. Neighbors: Norway (W), Denmark (S), Finland (E). Government: Constitutional monarchy.

SWITZERLAND

Embassy of Switzerland: 2900 Cathedral Avenue NW, Washington, DC 20008.

Phone: (202) 745-7900. Fax: (202) 387-2564. Website: http://www.swissemb.org.

Capital: Bern (administrative), Lausanne (judicial). National Day: August 1. Currency: Franc. Language: German, French, Italian, Romansch (all official). Religion: Roman Catholic (48%), Protestant (44%). Location: Alps, central Europe. Neighbors: France (W), Italy (S), Austria (E), Germany (N). Government: Federal republic.

SYRIA

Embassy of the Syrian Arab Republic: 2215 Wyoming Avenue NW, Washington, DC 20008.

Phone: (202) 232-6313. Fax: (202) 234-9548. Website: http://www.syriaksday.com.

Capital: Damascus. National Day: April 17. Currency: Pound. Language: Arabic (official), Kurdish, Armenian. Religion: Sunni Muslim (74%), other Muslim (16%), Christian (10%). Location: Middle East, at east end of Mediterranean Sea. Neighbors: Lebanon, Israel (W), Jordan (S), Iraq (E), Turkey (N). Government: Republic (under military regime).

TAIWAN

Taipai Economic and Cultural Office: 4201 Wisconsin Avenue NW, Washington, DC 20016.

Phone: (202) 895-1800. Fax: (202) 966-0825.

Capital: Taipai. National Day: Currency: New Taiwan dollar. Language: Mandarin Chinese (official), Taiwanese. Religion: Buddhist, Taoist, Confucian (93%), Christian (7%). Location: Off southeast coast of China, between East and South China Seas. Neighbors: Nearest is China. Government: Democracy.

TANZANIA

Embassy of the United Republic of Tanzania: 2139 R Street NW, Washington, DC 20008.

Phone: (202) 939-6125. Fax: (202) 797-7408.

Capital: Dar es Salaam. National Day: April 26. Currency: Tanzanian shilling. Language: Swahili, English, Arabic. Religion: Mainland—Christian (45%), Muslim (35%), indigenous (20%); Zanzibar—Muslim (99%). Location: Africa. Neighbors: Kenya, Uganda (N), Rwanda, Burundi, Congo (formerly Zaire) (E), Zambia, Malawi, Mozambique (S). Government: Republic.

THAILAND

Royal Thai Embassy: 1024 Wisconsin Avenue NW, Washington, DC 20007.

Phone: (202) 944-3600. Fax: (202) 944-3611. Website: http://www.thaiembdc.org/.

Capital: Bangkok. National Day: December 5. Currency: Baht. Language: Thai, English, Lao, Chinese, Malay. Religion: Buddhist (95%), Muslim (4%). Location: Southeast Asia. Neighbors: Laos (N), Cambodia (E), Malaysia (S). Government: Constitutional monarchy.

TOGO

Embassy of the Republic of Togo: 2208 Massachusetts Avenue NW, Washington, DC 20008.

Phone: (202) 234-4212. Fax: (202) 232-3190.

Capital: Lome. National Day: April 27. Currency: CFA franc. Language: French (official), Ewe, Mina, Dagomba, Kabye. Religion: Indigenous (70%), Christian (20%), Muslim (10%). Location: Southern coast of West Africa. Neighbors: Ghana (W), Burkina Faso (N), Benin (E). Government: Republic.

TRINIDAD AND TOBAGO

Embassy of Trinidad and Tobago: 1708 Massachusetts Avenue NW, Washington, DC 20036.

Phone: (202) 467-6490. Fax: (202) 785-3130. E-mail: embttgo@erols.com.

Capital: Port-of-Spain. National Day: August 3. Currency: Dollar. Language: English (official), Hindi, French, Spanish. Religion: Roman Catholic (32%), Protestant (28%), Hindu (24%). Location: In Caribbean, off east coast of Venezuela. Neighbors: Nearest is Venezuela (SW). Government: Parliamentary democracy.

TUNISIA

Embassy of Tunisia: 1515 Massachusetts Avenue NW, Washington, DC 20005.

Phone: (202) 862-1850. Fax: (202) 862-1858.

Capital: Tunis. National Days: March 20, June 1. Currency: Dinar. Language: Arabic (official), French. Religion: Muslim (98%). Location: Northern coast of Africa. Neighbors: Algeria (W), Libya (N). Government: Republic.

TURKEY

Embassy of the Republic of Turkey: 1714 Massachusetts Avenue NW, Washington, DC 20036.

Phone: (202) 659-8200. Fax: (202) 659-0744. Website: http://www.turkey.org.

Capital: Ankara. National Day: October 29. Currency: Lira. Language: Turkish (official), Kurdish, Arabic. Religion: Muslim (99.8%). Location: Occupies Asia Minor, stretches into continental Europe, borders on Mediterranean and Black Seas. Neighbors: Bulgaria, Greece (W), Georgia, Armenia (N), Iran (E), Iraq, Syria (S). Government: Republic.

TURKMENISTAN

Embassy of Turkmenistan: 2207 Massachusetts Avenue NW, Washington, DC 20008.

Phone: (202) 588-1500. Fax: (202) 588-0697. Website: http://www.turkmenistan.org.

Capital: Ashgabat. National Day: October 27. Currency: Manat. Language: Turkmen (official), Russian, Uzbek. Religion: Muslim (87%), Eastern Orthodox (11%). Location: Central Asia. Neighbors: Kazakhstan (N), Uzbekistan (N, E), Afghanistan, Iran (S). Government: Republic.

UGANDA

Embassy of the Republic of Uganda: 5911 16th Street NW, Washington, DC 20011.

Phone: (202) 726-7100. Fax: (202) 726-1727. Website: http://www.ugandaco.ug.

Capital: Kampala. National Day: October 9. Currency: Shilling. Language: English (official), Luganda, Swahili. Religion: Christian (66%), indigenous (18%), Muslim (16%). Location: East central Africa. Neighbors: Sudan (N), Congo (formerly Zaire) (W), Rwanda, Tanzania (S), Kenya (E). Government: Republic.

UKRAINE

Embassy of Ukraine: 3350 M Street, NW, Washington, DC 20007.

Phone: (202) 333-0606. Fax: (202) 333-0817. E-mail: infolook@aol.com. Website: http://www.ukremb.com.

Capital: Kiev. National Day: August 24. Currency: Hryvna. Language: Ukrainian (official), Russian. Religion: Mostly Ukrainian Orthodox, some Ukrainian Catholic. Location: Eastern Europe. Neighbors: Belarus (N), Russia (NE, E), Moldova, Romania (SW), Hungary, Slovakia, Poland (W). Government: Constitutional republic.

UNITED ARAB EMIRATES

Embassy of the United Arab Emirates: 1255 22nd Street, NW, Suite 700, Washington, DC 20037.

Phone: (202) 955-7999. Fax: (202) 337-7029. Website: http://www.uaedream.com/-government.

Capital: Abu Dhabi. National Day: December 2. Currency: Dirham. Language: Arabic (official), Persian, English, Hindi. Religion: Muslim (96%), Christian, Hindu. Location: Middle East, south shore of Persian Gulf. Neighbors: Saudi Arabia (W, S), Oman (E). Government: Federation of emirates.

UNITED KINGDOM OF GREAT BRITAIN AND NORTHERN IRELAND

British Embassy: 3100 Massachusetts Avenue NW, Washington, DC 20008.

Phone: (202) 588-6500. Fax: (202) 588-7870. Website: http://www.britain-info.org.

Capital: London. National Day: June 15. Currency: Pound. Language: English, Welsh, Scottish, Gaelic. Religion: Anglican, Roman Catholic, other Christian, Muslim. Location: Off northwestern coast of Europe, across English Channel, Strait of Dover, and North Sea. Neighbors: Ireland (W), France (SE). Government: Constitutional monarchy.

URUGUAY

Embassy of Uruguay: 2715 M Street, NW, Washington, DC 20007.

Phone: (202) 331-1313. Fax: (202) 331-8142. Website: http://www.embassy.org/-uruguay.

Capital: Montevideo. National Day: August 25. Currency: Peso. Language: Spanish. Religion: Roman Catholic (66%). Location: South America. Neighbors: Argentina (W), Brazil (N). Government: Republic.

UZBEKISTAN

Embassy of the Republic of Uzbekistan: 1746 Massachusetts Avenue NW, Washington, DC 20036.

Phone: (202) 887-5300. Fax: (202) 293-6804. Website: http://www.uzbekistan.org.

Capital: Tashkent. National Day: September 1. Currency: Som. Language: Uzbek (official), Russian. Religion: Sunni Muslim, Eastern Orthodox. Location: Central Asia. Neighbors: Kazakhstan (N,W), Kyrgyzstan, Tajikistan (E), Afghanistan, Turkmenistan (S). Government: Republic.

VENEZUELA

Embassy of the Republic of Venezuela: 1099 30th Street NW, Washington, DC 20007.

Phone: (202) 342-2214. Fax: (202) 342-6820. Website: http://www.embvenez-us.org.

Capital: Caracas. National Day: July 5. Currency: Bolivar. Language: Spanish (official). Religion: Roman Catholic (96%). Location: Caribbean coast of South America. Neighbors: Colombia (W), Brazil (S), Guyana (E). Government: Federal Republic.

VIETNAM

Embassy of Vietnam: 1233 20th Street NW, Suite 400, Washington, DC 20036.

Phone: (202) 861-0737. Fax: (202) 861-0917. Website: http://www.vietnamembassy-usa.org.

Capital: Hanoi. National Day: September 2. Currency: Dong. Language: Vietnamese, French, Chinese. Religion: Mainly Buddhist and Taoist, also Roman Catholic, indigenous. Location: Southeast Asia. Neighbors: China (N), Laos, Cambodia (W). Government: Communist.

YEMEN

Embassy of the Republic of Yemen: 2600 Virginia Avenue NW, Suite 705, Washington, DC 20037.

Phone: (202) 965-4760. Fax: (202) 337-2017.

Capital: Sanaa. National Day: May 22. Currency: Rial. Language: Arabic (official). Religion: Mostly Muslim. Location: Middle East, south coast of Arabian Peninsula. Neighbors: Saudi Arabia (N), Oman (E). Government: Republic.

YUGOSLAVIA **(Closed as of March 31, 1999)**

Embassy of the former Socialist Federal Republic of Yugoslavia: 2410 California Street NW, Washington, DC 20008.

Phone: (202) 462-6566. Fax: (202) 462-2508. Website: http://ourworld.compuserve.-com/homepages/wyuembassy.

Capital: Belgrade. National Day: June 28. Currency: New Dinar. Language: Serbo-Croatian (official), Albanian. Religion: Orthodox (65%), Muslim (19%), Roman Catholic (4%). Location: Balkan Peninsula, southeast Europe. Neighbors: Croatia, Bosnia, Herzegovina (W), Hungary (N), Romania, Bulgaria (E), Albania, Macedonia (S). Government: Republic.

ZAMBIA

Embassy of the Republic of Zambia: 2419 Massachusetts Avenue NW, Washington, DC 20008.

Phone: (202) 265-9717. Fax: (202) 332-0826. E-mail: zambia@tmn.com. Website: http://www.zambia.sadc-usa-net.

Capital: Lusaka. National Day: October 24. Currency: Kwacha. Language: English (official), Bantu dialects. Religion: Christian (50–75%), Hindu and Muslim (24–49%). Location: South central Africa. Neighbors: Congo (formerly Zaire) (N), Tanzania, Malawi, Mozambique (E), Zimbabwe, Namibia (S), Angola (W). Government: Republic.

ZIMBABWE

Embassy of the Republic of Zimbabwe: 1608 New Hampshire Avenue NW, Washington, DC 20009.

Phone: (202) 332-7100. Fax: (202) 483-9326.

Capital: Harare. National Day: April 18. Currency: Dollar. Language: English (official), Shona, Sindebele. Religion: Syncretic (Christian-indigenous mix) (50%), Christian (25%), indigenous (24%). Location: Southern Africa. Neighbors: Zambia (N), Botswana (W), South Africa (S), Mozambique (E). Government: Republic.

Appendix 2

Resource Listings and Suggested Reading

The following resource listings are provided as additional sources to discover more about diplomacy in general, Washington diplomatic life over the years and different avenues for diplomacy in the new millennium.

Agencies, Institutions and Organizations

CSIS (Center for Strategic and International Studies)
1800 K Street NW
Washington, DC 20006
(202) 887-0200
http://www.csis.org

The Electronic Embassy
http://www.embassy.org

The Export-Import Bank of the United States
811 Vermont Avenue NW
Washington, DC 20571
(202) 565-3946
http://www.exim.gov

The Goodwill Embassy Tour
Davis Memorial Goodwill Industries
2200 South Dakota Avenue NE
Washington, DC 20018
(202) 636-4225
http://www.dcgoodwill.org
Annual Event: Held the second Saturday of every May

The Hospitality and Information Service (THIS)
(an affiliate at Meridian International Center)
1630 Crescent Place NW
Washington, DC 20009
(202) 232-3002
http://www.meridian.org

Institute for the Study of Diplomacy
Edmund A. Walsh School of Foreign Service
Georgetown University
Washington, DC 20057-1025
(202) 965-5735
http://www.georgetown.edu/sfs/programs/isd

Johns Hopkins University
Paul Nitze School of Advanced International Studies
1740 Massachusetts Avenue
Washington, DC 20036
(202) 663-5600
http://www.sais-jhu.edu

The International Monetary Fund (Washington Bureau)
700 19th Street NW
Washington, DC 20431
(202) 623-7000
http://www.imf.org

Meridian International Center
1630 Crescent Place NW
Washington, DC 20009
(202) 667-6800
http://www.meridian.org

The Ronald H. Brown Foundation
2010 Massachusetts Ave NW, Suite 210
Washington, DC 20036
(202) 835-0700
http://www.rhbf.org

The United Nations
New York, NY 10017
(212) 963-1234
http://www.un.org

United States Department of Commerce
14th and Constitution Avenues NW
Washington, DC 20230
(202) 482-2000
http://www.doc.gov

United States Department of State
2201 C Street NW
Washington, DC 20520
(202) 647-4000
http://www.state.gov

The World Bank (Washington Bureau)
1818 H Street NW
Washington, DC 20433
(202) 477-1234
http://www.worldbank.org

Suggested Reading

Baldridge, Letitia. *Complete Guide to the New Manners for the 90's.* New York: Rawson Associates, 1990.

———. *Of Diamonds and Diplomats: An Autobiography of a Happy Life.* Boston, Mass.: Houghton Mifflin, 1968.

Gingrich, Newt. "Diplomacy in the Information Age." Institute for the Study of Diplomacy: School of Foreign Service, Georgetown University, Iden Lecture, October 7, 1997.

Herz, Martin F. *The Modern Ambassador: The Challenge and the Search.* Washington, D.C.: Institute for the Study of Diplomacy, 1983.

Kissinger, Henry. *The Kissinger Transcripts: The Top Secret Talks with Beijing and Moscow.* New York: The New Press, 1999

———. *Diplomacy.* New York: Simon and Schuster, 1995.

Loeffler, Jane C. *The Architecture of Diplomacy: Building America's Embassies.* New York: Princeton Architecture Press, 1998.

Mak, Dayton. American Ambassadors in a Troubled World: Interviews with Senior Diplomats, Westport, Conn.: Greenwood Press, 1992.

Miller, Hope Ridings. *Embassy Row: The Life and Times of Diplomatic Washington.* New York: Holt, Rinehart and Winston, 1969.

Pearce, David D. *Wary Partners: Diplomats and the Media.* Washington, D.C.: Institute for the Study of Diplomacy, Georgetown University, 1995.

"Reinventing diplomacy in the Information Age." Center for Strategic and International Studies, October 9, 1998.

Roosevelt, Selwa. *Keeper of the Gate.* New York: Simon and Schuster, 1990.

———. *Diplomatic Immunity and U.S. Interests.* Washington, D.C.: U.S. Department of State, Bureau of Public Affairs, Office of Public Communication, Editorial Division, 1987.

Sullivan, Joseph G. *Embassies Under Siege: Personal Accounts by Diplomats on the Front Line.* Washington, D.C.: Institute for the Study of Diplomacy, Georgetown University, 1995.

Appendix 3

Protocol: Diplomatic Do's and Don'ts

The Ambassador

Addressing the ambassador in person:
Your Excellency or Ambassador (Surname) or Mr./Madame Ambassador

Addressing the ambassador in correspondence:
Your Excellency or My Dear Mr./Madame Ambassador

Addressing the envelope:
His/Her Excellency
Full Name (No Prefix)
The Ambassador of (Country)

Place card for the ambassador:
The Ambassador of (Country)

If the ambassador has another title (Sir, Lady, Marquis, Baron, Colonel, etc.):
His/Her Excellency (Proper Title, Full Name)

The Ambassador and Spouse

The diplomatic couple in person:
Your Excellency or Ambassador (Surname) or Mr./Madame Ambassador and Mrs./Mr. (Surname)

The diplomatic couple in correspondence:

Your Excellency and Mrs./Mr. (Surname) or My Dear Mr./Madame Ambassador and Mrs./Mr.

The diplomatic couple on the envelope:

His/Her Excellency
The Ambassador of (Country)
and Mrs./Mr. (Surname)

Place cards for the diplomatic couple:

Ambassador (Surname), Mr./Mrs. (Surname)

Diplomatic Do's and Don'ts

- Don't use the title *Ambassadress* or *Mrs. Ambassador*
- Don't expect the ambassador always to be a male.
- Don't be surprised if the ambassador comes early and does not stay, or arrives late (they often have several events a night).
- Do learn how to pronounce the ambassador's name and country correctly.
- Don't expect the ambassador to attend a weekend event.
- Don't automatically expect an ambassador to make a speech. (Ask before the event; explain audience, purpose, etc.)
- Do acknowledge the ambassador's and diplomatic spouse's presence.
- Do remember that "casual" in diplomatic circles simply means "not formal."
- Do expect ambassadors to wear their medals and ribbons *only* for "white-tie" occasions.
- Do check diplomatic couple's drink and food preferences in advance (e.g., vegetarian, nonalcoholic).
- Don't dress more elaborately than the ambassador or the spouse. (For

example, if you were to wear a sari to an Indian, Pakistani or Sri Lankan event, it should not have more gold on it than the ambassador's or the ambassador's spouse.)

- Don't be surprised if the ambassador is unable to attend an event at the last moment and even sends someone else. (If your invitation is *only* for the ambassador, not the DCM or another representative, make that clear to the ambassador's staff.)

- Do send a thank-you note when you are the guest.

- Do learn about the ambassador's country prior to an event.

Index

Italic page numbers indicate a photograph.

Photo by Didi Cutler.

About the Author

Gail Scott, award-winning Washington TV anchorwoman, has always been involved with the intriguing lives of Washington's diplomatic corps. Having covered the White House, Congress and Embassy Row, Ms. Scott's unique storytelling style has taken her to Europe and on to the pages of *The Washington Post.* Living in Georgetown, the colonial district of Washington, Ms. Scott lives and writes among the diplomats and the students studying this new era of public and commercial diplomacy. In between writing deadlines, she speaks internationally and advises global executives on personal and corporate media issues. A native Washingtonian, she often travels to be with her daughter, Indrani, wherever she is in the world.